TRANQUIL PRISONS:
CHEMICAL INCARCERATION UNDER
COMMUNITY TREATMENT ORDERS

Under community treatment orders, antipsychotic medications are frequently imposed on psychiatric patients deemed dangerous to themselves or others. This practice is based on the assumption that the prescribed treatment is safe and effective and is medically necessary. Under recent mental health laws, patients may be required to remain on prescribed medications after leaving hospital. However, many psychiatric survivors attest that such treatment, often used for the purpose of restraint, can feel like a form of torture. The consequences of withdrawal can also be severe.

In this unique academic study of psychiatric treatment, Erick Fabris, himself a former psychiatric patient, discusses the use of chemical agents for treatment of mental illness despite the availability of suitable alternatives. He observes that patients often become dependent on psychiatric drugs, many of which have serious side-effects such as restricted movement and impaired cognition and communication. Calling for greater professional accountability and more therapeutic choice for patients. *Tranquil Prisons* is a bold, in-depth examination of a largely neglected but important social issue.

ERICK FABRIS is a lecturer in the School of Disability Studies at Ryerson University.

ERICK FABRIS

Tranquil Prisons

Chemical Incarceration under Community Treatment Orders

UNIVERSITY OF TORONTO PRESS
Toronto   Buffalo   London

© University of Toronto Press Incorporated 2011
Toronto Buffalo London
www.utppublishing.com
Printed in Canada

ISBN 978-1-4426-4376-5 (cloth)
ISBN 978-1-4426-1229-7 (paper)

∞

Printed on acid-free, 100% post-consumer recycled paper with vegetable-based inks.

Library and Archives Canada Cataloguing in Publication

Fabris, Erick, 1968–
Tranquil prisons : chemical incarceration under community treatment
orders / Erick Fabris.

Includes bibliographical references and index.
ISBN 978-1-4426-4376-5 (bound).   ISBN 978-1-4426-1229-7 (pbk.)

1. Involuntary treatment – Moral and ethical aspects.   2. Involuntary
treatment – Law and legislation – Canada.   3. Psychotropic drugs –
Physiological effects.   4. Mental Illness – Chemotheraphy.   5. Psychiatric
ethics.   I. Title.

R727.35.F32 2011   174.2'9689   C2011-902182-X

This book has been published with the help of a grant from the Canadian
Federation for the Humanities and Social Sciences, through the Aid to
Scholarly Publications Program, using funds provided by the Social
Sciences and Humanities Research Council of Canada.

University of Toronto Press acknowledges the financial assistance to its
publishing program of the Canada Council for the Arts and the Ontario
Arts Council.

Canada Council   Conseil des Arts   ONTARIO ARTS COUNCIL
for the Arts   du Canada   CONSEIL DES ARTS DE L'ONTARIO

University of Toronto Press acknowledges the financial support of the
Government of Canada through the Canada Book Fund for its publishing
activities.

Contents

Acknowledgments

This book is written for people who have been imposed upon or sometimes feel disordered or disoriented, but also for families and friends and anyone concerned with 'us.' I invite you to share this book with a counsellor, doctor, family, and friends. Whatever mistakes you find in it are mine alone, and I welcome your helping me to find them. I also invite you to read any part of the book in any order, unless you want to thoroughly critique it in which case you might want to read it all in order. It took many years to complete this book, for various reasons, not least of which is the effect of my own incarceration and forced care. I am fortunate to have a family who loves me and friends who have nudged me through the pain of that experience.

I need to acknowledge psychiatric survivors who have struggled together despite indifference to our issues, and people who resisted but did not survive. A dear friend of mine who committed suicide recently is still in my thoughts. I also think of others who have died over the years, and how they, too, had moments and hours of happiness despite their situation. I also need to acknowledge other people who struggle, especially the First Nations people here on Turtle Island, and other Indigenous and racialized people, and my Queer and disabled friends and activists.

I also want to thank people who have helped me with my writing, especially Nancy Jackson, whose guidance made this book possible from the start. Bonnie Burstow and Tanya Titchkosky have helped me better define research and representation questions, though in very different ways. Several friends have given of their time. The University of Toronto Press gave me gracious support. Their wonderful senior editor, Virgil Duff, I cannot repay with mere thanks.

I wish to thank a few friends also: Jeremiah Bach, Loredana Bruni, Lucy Costa, Marion de Vries, Loree Erickson, Lana Frado, Rachel Gorman, Aubrey Lake, Geoffrey Reaume, Lena Richardon, Rett Rossi, Tina Shapiro, Lauren Tenney, Jijian Voronka, and Andrea White. Thank you to my dear parents and brother for everything, and to our extended family, our respective families and relations for all their love.

This book deals with difficult subject matter. Some content may be disturbing.

TRANQUIL PRISONS:
CHEMICAL INCARCERATION UNDER
COMMUNITY TREATMENT ORDERS

1   Chemical Incarceration

Toddlers are being prescribed psychiatric medications today. So are school children considered disorderly or lacking in attention. Captured animals and pets, and adults of all ages are also given 'psych meds.'[1] Under certain conditions, some of us are given drugs by force, such as corrections system inmates and political prisoners, 'aggressive' people in care homes, and psychiatric patients who are considered dangerous or incapable of taking care of themselves.

Patients may choose treatments in consultation with a doctor, but what standards does the state use when it imposes medicine? The purpose of medical force is to make therapy possible and help patients 'recover.' But forced treatment can backfire, at least from the patient's perspective. To subdue violent or hapless people with drugs may seem necessary or preferable compared with other restrictions, but such drugs can exacerbate violence and dependency, cause withdrawal reactions, or simply fail to work. Yet to many psychiatrists and patients, psychiatric drugs seem indispensable for calming people or helping them cope.

Informed choice is key, but routinely imposing drugs as restraints complicates choice. What is the difference between treatment and restraint? In the case of correctional prisoners, drugs are applied for the purpose of behavioural control, usually without diagnosis. In the 1950s, in psychiatric wards where it all began, patients could be so drugged as to not be able to function outside of the hospital (Scull, 1984: 93–4). In

---

1 Quotation marks are generally used to identify common terms in psychiatric settings.

psychiatric wards today the patient is sometimes heavily tranquilized and given a similar drug as therapy. This is not everyone's experience of treatment or even of compulsory care, but as a common occurrence it concerns us all.

Psychiatrists say the reason for such force is that people with some mental disorders (especially 'psychotic disorders') may not know they are ill and may become a danger to themselves or others. 'First episode psychosis' can be frightening. Psychiatrists argue that the patient is unable to attend to work, life issues, and health. 'She's not just being eccentric,' they say. 'Try and talk to her. She won't listen. She gets herself into serious trouble. Call it spiritual or whatever, but the person can't cope with life.' To medical practitioners, bizarre beliefs and sensory hallucinations, the hallmarks of what are called 'the psychoses' ('schizophrenia' and 'bipolar affective disorder') implicitly suggest a biological abnormality that disturbs personal 'balance.' The medical way to nudge a person back to 'normal' is to suppress symptoms using medicine. As for side effects, there are medications for problems like nervous tics.

Interventions for psychosis should occur in emergency rooms, not jails, says psychiatrist E.F. Torrey (1997). Under most laws, a psychiatrist is required to ask a patient if she will accept treatment. If she denies that she has a problem (perhaps she ignores the psychiatrist altogether), she is said to lack 'insight' into her illness and can be declared legally 'incapable' or 'incompetent' to make treatment decisions. In fact, many psychiatrists think this legal requirement should be eliminated when the signs of psychotic illness are noticed (O'Reilly, 1998). The person may be restrained if necessary and given an 'antipsychotic' drug to calm her. How this is done depends entirely on individual clinicians' practices, though sometimes there are hospital policies in place to guide them. This form of intervention is considered a first stage of treatment, the 'stabilization,' though psychiatrists also call it 'chemical restraint.' When the patient seems lucid, the dosage can be dropped to a 'therapeutic dose,' and the person is readied for release as an 'outpatient' (hopefully with supports like housing, food, and other needs managed by social workers).

But what if the patient still denies that she has a problem or doesn't want to take medication for other reasons? Recently many local laws have been bolstered so that psychiatrists can legally impose (any) treatment and appointments on 'outpatients,' whether or not they refuse medication or act aggressively. For example, in Canada, hospital leave agreements and Community Treatment Orders (CTOs) are used not only to enforce treatment outside of hospitals but for quite arbitrary reasons. In the province of Ontario, more than 1,700 of these orders are used every year and the number seems to be rising. Legal safeguards have been ignored, according to mental health workers and lawyers, and so have patients' treatment choices. Elsewhere CTOs and similar measures are being used more and more broadly, and they are often regarded informally as therapeutic devices rather than as legal restrictions – this applies to the United States where they are called Involuntary Outpatient Committals (IOCs). Police can be called to enforce such arrangements by returning a patient to a physician. Families can even be enrolled to monitor the patient. Such coercive responses bring serious implications.

One of the implications of using coercion and force so readily is that the patient can resent it and start to distrust the therapy. And even if restraint is intended to be 'therapeutic,' it could be misapplied or abused and lead to serious problems including illness and death.[2] In fact, psychiatric restraints research, which I will review in chapter 3, has often indicated that clinicians need to stop relying so much on physical and chemical restraints; many workers are simply using restraints for convenience. Some articles even call for patients' direct input into restraints research, education, and policy development.

This book was written by someone who was restrained and forcibly treated. While there are people who accept such state-sanctioned treatment, not all of us do. I submit that forced drug treatment is no treatment at all, given the lack of efficacy and safety of psychiatric treatments alone, and the casual use of drugs to restrain.

'Treatment' masks coercion in forced interventions. Drugs can bring physical impairments and restrictive effects. This can lead to distress and danger through withdrawal or even to sudden death. As Grace Jackson shows, 'antipsychotic' drugs are always toxic and destroy brain tissues even at 'therapeutic doses' (2005). Imposing such drugs, whether as a treatment or as restraint, is destructive and excessive for

---

2 Death can be described by authorities as a product of 'therapeutic misadventure,' as in Ontario's Alviani inquest; see Simmons (1990), and also Weiss (1998). Dotinga (2007) reports a reduced life span for patients on long-term 'antipsychotic' drug use not attributable to other risks like smoking; see also Joukamaa et al. (2006) and Whitaker (2010).

the purpose of preventing violence and aggression.[3] But because this standard of care is imposed on most patients when other interventions are possible (though rarely provided), I argue that the risks outweigh the benefits, especially over time. More importantly, if we consider control to be a purpose of treatment, we enter a non-therapeutic discussion about who and what to control/treat.

To show how talk of treatment can disguise coercion, I use Ontario's Community Treatment Orders as a case study.[4] Because these orders are legal rather than informal coercions, they provide much material evidence of punitive control. Though orders are considered a less restrictive option than incarceration, over several weeks or months they reach the same goals as incarceration. Drugs control the nervous system to restrict bodily movement and communication with others, which are two basic conditions of incarceration, as Erving Goffman said in his book *Asylums: Essays on the Social Situation of Mental Patients and Other Inmates* (1961). Thus imposing toxic 'antipsychotics' for long periods should at least be considered a physiological mode of detention, what I am calling *chemical incarceration*. Such a practice should not be an acceptable method of constraint, and it should demonstrate a breach of ethics in either treatment or restraint policy.

To make this argument, I cannot simply rely on medical science. Medicine is important for understanding how drugs work on the body, in their function as restraints especially, but sociological research is needed to show how laws authorize such restraint, and how workers deliver it. People's everyday experiences are the most important empirical grounds for my research and argument. To understand the use of compulsory treatment requires research that is both scientific and personal. Ethnographic research bridges this divide. Ethnographic research uses rigorous methods to observe and describe people's relationships, what people say and do, while remembering that the researcher is also part of the situation.[5]

---

3 Most patients are not aggressive, and 'the mentally ill' are generally less violent than others (Steadman et al., 1998). E.F. Torrey (1997) and others in transactions with drug companies often say violence due to mental illness is rampant, an issue to which I will return.
4 The Ontario government calls Community Treatment Orders a 'treatment modality' (Dreezer & Dreezer, 2007).
5 Ethnography, John van Maanen says, 'rests on the peculiar practice of representing the social reality of others through the analysis of one's own experience in the world of these others. Ethnography is therefore highly particular and hauntingly personal,

To explore the world of forced treatment means working from a perspective that considers psychiatric researchers as well as patients. Most clinicians give some version of the above 'capture' narrative (the psychotic who is out of control and refuses life-preserving medication). But there is a minority opinion that drugs are not essential even in such circumstances; see, for example, Peter Breggin (1991), David Healy ([2001] 2009), Grace Jackson (2005), and Courtney Harding (1987). Such research has been instrumental in convincing the courts, and even the United Nations, that forced treatment is not generally beneficial; indeed, it is a form of torture, as ex-patient lawyer Tina Minkowitz argues.[6] Other former patients argue for coercive treatment in limited situations.[7] But the life stories of people who receive psychiatric interventions and arrangements, especially 'psychiatric survivors'[8] (Gotkin and Gotkin, 1975; Chamberlin, 1978), are most important to understanding forced treatment. Rather than using their lives as data for argumentation, this book begins from personal knowledge as most important to questions of coercion.

The use of such 'insider' knowledge in social or ethnographic research is a key to Dorothy Smith's *Institutional Ethnography* (2005; see also Campbell & Gregor, 2002). Smith's methodology inspired my own (a methodology is a theory of knowledge that underpins a set of methods for collecting data). Smith shows ethnographers how to link people's everyday experiences to 'practices of power' by state institutions, including psychiatry. This helps people reveal what she calls 'problematics' (kind of like puzzles or knots) that reveal society's 'relations of ruling.' Such problematics can be used to 'map' how ruling systems work. These maps help people resist 'extralocal' forces that impinge on their everyday experiences and struggles (Smith, 2005).

---

yet it serves as the basis for grand comparison and understanding within and across a society' (1988: ix).

6 Minkowitz (2006/07) and others provided evidence that convinced the U.N. Rapporteur on Torture to state that coercive treatment can be a form of torture that infringes on the rights of the mentally disabled.

7 Lawyer and therapist Elyn Saks (2003) received forced treatment and credited it for saving her life. She believes coercive interventions should only be imposed once, however. If a treatment doesn't work, the patient's objections should prevail. People who want forced treatment can have it arranged in legal provisions like 'advanced directives.'

8 Psychiatric survivors are people who have *survived* imposed biological psychiatric treatments and other institutional arrangements (see Chamberlin, 1978).

Our stories are important, but I am not interested in turning the ethnographic gaze directly onto survivors. Because subjects of Community Treatment Orders are in compromised positions under mandatory treatment, I decided to interview mental health workers instead. I asked ten workers about patients' experiences under CTOs. So this text brings several perspectives, among them the perspectives of patients and workers. I do not try to prove or disprove workers' perceptions; they are, indeed, consistent with hundreds of opinions made available to the Ontario government's Community Treatment Order review. Unlike the government's review, however, I quote mental health workers' perceptions at length to provide a deeper and broader analysis.

What kinds of stories were told? The government report says a woman who was put on a Community Treatment Order by her abusive husband felt she was in even greater danger than before. An advocate reported that a patient was made to take pregnancy tests periodically as part of her 'treatment plan.' One of my informants told me of a 90-year-old man who was put under orders to move him out of an institution that he had called home for decades. These are not the worst examples. There are positive accounts, too. Some patients choose treatment orders simply to get 'services' like housing. But I will suggest the surplus of negative stories indicates not just a psychiatric 'system' that is dysfunctional. It is a group of programs committed to care and control, a potential contradiction that goes unquestioned in practice. Practitioners do not often study psychological outcomes of psychiatric coercion, such as on treatment efficacy or recovery.

What is the basis of psychiatric coercion? I have asked this question in one form or another since being 'hospitalized' years ago. What I hid away under treatment, what I tried to pretend did not exist under constant monitoring, was a part of my life that was very important to me. That forbidden reality I call a Mad consciousness,[9] and without it I think we would have little reason to challenge forced treatment. We

---

9 I use the proper noun Mad, with others, to reframe the topic of forced treatment. I do not mean to say that madness exists as an essence, or to personify 'madness,' or to normalize what has been abnormalized, or to adopt Queer, Deaf, and autism community tactics without acknowledgment. Rather, I want to imagine 'mad' or 'ill' conceived experiences to be consciousness, at least in a very broad sense, and to acknowledge stories of our experiences as Mad people's historical consciousness. We may actually find importance, meaning, and knowing in our experiences, and we may reconsider disorientation, distress, and pain without the use of mental experts. I will return to Mad consciousness, identity, and subjectivization in the next chapter.

could only question the methods and outcomes of forced treatment on bodies that have lost consciousness. Without recognition of Mad people's realities, historically and interpersonally, we talk of suppressing symptoms while inadvertently oppressing 'mad' or 'ill' bodies in our midst. We never think of 'them' as people who remember what we do to them in a crisis. Authorities can 'improve' instruments and procedures of restraint, or usually just the rhetoric of treatment, but I will argue 'the seriously mentally ill' and specifically people who are 'actively psychotic' should not receive coercive treatment not only because of the dangers of present-day drug therapy (who knows what the future holds), but because our experiences can be important to us. We may not need a cure when our 'untreated' experiences can be meaningful (see Shimrat, 1997; Leibrich, 2001). This need not preclude public safety.

In this chapter I have introduced a complex set of subjects from violence risk to psychiatric survivor and Mad identity. This book cannot instruct the psychiatric system regarding care and control. It can only hint at colloquial or alternative practices in the concluding chapter. I would not blame individual workers who are trying, and surviving themselves. I am also not trying to incite people to become distressed or act violently; I think of 'madness' as quite sound. I am not against medicine or drugs on the whole. I like science and reason.

In the next chapter I will take up personal experiences, matters of restraint, and social discourses of madness. I will use a methodology called narrative inquiry (Conle, 1999) which provides a more personal means of exploring how Mad people are discriminated against through *sanism*.[10] In chapter 3, I explore how I dealt with forced treatment in my activism and as an advocacy worker at the 'Queen Street' institution here in Toronto. Afterwards I review the literatures on 'mentally ill violence' and psychiatric restraint. This sets the stage for workers' perceptions of CTOs in chapter 4, prefaced by a recollection

---

10 'Sanism' was coined by Mortin Birnbaum, an activist lawyer of the 1960s, in conversations with Florynce Kennedy, a notable African-American feminist lawyer (Birnbaum, 2010). The term was popularized by Michael Perlin (2000) and others and means prejudgment or prejudice against mentally ill people. But as I regard mental illness and madness to be concepts that are discriminatory in themselves, constructing difference and distress as problems or diseases of thought, I use sanism to mean the very construction of difference as 'madness,' and the dividing of minds and bodies into mad and sound. Sanism is a form of oppression that construes delusion as the root cause of distress and danger, and thus allows for institutional theories of madness and ultimately punitive arrangements like CTOs.

of my methodological choices. Local mental health workers' perceptions will be briefly compared with the government review and the
professional literature in regard to compulsory psychiatric treatment.
Readers who want to read about CTOs specifically should skip to
chapters 4 and 8.

In the following chapters, I broaden this interpretive inquiry to
Western historical and Canadian juridical decisions regarding forced
treatment (chapter 5). I review the pharmacological action and medical
application of neurological restraint using antipsychotic drugs and people's related experiences, including my own (chapter 6). This provides
for my argument that toxic chemicals restrain by fatiguing the body
generally, but also specifically targeting numerous brain functions.
Over months, such chemical restraint should be considered a form of
detention, not a compulsory 'treatment.' This practice initiates a process
of institutionalization and dependency that can be compared and con-
trasted with that of Erving Goffman's time, half a century ago (chapter 7).
People on the ground reveal how chemical incarceration and institutionalization are implemented in educational, correctional, and other
institutions, and are differently applied according to categories of class,
gender, sexuality, race, ability, legal status, and age (chapter 8). This
provides for a conclusion not only regarding the destructiveness and
uselessness of forced treatment, but the need for new ways of regarding
and responding to distress and difference (chapter 9).

In summary, my book explores how talk of treatment obscures the
use of restraint in care. In the case of Community Treatment Orders in
Ontario, excessive practices of restraint and a culture of control are well
documented legally, clinically, and in everyday experience. Such 'treatment modalities' as CTOs are imposed on people who have broken no rule
except to be considered 'mad.' 'Orders' to accept medication constitute
a long-term restraint, or chemical incarceration, at least when applied
for their stated purposes. Chemical incarceration can break bodies and
minds to suppress potential danger, inconvenience, or disability. It
should be abandoned by taxpayers, governments, and clinicians as
excessive and abusive.

I will also deal with several major opposing arguments to such ideas:
the apparent lack of alternatives available to clinicians, the touted
'safety and effectiveness' of drugs, the problem of 'psychotic' violence
and dangerous behaviour, and some patients wanting to take drugs or
accepting them by force in emergencies. Again, it is beyond the purpose of this book to tell clinicians or patients what they should do to

control symptoms, collaborate in treatment, invent new ways to interact, or prevent dangerousness – however they define it. But the issues
raised in this book, by a former patient, are meant to inform discussions
by clinical and social researchers, mental health practitioners, lawyers,
lawmakers, therapists, counselors, educators, and the public.

2 Mad

Living unlikely moments, impossible sides.

New selves, again. I changed my mind, many times before. I came back.

But now, there is a chance. Maybe the escape is here.

Or here. I am ready.

So far from home, a question, lines round the world. No friend laughs and enters this strange life. No knowing smiles across the counters of exchange: money is love. Not even smirks, no disapproval, like in the Burnaby Mall. I asked them if they knew who built this place. Too much that was, a simple question. A complex face.

Now my life is being decided for me as I wait.

I was recalled to the bakery in haste. The baker man with white flour hands told me to stand outside. Away from the customers, lest they see, I wait in the snow. Is that a point there? No points. Not yet.

His pity is stern, waiting, cautious. He's not listening or asking questions. I'm a wreck to him. I watch his watchfulness. I have no time to respond. I simply cannot insist, 'I'm still in this body here.'

How do I explain myself? 'It's only me. There is no confusion.'

There is no way to explain. I need to dance.

So I spin.

My arms are out.

They must think I'm ... crazy. I just need to make a small bridge and ... maybe.

An ambulance attendant steps up. He approaches warily. I do not look at him. I am trying to receive my intuitions.

He stands next to me, not facing me, as if a friend. I look at his insignias, his symbols, harkening back to secret orders. St John of the Cross. Europa. Ganymede.

He asks whether I will come with him or with the police. He has spoken. And the world is all broken.

All my thoughts work through his statement.

I rationalize my declaration: there's no time this time. Social demands. Maybe his priests will help me understand.

There. I accept. I said it, 'Yes.' I am escorted into his white van, a striking blue 'star of life.' The window.

I stare at it. Is it real? Memory washes over me.

We drive. No siren to scare the patient. This would all be so humiliating if it weren't happening in so many dimensions. The ambulance man sings softly all of a sudden. A nursery rhyme; I keep my eyes off him to prevent misunderstandings. No anger, no fear.

Next, I am escorted into an emergency ward in a wheelchair. I obligingly put on a light blue gown. I am escorted to the back. Room 6. I sit. I wait again. What's next? I imagine they will run tests, ask me to tell my story. They will probably say, 'Schizophrenic.' All these years of evasion. Finally my problems will be laid out, positively assessed with modern science instruments.

Was it inevitable? My mother was caught. Like her, I started to change, sensing life, all-around like-it-is. My senses interconnected. My mind liquid. My body awake. Symbols are objects. Objects are lives, to breathe and hold dearly.

But this change, this chance at meaning, in the cracks and lines, is just logical error to the ambulance man. Random decision making. Excitation. Distractedness. (Chemical imbalance. Neuronal dysfunction. Mental disorder. Genetic predisposition. Biopsychosocial disability.) My transformation belies a danger, to myself, to others, and their property. My mutability denies what is real.

Yet I have been through this before. It has never led to danger. I wanted to be here. This is a real place. We can come and leave. We can approach and go.

Who would agree with me in this new ocean city, all alone? This darkened corridor in the back of emerg is my whole life now.

After what seems like twenty minutes, I come out of my room to ask if anyone will see me. I call softly, 'Is anyone there?' It seems quiet. I take a few steps forward. Shadows shift behind plants and counters, like a world being shuffled.

A second later I am surrounded by waving arms and bodies, pressing in on me without touch.

Six males of different sizes, aggressively hunched. Yelling!

'Get back in the room, please! Get back in the room!' Their voices rise. My hands go open.

I try to reassure, 'Okay, okay.' Surrender. They holler and walk me back to the room.

Room '6,' I notice the numbers again. Like the Mall, the sixth gate. I hesitate over the threshold and enter in three steps. Right over the line, left and withdraw, right for . . . this.

I have kissed off the past. An uncertain future comes. Call it magic but the word is not enough. Call it childish but I know I'm twenty-four. I will remember this.

The room is just large enough for a gurney. I am positioned into a flat, prone position. They roughly bind my arms to the metal railings using leather straps. My right wrist is strapped above my head, the left wrist to my side.

Where have I seen this pose before? But I am in it. I try to tell them I have been in such a situation before, when I was seven. They are busy working on me. There is no time for bedside manner. A nurse approaches on my left. I try to say something but she just stabs a large needle into my left thigh, deeply. She injects a fierce, burning pain.

I wince and lie still. I'm quiet like a trapped thing. She swabs the pricked wound with alcohol. The orderlies drop their hands and leave like someone called them away suddenly. I am barely breathing from fear. I lie as still as I can, anything to prevent more. The nurse finally goes, too.

Alone. I begin to shiver with cold. The drug takes effect. I'm drowsy. A moment passes, maybe two. Hard to tell now.

My partner suddenly walks in, a look of horror.

I complain softly, 'Look at what they're doing to me. I'm an animal.'

'Listen!' she exclaims in a whisper, 'Whatever they ask you, say no!'

A white-smocked pretty woman enters, her blonde hair pulled back tightly. She wears small wire-rimmed glasses. She allows my partner to attend. She speaks the words on the clipboard, her ten questions.

'Have you been depressed recently?' she asks. The question is not judgmental, it is not emotional, or consoling; it is clinical.

'No.' I respond, like my tonsils are being checked.

'Have you had strange thoughts?'

'No.' I am glad to be saying that, playing through the exercise as instructed. I do not say about the ravens, or the feeling of wings on my face, or knowing when the lights will change. I do not say about running on empty for miles just to choke nine metres from the gas station.

I do not say about Death in the delivery van, or in the news. I do not say about the numbers, how they were happening and I was noticing.

A few more questions and consciousness breaks. I fall into a dreamless sleep before she finishes. Fourteen hours later? I'm awoken by noise. The snoring of older men in a dark room makes me start.

My throat is parched by hours of what they will call 'dry mouth.'

Trolleys rattle above us in a kind of distance, echoing. Thankfully, I see some light, the door.

I walk out of the room after some time has passed, shivering and thirsty. I poke my head around the corner and there is a large counter, almost as tall as me. I approach and notice a woman behind it, a nurse, I gather.

'Can I have some water please?' I ask, straining from fatigue: be polite. The nurse produces a 250 mL cup of grapefruit juice like a matter of fact. I am startled at the smallness of it. I drink it easily and ask for another. She seems frustrated, but I receive a second cup. I stop while I'm ahead.

I notice no one is talking. Some are sitting. Some are standing. Like a set piece. Some are eating. Some are slouched in abandon, lethargic. Some are pacing in slow motion but with quivering hands.

A few hours later, it seems, I ask the big question. 'Um ... can I just ask ... what should I do if I want to ... leave?' The nurse smirks with eyebrows perked up. 'Oh this one is smart!' she says to her friend, half-sarcastic, half-interested. Minutes seem like hours, hours like days, and my body feels like sleep without the rest. My mind is slow without the peace.

A common story. Carola Conle (1999) says that stories have the potential to cross many divides, if respected and shared mutually. She used to ask us not to freeze the story with analysis or argumentation. Instead, we can let stories teach us, such as by asking what happened in some small part of the story, or what happened next (not by asking what does the story mean). Analysis is useful, but stories can provide us with a living framework, a way of connecting ideas and people without relying on technical or analytical procedures.

By using personal narrative, I wish to provide some background for my argument. Argument can seem meaningless without context. I do not use narrative for or against analysis or science. This book can be read as narrative and as argument; however, I think it is also a kind of soliloquy. It serves a different function than to prove or show. As soliloquy, it functions like testimony, for whoever is listening, and for others with similar experiences.

In part, my intention is to show how mad or labelled folk are, indeed, present of mind, though perhaps less able to act when treated as different or as gaps in consciousness. Notice that this narrative of 'madness,' which can be read as 'sound' or 'mad' depending on how much empathy you have for the story, does not represent the crucial 'gap' in thought here. Rather the drugging event is making a gap, is intervening in the 'madness' story which is usually taken as the gap. By rendering madness as unconsciousness, the clinician tries to rule the gap or the divide that separates us.

In this chapter I am using a personalized form of narrative inquiry to present this 'gap.' I needed a self-reflexive methodology to uncover questions about consciousness that underpin psychiatric intervention. This was not a way to suspend argumentation, but to bring into relief certain limiting structures in talk of madness. Linguistic and social structures or limits bring legal and medical arrangements.

Narrative self-inquiry is also a way of getting to know another person. There is in many stories a key concern that gets people talking, and the rest of this chapter is an attempt to find that key concern, using more stories. But beware, some of it may seem murky at times; for those who want to get to the point, the next chapter, and the next, will help. To find a central theme or key I invoke narratives already given by existing explanatory models. In this chapter some madness discourse models are quickly described for a rearticulation of the story of drugging.

Another way of reading this chapter is to see *sanism* examined as a primary rationale for imposing treatments. This is broken down into sections: first a biopsychiatric explanation, then a physio-psychological, and then a philosophical-discursive move, and finally my own version of wearing sanism inside out in a concluding story of self. This chain of descriptions of sanism informs a Mad consciousness especially regarding the subject of restraint. It relates basic principles of sanism to what comes next in the book, such as regards restraints and violence described in professional and clinical discourse.

This is but one analysis possible. For the rest of this book, while I will continue to submit how I define my terms and set out argumentation, I also move through many kinds of data. As a generalist it is not my intention to provide exceptional detail in each of the questions revealed in this research. The purpose of this book is to provide an academic rendering of general issues relating to experiences of drugging. But it is not represented here as a strict design or a plan, such as to master a terrain of 'the drugging experience.' Instead, the narrative is allowed to resurface and even direct the course of inquiry.

A research question: what hit me? I ask because I want, even need, to know. What happened? How did it happen? Why?

Answer 1: Don't ask. Do. Explanation is useless.

End of story. See you at the market. Of course, you realize the market, sports, politics, all of our doings communicate as stories.

If you're wondering what happened next, I wanted to know what happened to me. I got out of the hospital after a month, thanks to my brother's careful negotiation with my doctor. I got out of drug treatment in about six months with the permission of another doctor. I only did this with the courage of others in the psychiatric survivor movement in Toronto, because while friends were supportive they could not have known what standard medical care was doing to me. I got into activism and advocacy for mental patient rights within a year (see my former employer online: the Queen Street Outreach Society, defunded in 2001, at www.qsos.ca).

The story goes on and it can be affixed to the stories of others, as well as to various literatures, from narrative research like that of Conle (1999) and Church (1996), to textbooks about psychiatric diagnoses (American Psychiatric Association, 1994), which are enacted or avoided quite differently by various workers in the 'mental health field' (Johnstone, 1989). Some workers have been on the receiving end of 'care,' like psychologist Rufus May (www.rufusmay.com), and medical doctor Tamarin Knight, who wrote *Beyond Belief* (2009), a book about not trying to correct beliefs and beginning from relating. Dan Fisher (2003) is a patient who became a psychiatrist. There is no 'us and them' in the simple sense, but attitudes, practices, and structures of control continue to operate to marginalize mad-conceived people.

The most personal part of my story, my beliefs while I was 'mad,' is the part that people would dismiss out of hand. My conservative side says that to put my story up like this invites trouble. Indeed, our stories have been used before, co-opted into the therapeutic touch. Our stories are often part of case files; excerpts may be taken to explain confusion in psychological terms, in philosophical terms. The 'system' needs to utilize madness stories to make its machinations more amenable to the human heart. But only pieces of this story will ever fit on the chassis of therapeutic justice.

My story is in pieces anyway, and will only be absorbed in pieces. The 'crazy quilt' of understanding can be reassembled again and again. It is not a final truth that anyone should accept at face value. It is not even an exacting linear critique of truths pretended by clinicians. There are many classical critiques (e.g., Conolly, 1856; Barton, 1959; Bateson & Ruesch, 1951; Szasz, 1960; Laing, 1961; Goffman, 1961; Foucault, [1961] 1965; Scheff, 1967; Basaglia, 1968; Chesler, 1972). Some of them even tell of patients' protests (Bateson, 1974). There are newer critiques, like Bentall's (2003) and Whitaker's (2001, 2010) that use medical and other standards effectively to dismantle psychiatric 'argumentation.'

It seems no explanation will change the system, perhaps because of an inherent economic imbalance (McCubbin, 1998). Sanism seems a good explanation for this imbalance, though as an explanation it will hardly change anything in itself. Perhaps this is the problem with explanation in the social world. The social is so complex, so changing, that explanation gets tumbled into what is being explained by others. So if explanation doesn't work, think of this text as a story of living, whatever our respective personal and mutual truths. It need not dictate what you think, and it cannot decide what you or I should do in any situation. As a story it simply tries to make an experience understandable. As such, it works at the level of art as well as explanation (Denzin & Lincoln, 1994; Conle, 1999; Abbott, 2007).

The question, 'What hit me?' has several answers.

Answer 2: Mental Illness

The story of 'mental illness' is quite popular as an explanation. I've heard it hundreds of times in many ways. It sometimes begins from evolutionary and developmental evidence. It often ends with lifelong impairment and sometimes with horrifying accidental death. The story could be shortened to the following.

Within the natural[1] cosmos grew animals that evolved into thinking people. People's bodily differences made some of them better suited to the environment, especially by thinking together in savvy groups. Weak

---

1 My story, and this book, is written in the naturalistic style. Nature is privileged as origin. This is not to ignore the centrality of language, and story, in understanding nature.

bodies with weak thinking organs and traits could not relate as well as others, and they did not survive as readily. Their brains failed to use electrochemical signals properly, and these chemical lines, or sequences in thought connection, are assumed to be broken when a person cannot communicate clearly. Twentieth-century storytellers helped us understand people we once called 'mad' to be 'mentally ill,' as follows.

The brain sometimes unfortunately receives and assembles environmental data incorrectly, laying the groundwork for 'delusion.' A self-correcting person recognizes data as inconsistent and asks for help. This perceptual and conceptual dysfunction mounts over time if a person does not maintain healthy habits. Eventually the brain is overwhelmed, perhaps by the impossibility of holding inconsistent positions, or by an environmental 'trigger' event. A crisis results. An implosion in reasoning results in outbursts. The person cannot understand why she is thinking incorrectly (or what others are saying, what seems to be happening). Or worse: the person assumes her thinking is quite correct and others are wrong. This 'psychotic' brain relates to its environment erratically using fantasies, images, myths, and memories. Some people call psychosis the waking dream, because the person is living as if the world is created by zer, them, him or her, and not the other way around.

Even the early theorists like Kraepelin, Bleuler, and others (if you're looking for Freud, he worked with 'neuroses' exclusively, hardly touched the 'psychoses'), knew that disorganized thinking would look different for each mentally ill person, and for persons with different social backgrounds (Bentall, 2003). But they thought the cause must be the same for everyone in the worst cases, given the similarities. They theorized madness as a lack of something – for example, biological constitution, regular health, rationality – and they worked to eradicate mental illness using scientifically valid treatments.

As an aside, to conceive of an opposite kind of world: imagine a social background in which 'fantasy' or 'dream' thinking is kind of normal for that world; there might be no interest in making communication or the environment conform to ideas of continuity in communicating. This does not preclude reasoning on anyone's part. People like me might seem less strange or awful. We might be allowed to take care of ourselves generally, and in emergencies be helped by intermediaries who know and respect us, but more importantly, we would not be seen as problems to be solved. This fantasy is not realized by psychiatrists, though they might say it is. Conversely, I would hardly fit into a dream-accepting society elsewhere (or in some imagined prehistory) because like others in the West, I am expected to discern fantasy from reality. But this other society in which fantasy does not close communication lines, in the brain, mind, or social situation, might not require such a division.

In any case, my own story above picks up in the 1990s. My incarceration happened after neurological disorders were quite well named and organized in the *Diagnostic and Statistical Manual of Mental Disorders*, which is the American Psychiatric Association's guide to 'mental problems' (*DSM IV-TR*, 2000; the *DSM-5* is in development as I write). After I was noticed to be living in a fantasy world, I was asked to provide 'self-reports' and was given psychological tests. Based on these, I received the diagnosis 'Psychosis, N.O.S.' or 'Not Otherwise Specified,' a catch-all category. They were still trying to figure me out, it seemed. Two weeks later they said in effect they had.

'Do you remember?' my psychiatrist calmly asked me. 'We met last week and you told me you were a little down because of the rain?'

'Yeah, it always rains here.' The ocean city had other charms.

'Well, that means you're not schizophrenic. Because you do exhibit affect, which is feelings, your psychotic symptoms[2] are a result of bipolar affective disorder. There are few depressive symptoms in your case.' He proceeded to explain that this illness is still mysterious, but that it is probably caused by neurons sucking up dopamine at the wrong rate, and that I am genetically predisposed to this dysregulation. It is passed down in families with the disorder. How did he know? I wondered.

He explained that with medication, I could suppress the symptoms (today, psychiatrists often call this 'recovery,' though this word was first adopted by survivors in the late 1980s to dispel psychiatric ideation that 'psychotics' are unsalvageable; see Deegan, 1988; Ahern & Fisher, 2001). There is much more anecdotal evidence now that supports untreated 'recovery,' including my own life story, for even the most 'severe and chronic cases' (people). I was already groggy on my loxapine (a newer 'antipsychotic' in 1993), and I didn't much like the prognosis. As much as I tried to make an appointment with a social worker and 'carry on,' the doctor suggested I stay put.

I wanted proof, perhaps a brain scan, or an electroencephalogram (EEG). They had ruled out physical problems like Lyme's disease from blood tests, I presume (I shouldn't). I wasn't really depressed though,

---

2 Examples: hallucination, delusion, thought disorder, 'pressured' or rapid speech.

hadn't been in five years, so I thought this was 'schizoaffective disorder,' a blend of schizophrenia and mood disorder? But bipolar Type I
allows for mostly 'manic' psychotic symptoms. I wondered about something. What if I had just conjured up my 'psychosis'?[3] What about my
wanting to 'go mad' as an adolescent? Did that not make this a kind of
neurosis (e.g., 'schizotypal personality disorder'? Minor hallucinations
are excluded in that diagnosis). In any case, wanting to go mad can be
explained as part of madness before 'florid symptoms' appear. So, if my
story can be reduced to a mental illness story, the exact type would be
'bipolar' (Bentall thoroughly interrogates and I think disposes of this
taxonomy in *Madness Explained,* 2003).

But this story has contradictions. The exact physiological 'markers'
for distressed mental states have not (yet?) been found (Valenstein,
1998; Greenman, 2004). These states seem dependent on social interpretation, that is, 'madness'/'illness' is socially defined, mediated, or
constructed, as sociologists would say,[4] and not reducible to particular brain functions observed in functional magnetic resonance imaging
(MRI) brain process scans, or brain shapes seen in MRI scans; Grace
Jackson (2005) interrogates this evidence.[5] This does not preclude biology, but qualifies it. As many now know, the brain tends to heal itself,
though this is not an excuse to do nothing.

Imagine advanced computational neuroscience revealing 'neuronal
assemblies' (Dobbs, 2006) that occur always in relation to 'psychosis,'
which can be 'genetically' caused or induced by drugs, injury, or various
other brain changes that we can only theorize at this time.[6] The scans
would show the physiological side of the phenomenon, but is the brain
somehow causing this 'correlate' behaviour? Causation demands splitting the body into a Cartesian body-mind. Perhaps we could blame all
mental (and by extension social) crises or conflicts on nature's mistakes,

---

3 'Psychosis,' in the medical literature, is marked by delusions and sometimes involves
   hallucinations or thought disorder. It is said to be caused by 'major mental disorders'
   such as 'schizophrenia' and 'bipolar affective disorders' but can also arise from other
   illnesses, brain trauma, psychoactive drug use, sleep deprivation, or torture (Waring,
   1987; Lee & Shlain, 1985).

4 See Pilgrim and Rogers (2005) on the lack of commensurability between sociology
   and psychiatry.

5 Brain-reading technology can, e.g., decode consonants and vowels in silent speech
   (Singer, 2009).

6 Perhaps we could look to quantum consciousness processes; see Pestana (2001) and
   Jibu (1997).

consider them mechanical errors, but not in a fantasy-accepting society I think. My point is that mental illness is not a simple fact but a social idea; it depends on diagnosticians' notions of behavioural exceptionality, biopsychological causality, as well as individualism and disability.

To conclude the mental illness tale: it is all in the brain, even if the brain is triggered. In other words it's something that's bound to happen to bodies like mine because of a genetic predisposition (a shape of the brain, a flow of a chemical, the harmonization of certain brainwaves, and so on). This story is supposed to nurture me, help me avoid the implications of moral madness, and perhaps give me hope that one day it will all go away, thanks to technology. Yet it makes managing my illness not unlike managing my spoiled identity, as Goffman would have said. The story continues. I still don't know what hit me.

Answer 3: Psychological Trauma

I am not a psychologist or psychoanalyst (these professionals are not authorized to prescribe medications like psychiatrists and general medical practitioners, though often psychiatrists have been psychoanalytically trained or informed), but I am somewhat informed about my own self. I am a slouch when it comes to Freudian, Lacanian, Kleinian, Kristevian, and other theories of subjectivity (I took a course on Jung and once took a half-course in social psychology). I have not followed Laing or other 'radical' theorists, though their ideas certainly trickle down to us, and yet came from sometime before them. I am rather proud of my non-psychological knowledge.

I will not try to dispel any conceptualizations of mind, psyche, or unconscious that are said to motivate people's actions – see critical psychologists like James Hillman and Michael Ventura (1992) or Ian Parker and Erica Burman, for deconstructions of therapeutic device – just as earlier I could not statistically marshal arguments against neurologists, behaviouralists, and psychiatrists who designate the 'corpus' or 'central nervous system' as their prime mover. My point is that if there are processes *behind* behavioural-social processes, they must be either quite simple or greatly unknowable in their complexity from the inside of human living.

First, there is a paradox created by saying that our interpersonally interpreted actions, which we read or understand through social standards like moral codes and rules of the road, are caused by something mysterious (perhaps something mysteriously mechanical). We are then somewhat bound by those initial descriptions of behaviour. The mysterious is the unknown and we might just as well 'perceive' the mysterious by interpretation (i.e., not 'positive' science), yet the mysterious becomes 'known' in theories of madness. Instead of applying positive science to or from existing interpretations of behaviour, we might reinterpret interpretations, including positive scientific observations regarding behaviour. In other words, the mechanical brain is somewhat known to us, in emerging brain sciences, but it too is interpretable and analysable as subject, as story. It is a part of the way we 'are,' just like diet and exercise make us up, and drugs.[7] We moralize through mechanics. Our interpretations of decisions and actions are not swept away by such mysteries or mystifications as the brain being the seat of judgment; our 'stigma' is not busted by medicine or science.

Psychosocial science that uses quantitative explorations of the psyche without a sense of how stories emerge in interpersonal and societal contexts may say that the mysterious will be revealed in the facts. The discernible body, readable according to patterns, is sometimes enumerated in statistical research using data streamed according to code, theme, or ideas (including themes that are not total or stable). These are 'correlated' to 'behaviours,' our anticipated intentions and actions. But the psychic archetypes of behaviour are not the prior facts that drive bodies, behaviours, and our decisions in every or many respects. Brain growth can certainly be influenced by thought, as neuroplasticity shows (see Libet, Freeman, & Sutherland, 1999). But prior thoughts (perceptions, emotions, conceptions) that influence later thoughts are conceivable as a mediation or cause of mental disorder when they are in logical error (Sass, 1994). As such, narrative is how we mediate 'madness.'[8] Interpretation of distress is most important to how collectives manage policy on madness.

---

7 How do we attribute certain behaviours to drugs, like 'suicidality' in the case of seratonin blockers, yet not to pre-existing mental or brain states? While pre-drugged exceptionalities in mood and behaviour might be attributed to 'natural' disarray, they can be induced 'artificially' and ramped up beyond usual behaviours with drugs or other methods. This observation does not commit us to 'correcting' minor exceptionalities, nor to believe that drug-conditioned behaviours would have appeared regardless of drugs, toxicity, and related issues.

8 I do not mean to suggest that narrative is the only way to find understanding; see Abbott (2007) or, conversely, King (1993). 'Madness' is a narrative, as experienced by us, and/or as imposed on us by others.

While my narrative could be reduced to a psychological cause, an unconscious dilemma, based on trauma perhaps, abuse, oppression, ill logic, or bad memory, I can still rewrite that memory to invert the process (as 'narrative therapy' is said to do) of the stare of the psychiatrist.

In my life, I have not been openly 'psychotic' since those days in the early 1990s, and again have not gone back on meds since, though yes I will use other substances to quell moods sometimes (nothing as powerful). Need I say choice, not drugs, is the important matter in imagining 'therapeutic value' and the reconciliation of conflicts? As for my 'recovery,' did I truly unseat my illness or trauma? Why not call that a mere change of mind? Trauma theory seems to explain our problems as injury or maladapted habits ('defences'), but this seems to reinforce the 'broken' image of our experience. Why is the broken image the given reality? It is not that our experience holds together despite abuse or oppression often, or that distress is the true social appearance of hurt. Brokenness is also the experience of injustice, a social issue.

Like any other theory of (dys)function, psychological theory such as 'trauma' seeks a prior cause to something exceptional (which might actually be quite ordinary). Experience binds to many kinds of appearances, and distress too can attach to anything. (If we can change our brains, how does that inform our understanding of social injury?) This is not to say that we command appearances or that our performances are unreal or premeditated. We are in a complex set of relations in which appearances cannot be mechanically explained in terms of injury alone. When psychology skirts causality, like in Jung's 'synchronicity,' psychology attempts and perhaps achieves by its own standards a magical conjunction with storytellers who work beyond explanation. I cannot understand its therapeutic and mystical claims together, but perhaps this is worthy of inquiry.

While I might accept that my narrative was the likely outcome of my immigrant experiences, or the anxiety of not knowing English, or my mother's 'mental illness,' or a fixation on some maternal lack, or a neglected childhood leading to bad programming, these explanations suffer a kind of morose philosophical fixation on causality and exceptionality (both are focused primarily on a particularity in my experiences that could be interpreted in many ways). They seem to seek a final resolution to technical problems: how do people go 'mad' and how can we stop it? These purposes ignore the social possibilities, the societal responsibilities, of personal interaction alone, and relate our experiences as tools in therapeutic and clinical methodologies. These relations

generate financial arrangements, make for false curative pronouncements, and reify universalizing and proscriptive power relations.

But political and interpersonal communication cannot solve human
conflict lone either. The question runs deeper. What hit me?

Answer 4: Ø

As if this couldn't get deeper. Psychological symbols become structural
or philosophical symbols. If the search for cause runs into questions
about what we are defining as 'different' or 'distressed,' perhaps there
is simply a limit to human understanding. Stories may end up in how
words are defined, or how they drop off into silences of voice, or
voids.

A lack of meaning is, in fact, what madness represents to many
people, so we are at a strange intersection in theory between logic and
chaos. What lies beyond order is unknown (but can be known), and
what lies beyond thought is unknowable, void. From a pragmatic point
of view, madness is nothing to think about at all because it is what we
label as beyond knowing or understanding. Yet if madness represents
nothing(ness), why do we try so hard to erase it from our minds? Why
do biological psychiatry, psychology, and psychoanalysis see psychosis
as absence of some kind, or an unconscious process, and seek to annihi-
late it? Biological psychiatric ideas were not validated in the laboratory
during the nineteenth and twentieth centuries. They grew from stock
conceptions and became philosophical, technical, and bureaucratic
grounds for therapeutic procedure.

Madness discourse offers many themes, from ridiculous to divine,
but the themes of absence and indeterminacy seem most characteristic and reductive. The expression 'losing one's mind' invokes loss or
absence. To describe madness we have terms for presences no longer
there, or potentially there but not 'real.' Reality is both perceived and
perceivable by others, by commonsense definers. Peel back the nuances
in description, the rules of sentence structure, to a structural motif of
presence and identity to be found in formal logic. Follow logic and the
question of being to logic's a priori beginnings, as philosopher Alain
Badiou does, and we find a powerful ontology about what counts
as being.[9] Badiou uses mathematical (set) theory to show that what

---

9 Ontology is theory on being and existence. Badiou's work (2006) tries to link French
   philosophy with quantitative-analytical work found in Anglo-American philosophy.

conditions presence is absence: 'being' depends on marking out what cannot be: 'The void of a situation is the suture to its being' (2006: 526). Extending this theory, rational social decisions depend on some bodies being marked as 'not all there,' 'lost,' or 'mad.'

The 'mad' body is often conveyed as not understandable, as lacking in cognitive capacity, as not socially present. The issue of understand- ability was grafted from phenomenology by psychiatrist Karl Jaspers in the early twentieth century, and certainly informs theory still. Presence of mind is regarded as the base of decision-making power. It is through the marking of a person as not-there that others who count, who mat- ter, are socially defined. It is through defining the 'mad' person as not- conscious, as in-a-world-of-her-own, that the group affirms centric consciousness. This group mode does not have to be sanist, necessar- ily. Historian Roy Porter quotes Restoration playwright Nathaniel Lee: 'They called me mad, and I called them mad, and damn them, they outvoted me' (2002: 88).

If being can be described by the presence of at least one thing or per- son or idea, non-being can be described as a kind of absence. Consider the tropes or literary themes given to us in simple figures. The figure 0 has zero, nil, or null value. The figure ? leaves explanation to contingency, or indeterminacy, or chaos, or some yet-unknown value. And paradox is another rhetorical figure in madness discourse, conveyed by the fig- ure of the empty set in mathematics, or ø ({}).[10] In the United Kingdom, something is 'at sixes and sevens' when one value system is incommen- surate with another. What counts in Western social space is value. A zero or unknown or empty or confused value marks out what is 'not' social. It, the mindless body, marks a void in social space to be filled or used. A body-mind that does not perform, that cannot represent itself in the language, lacks the order or value to be present and will be exempted from communication and decision making. Moreover, while its slippage could easily be seen as freedom from order, order is imposed anyway, by 'sound' or right-thinking people with more value.

But though some clinicians talk about patients in the room as if they were not there, the body-as-person is still present somehow. In memory or an uncertain future, that body could make sense differently. The idea that a person is void or lost denies her being. The idea of 'madness' as absence of mind denies our already existing social location, connection,

---

10 An empty set exists yet has no elements, like the set of octagons with nine sides, or hypodermic needles that are not hollow (actually the latter is possible).

and language. So 'mad' is reduced to non-being and filled up with something like stillness and awaiting, in the body-brain automaton of modern medical intervention.

Again, the philosophical, which I have barely touched on here, leads back to social questions for me. What hit me?

Answer 5: Madness Discourse as Sanism

The word 'madness' unlocks my story like a key, or locks it up like a safe. It readies the story for interpretations that would dismiss my pretence, agency, and will. Without 'madness,' the story could read like most other coming-of-age tales.

So what does the word mean? Madness discourse (or communication) generally insists on 'madness' as abnormality. To distinguish something, or someone, as 'mad' implies that someone or something fell from a socially graced or normal state. The more we talk about 'madness,' the more we reinforce an idea of normalcy. Yet people rarely express surprise at finding something normal (it's an unfindable ideal as disability activists say): 'He was so normal, I just couldn't believe!' Instead we fall over ourselves laughing, screaming, or crying when we identify 'madness.' 'She was like psycho!' 'Dude, that shit is nuts!' 'I'm so crazy in love!'

Madness discourse, then, is a kind of modifying discourse that says something is not normal. It is beyond the limits of the known or predictable: 'extreme' or 'different' in some way. This is ironic when there is no simple 'known' normalcy. Indeed, madness discourse rarely refers to 'the mentally ill' directly or specifically anymore, especially as a result of the ascendancy of the medical nomenclature. Abnormality can be attacked without fear of insulting the mentally disordered: they/we are abnormal and don't even guess it! Even if sanism insults us all, no one expects people in mental health facilities to start committees to correct people on their use of the word 'mad' or 'crazy' (the mental health charities are supposed to do that). The 'mad' can't speak for themselves is the standard rebuttal. The 'recovered' are no longer mad and therefore can't speak of 'madness' any more than others can. While this paradox seems to bar 'mad' people from our own experience and polity or relations, Mad people might redirect the problem with the old chestnut, though still applicable, 'What is mad?'[11]

---

11 Anatoly Liberman (2007) provides an etymology of the word 'mad' that runs back through German and Gothic (words meaning 'adulterate, exchange, gift, folly') to Latin (*mutare*, meaning 'to change'). The word 'crazy' comes from pottery's 'crazing

I would like to interrogate the word 'mad' a bit, without deferring to the progressive literature. I want to have some distance from madness discourse, nice and nasty, in order to assay it, only because I'm tired of hearing the word and rolling my eyes. As others have commented, the usage is so ubiquitous as to lose all meaning, which echoes its definition as 'lacking meaning' (whereupon endless regress begins).

If we consider how the word 'mad' is used in everyday conversation, we find it usually alludes to ideas well outside the psychiatric or psychological categories, a kind of arcana of strangeness. Discourses of madness as void or as indeterminate lead to all kinds of uses in social situations.

When we move closer to interpersonal talk, themes of void and chaos can be applied to people (us) as if they (we) embodied them. These varied utterances can be separated out into discourses or themes. For example: madness-as-lack ('she just lost it,' 'totally gone,' 'not there'); confusion ('makes me dizzy,' 'spinning,' 'all over the place'); incoherence ('can't understand a word he's saying'); absurdity ('over the top,' 'wack-a-doo,' 'cracker-jack'); suffering ('not just sad, clinically depressed'); nature ('just freakin' wild,' 'crazy like a fox'); illness ('sick in the head'); degeneration ('nineteenth nervous breakdown'); injury ('they're broken,' 'fucked up'); death ('zombielike,' 'psycho killer'); loss ('couldn't cope with him leaving'); love ('crazy for you'); mystical ('crazy coincidence,' 'crazy truth'); exceptionality ('mad skillz'); creativity ('crazy artist up all night'); spiritual ('street preacher,' 'crazy energy'); emotion ('hysterical,' 'crying our eyes out'); biology ('raging hormones,' 'clinical depression'); cool ('cra-zy guitarist, man'); busy ('crazy with people in there'); otherworldliness ('living in a different world'); stupidity ('numb nuts' and often mental (psychiatric and intellectual) disabilities are spoken of as interchangeable); disorientation ('out of control'); imbalance ('not quite right,' 'off-kilter'); incapacity ('he's unable to drive in that condition'); failure ('couldn't hold herself together,' 'went crazy in the end'); immaturity ('started barking at the dogs'); sales ('crazy crazy crazy march midnight madness blowout'); human condition ('we're all a bit nutters'); risk ('don't go off half-cocked'); violence ('out of nowhere,' 'holding it all in till he burst,' 'gone berserk'); excitement ('crazy times'); and the list goes on. We use the

---

of the glaze,' meaning crackling, from a Scandinavian word meaning 'break.' However, Liberman is careful to point out that meanings are not simply transferred, and 'crazy designs in the history of words are the rule rather than an exception.'

word 'crazy' as a substitute for any number of ideas, suggesting that the word is becoming a placeholder like 'like,' or a modifier like 'very' in early twenty-first-century English.

From a psychiatric survivor perspective, emotional acts are often attached to madness: excitability-as-madness ('did you see him jumping on the couch?'); sadness-as-madness ('they cried like a banshee'); badness-as-madness ('psycho!' 'he was a zombie').

All this is to say that madness discourse plays a social function. It insists on certain norms. It tacitly identifies actions, ideas, and people who fall outside those norms. Yet it also tries to hide its action as it becomes a word of exceptional commonality and adaptability. This is not to say that people have planned all this or that structural forces in the language make it necessary. I am simply noticing this trend as I ride the bus and walk down the street. What's wrong with that, you might be wondering? Language changes. Words become popular. Again, my interest is not to change language or proscribe its use, but to be aware of how it is used and invite others to become aware of it also. A more distanced position may help people be less vulnerable to dismissive talk.

Also, I do not mean to say that medical terms that arose from madness discourse are more exact. Words like psychotic, delusional, hallucinating, and others are difficult to define, as critics have said; for example, on delusion see Georgaca (2000) and Knight (2009). They do not describe simple facts ('the person was shaking his fists quickly'). They describe evaluations also ('he shook his fists furiously'). So madness discourse, including psychomedical usage, indicates a leveraging and a hierarchy in normalcy, a kind of competition for sanity, 'mental health,' and all its benefits ('I've been crazy, but not that crazy').

The idea of madness introduces a category of ideal 'sound' mind that cannot be rendered. The splitting of social life and interactions into 'mad' and 'sound' (sane and insane, healthy and ill, rational and irrational) is necessary for the containment of certain acts and experiences. This hegemonic, ideological, or dividing move has been called *sanism* (Perlin, 2000) and *mentalism* (Chamberlin, 1978), though the latter can be regarded as a more general form of discounting any mental 'difference.'[12] It might also be called *European androcentric rationalism*,

---

12 People resist oppressions on the basis of class, race, gender, sexuality, belief, and other schemes including disability. The latter oppression can be subdivided into physical, perceptual, and mental categories of 'ableism.' Mental disability is subcategorized into intellectual and psychiatric disabilities (viz. 'mentalism' and

but while this identifies an oppression it does so without clearly identifying its expressed target, madness.

As psychiatric survivor and historian Geoffrey Reaume shows in his work (e.g., 2006), people considered mad have long been trying to communicate their perspectives and experiences. Margery Kempe, who in the 1430s wrote about her own spirituality (1982), is the first known English autobiographical writer. John Perceval reformed legal rules regarding 'lunatics' in mid-nineteenth-century England in ways that activists today might only dream of (Hervey, 1986). Mad people's causes do not depend on antipsychiatrists or progressive therapists; we provided the grounds for those twentieth-century reactions to bio-determinism. While the Mad movement is hardly militant, it is not easy to root out, as evidenced in the thriving mental health consumer movement[13] and its germination in the psychiatric survivor movement (Chamberlin, 1978; Shimrat, 1997).[14] Thus, from the perspectives of contemporary survivors (e.g., Gibson, 1976; Capponi, 1992; Beresford & Wallcraft, 1997; Deegan, 1997; Cohen, 2001; Carten, 2006), medical force is more than a problem about what to do with 'the mentally ill.'

'sanism'). There are psychosocial and *bio*psychosocial models of psychiatric disability. These might be used to explain the positions of people who call themselves 'psychiatric survivors' and 'mental health consumers' respectively. The survivor movement appears to share goals consistent with the anti-prison movement (seeing madness as a social construction), while radical consumers or 'users' might be compared to 'neurodiversity' activists (for whom neurological difference is no reason to deny rights). A Mad polity might combine survivor and consumer/user positions (and include other labelled positions like that of 'addict') to provide a theoretical ground that does not ignore distress (as survivors are sometimes perceived to do) or treatment refusal (as consumers are sometimes said to do). The issue of reduced responsibility (e.g., 'the insanity defence') could be addressed by a Mad polity that is oriented to questions of societal responsibility.

13 Mental health consumers and users advocate for inclusion of the patient in psychiatric care and decision making (this does not preclude them from feeling put upon by certain practices, or discriminated against generally, or even feeling they have survived certain abuses).

14 Psychiatric survivors advocate for new ways of dealing with distress and difference generally, as psychiatric treatments have been brutalizing and irrational (this does not preclude them from using psychiatric treatments, services, or theory, especially when negotiating their status or treatment as a formality). Academics who have written about the movement include the following: Emerick (1989), Church (1996), Duerr (1996), Everett (2000), Sayce (2000), Cohen (2001), Morrison (2005, 2006), and Adame (2006).

Mad People's Thought

How do mad-conceived people defend themselves against sanism, the dividing of thought into mad and sound? Is there an autonomous position that is not reducible to either of these two categories? If we deny any 'mental' exceptionality, what language would we use to speak of our experiences? How can we argue for the importance of emotional and mental differences, and for the need to respect distress and lived experience, without naming them and therefore appealing to reason that marks them out for the void? We are not even credited with having experience; we are thought to have lost our minds, to be unreasonably emotional, possibly at the worst of times, a kind of philosophical exemplar of inaccessible life: 'The mad are among God's blasphemies or as I say, nature's freaks. Or they are, instead or as well, mutants produced by a hostile environment, human or otherwise. They are not only different from us but an insult, a disturbing affront, to things we hold dear' (Canadian philosopher Brian Grant, 1999: 96).

Some might say we should run to the defence of emotion, distress, animal nature, bold expression, and uncompromising unreason. These are necessary grievances. But what tool would we use? Representation seems to be a significant problem. In art school I remember reading about movements against classical and rationalist aesthetics (philosophies of representation): Romanticism, Expressionism, Art Brut, Surrealism, Dadaism. These movements conveyed madness in many different ways, and they have had an effect in Western culture, yet they have not moved us to defend distress as we do art.

There is conversely a kind of therapeutist (Myers, 2002) apology for the mad person in some progressive positions that does not allow us to move beyond the dichotomies. The modern movement for therapy insists not all is lost. 'Many successful people are mentally ill.' 'Mental illness exists on a continuum with health.' 'Mental illness is a problem with living.' 'Madness is sound in a mad world.' But this again relegates our experience to that of the supplicant, the victim, the wistful dreamer, and reifies the dichotomy.

There may be a different way of conceiving interpersonal realities. One of these is to conceive of a history of madness with 'mad' people in it. To do so we need to regard everyone's self-narrative as central to encompassing social engagement. 'The experience of unreason cannot simply be forgotten; we must form a new idea of reason' (philosopher Maurice Merleau-Ponty, 1964). Madness is sound, but not because we live in a mad world (there is nothing mad about it either).

We have identity *in* 'mad' experience, in difference, not despite it. I would like to suggest that madness is not only excusable, interesting, or a version of rationality under pressure. Madness is an embodied way to know. It is intelligent, searching, and valuable. It is not regression, but a conscious reaching out, as is technical work, healing love, or creative feeling. Purpose is not impossible in 'madness,' but it is also not easily described in a non-normative relation to the world. Again, this is not a call to violence: we must redefine our collective ideas of what we consider deluded.

In the following narrative that partakes fully of madness discourse, I try to express one version of Mad consciousness.[15] It is in many ways not what I would say myself because it gratuitously uses sanist language to get a point across that would not be required in a non-sanist world (which is admittedly an idealization).

In my life, I did not descend into madness, I embraced it like a mother. My mother was mad in my youth, staring off into space, talking to herself, sometimes smiling at me. I embraced her. But after she left, I wanted to know her dearly.

And so I eventually found a way to join her through madness. It was no accident. It was something I wanted to know. This may seem like regression; it certainly ended badly with incarceration and drugging. But it was, at least for me, a natural want, a natural way.

Yes, there was a certain risk, of losing control, of becoming dangerous, and at times I feared my own thoughts. Imagination is horrifying (this is how I would think of these thoughts). I would ease off slightly, retrace my steps, stay in, and slowly take up work and family rituals to return to normal.

The first time this happened was more by accident; I was sixteen. It lasted a few days. I called it 'accelerating,' not knowing it could have been labelled 'hypomania.' With today's 'early interventions,' I would have very probably been given medications and told it was an illness.

---

15 Consciousness might be considered self-reflective capacity, as in Julian Jaynes' philosophy (1990). I would question whether self-consciousness is truly continuous in a life of distraction or simply the concept to describe a fleeting recognition of what we are. Similarly, Mad as a category does not emit madness as a category, but reflects it.

But by opening myself to this way of sensing, by tuning into my body as a way of knowing, and not considering it madness or badness, I got through the internalized structures I was raised with, and attached myself to the being of objects, the soliloquy of sounds, the shifts of meanings all around us.

But I was worried that I would lose myself to it all, and so I convinced myself to go back to the production line of high school. I veered from a full embrace of madness.

I returned four years later, staying for two months, and welcoming others into an appreciation for simple chance. Eventually I closed myself off from it again. (I did not lose enough time at school to ruin my career, so to speak, and so for me this was a fulfilment of sorts.)

Four years later, I entered madness full force in a year of great disappointment with my life. I decided I would be the madman and let myself go. This time I was detained for a mental illness. I worried that it was the reality I had refused to acknowledge. I was simply deluded.

A psychiatrist might suggest that I was actually on a unipolar cycle with a four-year amplitude. But I escaped the cycle, if there was one. I embraced madness one year later, after I got off my 'meds.' I needed to make the experience my own again after hiding it away in the hospital ward. To be pushed down naked, told my wonderment was a disease, was too much.

This would be the last time, though there have been many waves ever since. I used sensory and sleep deprivation, eating dysregulation, cognitive distraction, and other methods to destabilize my orderliness. And later I recovered my social face with repeated activities, orderly schedules, light conversation, fluffy reading, more eating, enforced laziness, and conformist radio program listening. I did it in a shorter time than my prior psychiatric treatment experience, despite madness being more frightening than before. There was also love to make the return something like a homecoming, a story I still love.

I did not master madness. I approached carefully and left carefully. Respectfully, I found it and it found me (it was not a simple achievement like taking drugs, and is not something anyone can do easily). One may confuse oneself, and one may distract oneself from confusion, using latent knowledge. Should people do psychotourism? Perhaps the problem is most people are pushed into madness before they are ready.

Madness is a subset of sanity. It is not only sensible, or rationalizable in any circumstance, it is necessary to order and consciousness. Its gap informs the way we configure memories into chapters. What is madness but a break from self-monitoring? What is sanity but a piece-meal assembly, a vain hope for a unified theory? What is conscious-ness but a harvest of racing thoughts, selective memory, incongruous perceptions?

A Mad polity does not eschew sanity, or join it in destroying irrea-son. A Mad sensibility recognizes an organic order to disarray, and welcomes distress as a process of healing. A Mad polity constructs, theorizes, links. It struggles to afford safe places for people to deal with distress. It does not try to change what is but creates anew. This is not a therapeutic plan; it links to other political movements that try to heal a violent world, though healing cannot be imposed. Confusion is met with listening and understanding.

In presenting this story, I search a way in which to remember, to live. I resist taking a revolutionary position because new systems are simply occupied by old players. This takes me to the foundations of madness language, which in later chapters will be translated into medical and other languages. To proceed with research on social relations around 'madness' requires a relationship not only to experiences but also to the languages about experience, but mostly to Mad people. To name madness experience requires a distancing move (and Foucault shows us we can never escape naming in theory). As a basic distancing tech-nique however, naming the naming is a means of relating our experi-ence, thus providing some escape from the determinism of concepts like brain and trauma as problems to be solved.

If we consider the perspectives of Mad people, the question of state-forced treatment is not just a medical, therapeutic, technical, or legal issue regarding 'misbehaviour.' It is a societal or relational issue that vexes us all. A Mad relation presents theory as lived, practice as felt, reason as ex-perienced through people. To contest force in psychiatric arrangements requires more than empathy or technique in the other's 'best interest,' and more than knowledge about us without us. We start from relating the wisdom of our own bodies, in brokenness or joy, and relate them to the rest of our lives. We may imagine new social relations that accom-modate distress despite the predominance of druggings and prisons as a form of response. Such hopes are reconsidered in the concluding chapter.

Thus Mad consciousness does not resolve into 'sound' or 'mad' rhetoric in rationalistic commonsense terms. It tries to create multiple, autonomous spaces to which people can retreat or join in with others. Mad relations try to provide an autonomous societal space, at least from which to conceptualize psycho-medical force as othering.

3   Restraints and Treatment

Conditional love is no love at all.
                    – Psychiatric survivor Leonard Roy Frank, *Frankly Quoted*

When I visit a family friend in Italy, she asks what I am doing in Canada. I explain that I am writing a book on psychiatric treatment, legally mandated treatment. This scares her a little because she uses psychiatric drugs for depression, and her family rather nicely makes sure she takes them.

'Medicines are meant to help people cope,' she points out helpfully. But she is intrigued and asks me to explain further. She orders a *caffè macchiato* in the sunny town square. I order an Americano, wearing my aviator sunglasses. She walks to our patio table with a stagger, slowly, painfully. She draws stares. Or maybe it's me. I stare back.

Her face is a mask. She is also peeved. The tense muscles are part of the effects of her medication. But her eyes are still alive and sharp. I don't want to scare her; she's been on psychiatric meds for most of her life. She has memories of being forced on it. Even to talk about the negative side of medications is to risk censure in many circles. But I decide my friend is not afraid. She is resilient and intelligent.

She knows English far better than I know Italian, so there is a chance that I can at least tell her how medications are critiqued by a minority of psychiatrists. And with a bit of humour the conversation moves along. I tell her about the government starting a new program in Canada to make people take treatments or police may bring them to hospital. She shakes her head.

'Not everyone follows the law,' I say.

'Do they flush their medications?' she asks.

'They can't. They are supposed to go for appointments. They get the needle instead,' I explain. 'This is the typical thing . . . *tipicale*?'

'*Tipico*. But the medicine is good for them,' she protests. I say not always. She says I don't know enough about it. I prepare a well-known study.

'A few years ago, the U.S. national mental health organization did a study, the largest study of its kind. Hundreds of willing patients were put on three new medications and one of the old medications. They were comparing antipsychotics.'

'What?' she asked.

'A medicine for psychosis, for when you hear voices, or you believe strange things.' I hate to be so simple, but we are negotiating a language difference.

'I'm not psychotic,' she says with a frown. Yet she's told me the name of the drug she's on, 'Aloperidol,' which is the old antipsychotic halo-peridol or Haldol™. But I know better than to mess with someone's identity.

'No, you're not. But you are taking a drug like those, an antipsy-chotic,' I say. She demurs with some seriousness. 'The study ended after a year and a half. Old or new drug, it didn't matter, three-quarters of the patients stopped taking their medicine. They said it didn't work, or it made them feel worse. Some of them just dropped out of the study. The medicine only works for a quarter of people, if it works at all.'

'I must be one of the twenty-five per cent,' she smiles. I laugh out loud. I've been through this conversation hundreds of times before. It never goes well if you can't laugh. 'Besides, all drugs have problems. They're not perfect.'

'These are some of the most powerful drugs known. They can cause diabetes or Parkinson's,' I say. Again, I am simplifying the information for the sake of conversation. She responds saying there are medications to reduce side effects. I suggest they should just drop the dose.

She lays down an ace. 'But what do you know? You're not a doctor!' I agree emphatically.

'You're right, I'm no doctor. But if your chances are twenty-five per cent, it just seems like common sense to drop the dose when things get worse.' I realize there are naturopathic remedies that are supposed to make things worse before things get better, but this is allopathic medi-cine. It is supposed to suppress symptoms.

'Well, it works for me,' she shrugs, her ace in the hole.

I respect choice. I have to if I can convince people they should have a choice. But choice can get complicated.

'That is most important,' I say.

Our conversation stops every few minutes. She needs time to rest, and now she stares off into space for several minutes. I look at her trembling hands, her expressionless face frozen into position. I don't have the heart to point it all out as part of our chat.

Neither do I want to remind her that she is still hospitalized occasionally, her meds increased temporarily, until she calms down, and then she is released again on a 'maintenance dose,' fearful of her next crash. This is mere withdrawal management from a druggist's perspective, an anticipated illness relapse from her doctor's perspective. Treatment failure is an unthinkable concept after all these years. She rouses again.

'What is this book about?' she asks.

'Psychiatric treatment.'

'My medications have saved my life.'

Beyond Experience

In the last chapter I worked from narratives towards very general ideas or expressions about madness. I suggested that a distance from madness discourse, which seeks to define and control what madness is or means, could provide a distance from sanism and its internalization. How sanism is externalized or socialized leads us to professional or industrial texts and conversations about madness.

In the conversation above, madness is managed by medication. Unexpected information is brought to bear on the issue of medication and illness. As therapy is the accepted role of medication, and control of illness is its reputed benefit, the idea of choice is possible. The benefit of treatment is evidenced in thousands of subjective accounts. In this chapter we will look more closely into the literature for the grounds used to initiate restraint and prepare for the next chapter's description of what actually happens in everyday psychiatric practices.

I may believe that the idea of madness as confusion is separable from issues like emotional or physical distress, disablement because of 'stigma,' and danger to self. However, most people do not. Most people believe that madness begets violence; they believe that strange ideas eventually lead to a chain of events: confusion, ambivalence, distress, irritability, aggression, and finally unpredictable violence – and that the most immediate, reliable way of addressing such violence, or preventing it in the first place, is by the use of antipsychotic medication. Such drugs work to focus attention (distract him or her from distractions, as I would say), make one lucid (respondent), and less impulsive or volatile. We will look at how they 'work' in chapter 6. But as a therapeutic 'agent,' neuroleptic drugs bring 'risks and benefits' that we usually weigh from a therapeutic perspective. There are endless therapeutic possibilities in administering such drugs, alone or in combinations, all potentially ethical in a collaborative effort (despite their toxicity).[1]

What about the restraining properties of this medication? We might compare these meds with other forms of therapy, but if they constitute the most scientifically significant, expedient, and reliable means of controlling mental illness symptoms as well as patients, what exactly are the 'risks and benefits'? It depends how we consider the question in relation to other questions. But what strikes me about my conversation with my Italian friend and many others is how the effect of tranquilization prevents people from recording information and basing judgments on memory. My friend can't remember many of the details I'm giving her. She is so passive, so amenable to the plans that others make for her, that she relents easily. This acquiescence might be seen as a return to healthy cooperation. What we would call passivity reduces symptoms. Behaviour and even beliefs can be constrained from the inside, albeit in a most crude way. If we consider passivity a mere side effect, we fail to consider it an effect of a chemical restraint, an unspoken and desired effect. This is not mind control exactly, or mental oppression broadly (which comes with the emotional violence of drugging, to be sure), but biological control.

Mental illness is not a figment, many insist. It is an empirical fact. We notice it in our social relations. It is researched physiologically as a neurological problem that is genetically traceable. Given its associated problems, like homelessness,[2] drug abuse, suicide, aggression, to say nothing of the bizarre ideas people may construe (which damage relationships) it must be a medical condition. There is no denying it

---

1 People can discontinue psychiatric medications even after years of taking them, though this is no simple procedure; see the 'mental health recovery' literature, and alternatives literature, e.g., Lehmann (2004). Sometimes, people manage the dosage themselves, or negotiate the dosage and make it a fraction of what they received before, which is enough to control withdrawal, or distress, as Mike Barnes wrote in his book, *Lily Pond* (2008).

2 For a recent review of the Canadian literature, see Frankish, Hwang, and Quantz (2005). For a Canadian survivor's perspective, try Pat Capponi (1992) and Ron Carten (2006).

sometimes bears its clinical appearance: the confused, erratic body that is out of control. Facial contortions. Ecstatic wonder or loss. These explosions in behaviour may be short-lived and episodic, even dependent on environmental pressures, but the cause is a simple problem in the body, in the gears of mentality, in our very genes, and it is possible that science may one day identify and prevent it directly. But for now, neuroleptization is the preventive antidote. Perhaps mental illness is like diabetes, a dysregulation that requires artificial balancing, or it is like fibromyalgia, a kind of general pain that is very real and requires certain therapies. Why shouldn't people take drugs to curb the pain until they regain their senses? The stakes seem high enough: ruin and violence.

We now begin a journey through the literature that will provide some grounding to my research and (from a scientific world view) test the assumption that mad people will become violent and must be restrained with chemicals. Accounting for perception does not ignore what experimental scientists or quantitative researchers do nor is it a form of bias in the sense that we perform experiments or analyses without rigour. Studies may not provide enough evidence for our cause, given the paucity of study, but they suggest at least in empirical terms that not all is well with some of the psychiatric narratives that we have thus far encountered.

Restraints

Yet, in the case of absolute madmen, as they are not answerable for their actions, they should not be permitted the liberty of acting unless under proper control; and, in particular, they ought not to be suffered to go loose, to the terror of the king's subjects. It was the doctrine of our ancient law, that persons deprived of their reason might be confined till they recovered their senses, without waiting for the forms of a commission or other special authority from the crown: and now, by the vagrant acts, a method is chalked out for imprisoning, chaining, and sending them to their proper homes.

– from William Blackstone's 1765–69 *Commentary on the Laws of England,*
quoted in Hunter and MacAlpine (1963)

The literature on coercion can help us define restraint, show its general parameters of use and abuse, and suggest ways of remedying reliance on restraints. A deeper history, of restraints, especially chemical restraints in the era of 'deinstitutionalization' during the 1950s, provides triangulation on workers' perceptions to be considered later. Even a quick review of the restraints literature will support my interest in moving beyond a therapeutic paradigm for studying restraints. 'Psychotic' violence studies come next, and later chapters will cover psychiatric coercion literature in general, and 'coercive community treatment' specifically. Anderson and Reeves explain that there are at least three types of restraint:

'physical, mechanical, and chemical. Physical restraint is defined as bodily physical force applied by others to limit freedom of movement, while mechanical restraint differs only in that a device rather than a person is used [e.g., straps]. Chemical restraint is defined in [Massachusetts, U.S.] statute and regulation as involuntary administration of medication for the purpose of restraining the individual. Medication used for the treatment of illness is explicitly excluded' (1991: 3). The authors mean medication is excluded from the definition of restraint, yet the same drugs are used for treatment and for restraint. Such definitions are not universal, but they indicate some common sense of usage. 'Environmental' restraint is yet another form, meaning a bodily seclusion or isolation.

Treatment and restraint are often defined as mutually exclusive, yet Richard Hunter (2000) finds a third area between them, 'management,' which he defines as giving some relief from 'symptoms.' Management does not provide new ways of living for the patient, or prevent difficulties over the life course as treatment does. Hunter reproaches the use of 'drugs and TV therapy,' but sees a place for management as a stop-gap measure. He uses the example of a patient whose management medication is eventually reduced. 'No amount of medication would affect his delusional system,' as we are often told they should, but in time several drugs were reduced 'to a minimal dosage of haloperidol, a level that controlled his hallucinations' (2000: 12). The patient's false beliefs could not be controlled, but his false perceptions could, and this allowed for therapeutic success.

While restraints research tends to bring out ethical concerns in many articles, some simply seek the most effective form of restraint. Yildiz, Sachs, and Turgay (2003) find that newer antipsychotics are better than the old 'in the treatment of acute agitation.' Again, the hazy line that separates agitation from illness and drugging from treatment begs the question. What is apparent is the primacy of the professional apparatus and perspective, which is concerned with the 'aggressive' patient.

For example, Currier and Allen (2000) say that psychiatry aims to be less coercive, but the state has cut costs by closing most hospital spaces: 'Consequently, the concentration of aggressive patients in the hospital has risen, and hospitals have become increasingly dangerous places. Concern has also heightened about violence committed by mentally ill persons in the community'; yet restraints' 'ultimate value remains unclear,' and patients 'perceive them to be coercive and traumatic' (2000: 717). Treatment is a necessity in the work of Currier and Allen.

A recent overview of the literature by Sailas and Wahlbeck calls for curbing the use of restraints: 'Lately, prominent international recommendations have aimed to restrict the use of seclusion and restraint, and reminded that they should only be used in exceptional cases, where there are no other means of remedying the situation and under the supervision of a doctor. The use of seclusion and restraint has remained prevalent, but there are several innovative programmes that have succeeded in controlling and reducing their use. Staff attitudes about seclusion and restraint have changed little in the last few years' (2005: 555). These authors suggest cluster-randomized trials, with 'customer' involvement in research design, as there is a need for novel, 'multiprofessional' approaches to curb restraints use. Professionalism can invite the 'layperson' in but it holds the reins on reform.

The restraints literature spans many institutional sectors including geriatrics, pediatrics, residential care, and psychiatry. Restraints are known to cause deaths, for example, due to incorrect application and accidental asphyxiation. The 1998 *Hartford Courant* exposed deaths caused by restraints in the United States, and estimated that 50 to 150 such deaths occur each year (Weiss, 1998). There has been a push to standardize protocols says Weiss, including staff debriefings after the use of restraints, but it remains to be seen how effective such policy can be in changing practices and resource allocation. Sixty people a year die in Ontario psychiatric facilities (which are not often used for long-term stays), according to advocate Linda Carrey (personal communication, 28 Aug. 2007).

Philip Fennel's exhaustive history of restraints provides some grounding for a critical analysis. He includes historical material on Victorian-era drugs used to calm patients in England, including but not limited to opium, morphine, ether, chloroform, chloral, cannabis, bromide, hyoscyamine, and paraldehyde (1996: 34–47). Each of these drugs came into popular use as a progressive treatment. Inevitably each fell out of favour after decades of producing negative effects, including madness

and death for thousands of patients. As today, their restraining properties were considered symptom control rather than bodily control:
'Under the guise of medical treatment, troublesome patients could be
paralyzed with powerful narcotics, and yet an asylum could appear
from the register of restraint and seclusion to be a very model of non-
restraint. With such powerful chemical restraints there was no need for
mechanical ones' (47).

Historical reforms come and go. Benjamin Rush is said to have freed
the mad in America with psychiatric care. Fennel explains that historians 'have tended to trace the beginning of modern psychiatry to
"Pinel's unshackling of the maniacal patients" in Paris in 1792,' though
it was actually Pussin who did this a few years later (1996: 2), and the
shackles did not stay off. In our own era, as Andrew Scull explains in
Decarceration (1984), 'deinstitutionalization' began as early as 1948, well
before the advent of psychiatric drugs reputed to have revolutionized
psychiatric medicine. The move to close the asylum was really a result
of government cost-cutting that sent thousands of institutionalized
patients into the streets without supports (Burris, 2004; Black, 1982).

Both Scull (1984) and Whitaker (2001) recount how the drug company Rhone-Poulenc found a phenothiazine derivative called chlorpromazine that bore tranquilizing properties, but no sedative (sleep) effect.
It was tested on 104 patients in 1950 before being approved for sale, and
then administered to two million U.S. patients within thirteen months.
Scull refers to clinicians like George E. Crane, who was among the first
to examine the negative effects of the phenothiazine tranquilizers (later
euphemistically called 'antipsychotics' and 'antischizophrenics' by their
manufacturers). Scull finds many badly designed studies from that era,
but a few well-designed studies, too. The latter show that placeboes
outperformed tranquilizers as treatments, but not as restraints: 'There
can be no question, for example, that "excessive doses of neuroleptics
produce severe reductions of motor activity and a general loss of spon-
taneity" – that they function, in effect, as "chemical straitjackets," Crane
says' (Scull, 1984: 87). (In chapter 6, I will explain how phenothiazines
do this, along with newer 'antipsychotics.') Scull continues: 'Drugs
failed to be very therapeutic in many circumstances. In their review of
studies of chlorpromazine usage to treat chronic schizophrenia, Glick
and Margolis report that the definition of improvement generally used
by these researchers allowed them to count as "improved" patients
whom drugs simply rendered less troublesome in a hospital context,
but who, it was conceded, were not fit for release' (87).

Scull specifies that 'the definition of "moderate improvement"' used by Blair and Brady was typical: 'Patients still suffer from serious psychiatric symptoms such as delusions and hallucinations, although these are diminished in intensity and severity. Their behaviour has improved and their social conduct is satisfactory, but they have limited capacity to adjust themselves to any environment other than to which they are accustomed. They are allowed the freedom of the hospital grounds on their own. They are capable of simple manual and occupational tasks under some supervision. They require a moderate degree of support from the nursing staff' (1984: 92–3).

Drugs advance what Barton (1959) once called 'institutional neurosis,' a disorder resulting from psychiatric institutionalization that prevented a return to the community. Scull quotes Crane: 'As for the quality of the patient's adjustment after he leaves the hospital, the results of drug therapy are even less encouraging: the majority of those who live in the community continue to be unproductive and are often a burden to their families' (Crane, 1973: 125; cited in Scull, 1984: 88). If we ignore many of the actually reported effects of drugging, we could say that families and patients merely came into conflict as a result of failed treatment. Quoting Maurice Rappaport's work, Scull concludes, 'his finding that patients on chlorpromazine perform significantly better in a hospital setting than do those on a placebo, whereas on the outside this relationship in almost precisely reversed, provides presumptive evidence in support of [his] position [that typical measures of improvement] "may simply not tap the kinds of factors important for successful functioning in the outside world"' (88).

What seemed to 'improve' the patient in the locked ward context did not 'work' in the community. To many clinicians already steeped in the clinical literatures, failure can be explained as a product of mental illness. How do we define improvement? This question leads to how we define illness, treatment, and restraint – and that depends on how we understand violence. Treatment is defined by clinicians, who tell patients that medicine will calm us and get us ready for the community as best as possible. Assumedly, medication would work in a shorter time than psychological treatment or simple social support alone.

Violence

In this section I analyse mad-violence literature as constituting the necessary grounds for drugging. I recognize not only that people labelled with psychoses are generally peaceable but that ordinary conflicts over personal autonomy are often read as delusionally violent.

In law and medicine the perturbed 'unpredictable' body is considered dangerous. It is prone to become aggressive when it is found incapable of managing simple tasks, judging social situations, and representing itself with the usual ease. Madness is a failure to control the self, the body, emotions, leading somehow to irrational violence. It could be argued that an unaccommodating world drives the self to danger, but the medical model roots this in the individual body. In this section madness – e.g., 'psychosis' – is conceived as a pretext to violence because of confusion itself, especially with hallucinatory delusions. It is shown to be a scheme or narrative, as borne out in the social science literature.

The idea that madness leads to violence is deeply entrenched in the 'psyche.' It might be assumed that we carry the memories of ancestors who were attacked by feral dogs every so often. This conception of madness as rabies or rage is what I consider a madness-as-violence discourse or narrative. If we apply this anti-sanist distancing, madness as violence can be explained by madness-as-distress discourse. A person may perceive or conceive things that frighten her or others, leading to outright fear and continued erroneous conclusions about the world. This should lead to a decision to do something harmful in self-defence. Horrifying voices or feelings can be enough to impel a person to act out spontaneously. She might fly out into the street attacking people in a panic. We might try to listen to her openly now that she is at her 'wits' end,' but we may be too late.

Discourses of madness-as-confusion are also useful in sustaining the idea of madness-as-distress leading to violence. We rely on them for a construction of 'psychosis' as irrational. For example, 'paranoia,' conceivable as an overactive self-defence, assembles perceptions of the world into confused plots that give rise to extreme emotions, threats, and attacks. Other forms of 'delusion' emphasize the self in the world, making ego larger than life in self-representations. 'Thought disorder' mis-assembles conscious thoughts and renders the person utterly unintelligible to others (her or his verbalization of thoughts could be described as scaffolding or backgrounding). And 'delirium' and 'dementia' result from mental submersion into a vapid emotionality, a kind of 'regression' to child life that was generally characterized in women as 'hysteria' (Chesler, 1972). Thus, confusion leads to unconscious distress, which leads surely to aggression.

'Hallucination' and 'illusion' cannot be forgotten, as they occupy a privileged position in madness discourse. While many 'normal' people 'see things' or 'hear things,' these events are usually experienced in periods of stress, bereavement, intoxication, or under the influence of psychoactive substances (including psychiatric drugs). The narrative of ongoing hallucination (each visage progressing to another in a kind of dream or nightmare story) can only be internally explained using the construct of 'delusional ideation.' The mind tries to explain dream sequences leading to mismatched plots and confusion leading to distress leading to danger in the social realm. This drama can be used as a schematic for how disordered perception leads to errors in judgment that eventually lead to aggression (and require restraint as a standard approach).

This schematic, however, is not borne out in the quantitative data, or in anecdotes of individuals able to ignore 'hallucinations' and temper 'delusions.'

First it must be noted that an extensive epidemiological overview of the literature suggests that neither 'mental illness' nor violence appear to be simple categories ready for statistical analyses (Arboleda-Flórez, Holley, & Crisanti, 1996). But clinicians are expected to make decisions to protect the public from harm, especially when called upon by courts, tribunals, and legislators (Pinard & Pagani, 2001). The search for predictive power has led to decades of statistical evidence showing that 'madness' and violence are not linked – the largest study being by Steadman et al. (1998).

'Dangerousness' in research is often defined not only as aggression or violence directed at others, but also as the intention to commit violence, causing injury to self, or lacking control that leads to property damage and loss of social esteem. The most advanced quantitative research in this area, like Steadman and colleagues (1998), has led to work called 'actuarial risk assessment,'[3] in which we learn from the actualities of the patients' prior behaviour. Grann, Belfrage, and Tengström (2000) found that actuarial risk assessment is better suited for predicting violent reconviction by people labelled 'personality-disordered offenders' (i.e., people labelled psychopathic, which is defined as amoral behaviour and lack of empathy by an otherwise 'normal' person) rather than

---

3 Examples include the Violence Risk Assessment Guide (VRAG), the Sexual Offender Risk Appraisal Guide (SORAG), and the Historical, Clinical, and Risk Management Factors Instrument (HCR-20), all of which perform far better than sheer intuition.

with 'major mental disorders' (i.e., people labelled with psychoses or mood disorders).

Researchers have noted that most 'mad' violence occurs near the time of incarceration or when families try to 'set limits.' A critical analysis might call this phenomenon mere conflict. A Mad analysis could call it self-defence. Note how Pinard and Pigani describe a person considered 'psychotic' and 'dangerous': 'Persecutory delusions are most likely to be acted upon, with the violent act being directed at the perceived persecutor. Violence is rationalized as an effort to protect oneself. It is not surprising that the accumulation of weapons is associated with paranoid features' (2001: 25). The flow of causality runs from paranoid features to accumulation of weapons to perceived persecution to violent act. Whereas actuarial risk assessment looks to the past for predictive capacity, this research looks to clinical 'features' to explain ongoing events. The reason a person accumulates weapons is 'persecution fantasy,' not any rational sense of endangerment, which fits nicely with an explanation of why this individual might resist medical help.

Despite problems with 'dangerousness' research related to psychoses, such as lack of 'inter-rater reliability' (the agreement between psychiatrists or raters on their semantics and predictions), and with society's demand for professionals to predict violent situations (psychiatrists may perform less reliably than a coin toss in this regard), the most comprehensive and critical empirical analysis that accounts for social factors in violence finds that an individual's 'psychiatric history' is not generally linked to violence. Even when violence is exacerbated by delusion for whatever reason, 'psychosis' is not statistically violent.

People classified as 'schizophrenic,' including 'paranoid schizophrenic,' are less prone to violence than people with other psychiatric diagnoses like depression, who in turn, are less prone than the 'general population' (Steadman et al., 1998). Note that Whitaker reports an increase in the rate of violence by 'mad' people since the introduction of psychiatric drugs (2001: 186). People labelled with 'psychopathy' are more prone to violence than any other group (including people labelled as having 'drug abuse' problems or a 'prior history of violence,' which are also predictors of violence). Again, psychopathic personality disorder is defined as antisocial, predatory behaviour.

The second group studied, with far less substantial risk, comprised a small number of 'psychotics' who experience 'command hallucinations' ordering them to harm someone. This is relatively rare, and not impossible to manage as voice-hearing groups show (see Romme and

Escher, 2000), and as clinicians are showing by using cognitive therapies and other interactive methods. Seeking a more positive link in the
'command hallucination' group, Junginger and McGuire (2004) found
violence is correlated to hearing a voice that is identifiable to the hearer
demanding violence. They consider this a significant distinction that
might help us understand and control aggressive 'illness.'

Their search for a psycho-medical identifier that predicts violence
has been contested by other researchers who remind them that 'demonstration of a correlation does not prove causation. Available research
suggests that violent behavior by psychotic patients results from a complex array of neurobiological, psychological, interpersonal, contextual,
and socioeconomic factors, to name a few' (McNiel, Eisner, & Binder,
2001: 385).

But the shortage or lack of a link may not matter. Unexplained danger lurks. Any explanation may be sought. While causal analysis is con-
founded by the lack of determinate data that would make 'psychosis'
or 'delusion' identifiable, volition or agency is generally denied in the
'mentally ill' person. Greed or rage may appear irrational, but violence
attributed to these 'normal' urges is managed by the courts and exploited
by the prison industry. Abnormal excess might certainly decrease inhibition, especially under the influence of drugs, according to Steadman and
associates (1998). But whereas confusion is often considered the moti-
vational factor leading to 'delusional' violence, even people who hear
'command hallucinations' usually refrain from attacking others indis-
criminately. This does not suggest that they should be ignored or have
no need for social connection; indeed, relationships help everyone.

The idea that 'mad' confusion (unlike regular confusion) invokes aggression regardless of context seems to depend almost exclusively on
the idea that a mistaken belief, not the decision to act, is the basis of
'inexplicable' violence. Yet many of us, including 'schizophrenics,' do
not act on belief alone, according to our data. Perhaps they all would,
with enough time under stress, but statistics from the age before 'medication' suggest otherwise, as Whitaker (2001) notes. He says violence
was less significant among mental patients of the pre-1950s era. So mistaken belief or mistaken perception and any related distress are not
enough to explain a loss of inhibition and violence. Aggression cannot
simply be attributed to a condition of the individual body either; social
factors must play some role.

Biological weakness, which is commonly believed to be the cause
of neurological disorder, may not explain violence by people who are

in distress. However, chemical intervention does seem to have a relationship to mad people's violence. While biology seems to be a rather narrow way of interpreting conflict and explaining violence, a recent study found that major tranquilizer use for suppressing aggressiveness in people labelled 'intellectually disabled' was associated with increased violence (Carey, 2008). Assuming context was accounted for in the study, it is possible that people react strongly to medication or to being medicated, or it could be supposed that 'intellectually disabled' bodies are different from 'mentally ill' bodies in some way, and they reject the curative effects of 'antipsychotics.' But this explanation relies on the idea that 'psychotic' and other body *types* are understood biologically, that their condition is a discrete physiological state correctable by drugs. A simpler explanation: major tranquilizers act on all bodies in similar ways (though never exactly the same for every body) and may lead to some of the violence (and distress) at present attributed to psychiatric patients and illness.

But while the industry searches for automatic neurochemical 'switches' involved in aggression, we often fail to understand the contextual and social roots of mad-labelled violence. Moreover, while people might be assisted in dealing with confusion or distress, reducing distraction using mental rest, and thus reducing the chance of aggression, we might also consider the political or social problems that seem to lead to distress. If chemical intervention actually does increase rates of aggression, clinicians might try alternative interventions, and even abandon drug therapy as a restraint (regardless of the little value placed on autonomy in therapeutic justice). Again, this would not mean an end to therapy, or to the possibility that people find ways to help one another in distress. Before we look at how such therapeutic interventions work out on the ground, let me introduce my own approach to such research.

The No Force Coalition

In this section I recount how my prior advocacy work informs my research. I describe it in some detail to provide a historical sketch of the period in which Ontario debated and elected Community Treatment Orders (CTOs), in 2000. There is also some demonstration of the critiques we made of them as psychiatric survivors and activists of many kinds.

When I first heard of Community Treatment Orders, or 'leash laws' as some psychiatric survivor activists referred to them, I was working as a 'peer advocate'[4] for a tiny program called the Queen Street Patients Council (QSOS, 2002a). The Patients Council concept, which was also implemented in England and the Netherlands, was an attempt to bolster patient participation in hospital programming in the late 1980s and 1990s, as called for by the Graham Report in Ontario (CMHA, 2010). That report found gaps in services and complaints of abuse. As a result of this initiative, patients and former patients were given the means to do direct concerted advocacy work (though there already existed a Psychiatric Patient Advocate Office, established in 1983). This ministerial concession was hardly welcomed by the hospital administration. The Queen Street facility administrators easily rebuffed our efforts and calls for policy change. They said in essence, 'Don't give us criticisms, give us answers we can use' – while refusing us at any turn. Even inside the system, we were working from outside the system.

Our pilot project got off the ground quickly and used resources effectively to accomplish the following: launch survivor protests, publish missives on abuses, help individuals confront staff decisions when no one else would, incorporate our board of mental patients and former patients, even act as an intervener at the Supreme Court of Canada on a case related to the rights of forensic psychiatry survivors. Jennifer Chambers led work on a series of initiatives, including a conference with the Urban Alliance on Race Relations and the Toronto Police Services to discuss the use of lethal force in confrontations with racialized survivors in 1999. We submitted numerous policy documents based on our discussions, held patient parties and information forums, and published *Psycho Magazine* (QSOS, 2002c). We did this using $60,000 a year.

My work with the council included a weekly social 'coffee hour' among other routines. I would go downstairs to the basement level where I walked through a long utility tunnel to the main kitchen. Robots that ran along painted tracks would use these tunnels to deliver food and drugs to each ward in the hospital complex. I would borrow one of the kitchen's eighty-cup urns and let the coffee brew for an hour while I worked in the little beige office they gave us. Then I would retrieve the urn and wheel it out to people lounging in 'the Mall,' a giant atrium in the gangway between units.

En route, I might see people roaming the hallways for lack of something to do on the wards. They propelled themselves slowly, with a

---

4 A 'peer' in this context is a term used for user/consumer/survivor/ex-patient.

wobbly countenance or with spastic gestures. These 'parkinsonian' movements were not caused by mental illness, as you might suspect, but by antipsychotic treatments (see chapter 6). People might talk to me about quite mundane matters, like what they ate, who visited them, or conversely very private matters, like who attacked them on the ward, or what ailed their bodies, or they sometimes shared the ideas that others disbelieved, misunderstood, or denied.

My own experiences in the psychiatric system greatly improved my effort in communicating with patients and supporting them in their self-advocacy. I did not talk down to them or dismiss their emotions. I did not try to amplify their emotions. I took beliefs I did not share or understand in stride without privately or publicly mocking them, and I listened for what I could help them with. However, I think individual advocacy was the least successful function of the Patients Council, given the power differential between patients and professionals who could determine patients' legal status, living environment, diet, treatment, and even daily allowance. Some were given three dollars a day, not even enough for a pack of cigarettes.

In 1997, four years into my work with the Council, the newspapers reported a number of incidents of violence attributed to 'the mentally ill.' On 20 February, former medical student Edmond Yu was shot dead by Toronto police for brandishing a ceremonial hammer, when they approached his poverty-stricken form on a streetcar. He had slapped a passenger and was made to stay in the back of the streetcar until the police arrived. Many people blamed the incident on Yu for 'shunning medication' (Cordileone, 2000; cited in Everett, 2001). The Chinese Canadian National Council held a rally of protest that summer with the Patients Council. Later the council participated in the inquest into Edmond Yu's death. This did not prevent the inquest from recommending the introduction of mandatory treatment for psychiatric 'outpatients,' those leaving hospitals.

In March that same year, Lucia Piovesan stabbed an infant despite repeated attempts by the child's parents to have her forcibly treated. The inquest into this event also recommended legally mandatory treatment. On 26 September that year, Herbert Cheong pushed a 23-year-old woman in the path of a rush-hour subway train. He was alleged to have a crack cocaine addiction, and a problem managing anger, yet he was not psychotic at the time of the incident, according to the court (as Scott Simmie told the Kirby Senatorial Report; Canada, 2005), but none of these explanations nor a possible psychiatric drug withdrawal were considered in media reportage (he had apparently asked for medical attention before the incident).

Such incidents are rare,[5] but the incident that would have historic implications for survivors in Ontario occurred on 1 August 1995. Jeffery Arenburg shot and killed a well-known Ottawa sportscaster, Brian Smith. Arenburg was subsequently diagnosed with 'paranoid schizo-phrenia.' It was reported that he believed that the media were transmit-ting messages to him personally. Arenburg was detained in a 'forensic' (i.e., criminal) psychiatric facility until 2006. Upon his release, he was allowed to live in the community without any drug treatment. After a year, attempting to ride a bus over the U.S. border, Arenburg was questioned by a border guard, refused entry, and searched. He struck the officer in the mouth and was arrested. He was not placed into cus-tody in Canada, but served a two-year sentence in Buffalo, New York (Thomson & Dimmock, 2007; Greenberg, 2008; Willing, 2009).

Whatever may be said of how institutions handled the Arenburg file, his victim would become the namesake of a new law to better control psychiatric patients by ordering them into treatment when they left hospitals. Brian Smith was survived by Alana Kainz, who is reported to have told her dying husband that she would change the system to prevent such attacks (Greenberg, 2008). She became one of the main proponents of 'Brian's Law,' which was passed in 2000, and when Kainz heard of Arenburg's release in 2006 she said, 'Please do not release him at this point. Somebody needs to take care of him, so he doesn't go off and kill someone' (Hayes & Wingrove, 2007). Kainz received a lot of support from Ontario legislators. When Arenburg was arrested in 2007, however, he was not put on a Community Treatment Order or committed to a facility. There was little debate in Ontario's Legislative Assembly about his fate.

In every 'mad violence' case, it could be argued that someone lashed out at the real world because he or she was living in a world of his or her own. Of course, many factors were involved, but 'delusion' is taken as the central factor in violent illness narratives. So in 1997, Liberal mem-ber of the provincial parliament Richard Patten drafted two private

---

5 There were six such incidents in Toronto from 1995 to 2000, as I recall, though three of them did not involve people given psychiatric diagnoses. Since then, subway push-ings (usually not lethal, and not the only attacks on subway platforms) have been reported on the following dates: 5 March 2002, 7 March 2002, 21 May 2008, 13 Feb. 2009, 28 March 2009, and 24 Dec. 2009.

member bills, Bill 78 and Bill 111, to introduce Community Treatment Orders in Ontario. Many psychiatric survivors and mental health consumers were incensed. These bills both failed in the Assembly, but Bill 68, Brian's Law, backed by the Conservative government in power, would receive broad support.

The Patients Council resisted Community Treatment Orders well before they were passed, saying that mandatory treatment would not solve its stated purposes. Jennifer Chambers wrote our 'Statement of Opposition' in 1998:

> Support for this legislation requires that scientific evidence, ethical and legal issues, and provincial consultations, be ignored. There is no lack of scientific evidence that these measures are unnecessary and harmful. As for the law – it is not surprising that the general public does not understand the Mental Health Act. It's shocking that Ontario doctors are so ignorant of the law that they lobby for powers that already exist [i.e., the power to detain based on a person's need for treatment in the non-immediate future]. We want to ensure that the public and the government are operating from better information, and are listening to a more broad-based voice on mental health issues. (QSOS, 2002d)

Based on existing evidence in mental health literature, the council argued the following: people considered 'psychotic' are not more dangerous than the general population, psychiatrists cannot predict dangerousness, most people were being detained without being 'dangerous,' 'homelessness' is not caused by mental illness though the opposite argument is supported in some studies, coercion wouldn't work to solve homelessness, housing is more important to survivors than psychiatric treatment, and most psychiatric crises are better understood as social situations or as direct or indirect results of poverty, discrimination, and other structural inequities.

Furthermore, 'antipsychotic' drugs, the treatment most often used for the group targeted, often do not work to curb hallucinations or other symptoms, and used as restraints they do more harm than good, causing 'lack of feeling, lack of will, a sense of gloom, unbearable restlessness such as leg movements even while trying to sleep, strange involuntary movements such as writhing, twitching, spasmodic movements, trembling, a rigid walk, inhibition of the gag reflex, etcetera' (QSOS, 2002d). But, generally the problem was not that patients refused treatment, rather that non-coercive support they needed did not exist. (Even when one wanted to curb self-destructiveness, the system was not there to help.) Meanwhile, any individuals who want to avail themselves of imposed treatment, if they become incapable of making treatment decisions, could do so in a legal statement of prior wishes (though in practice, any kind of treatment can be denied to those who ask for help). The Statement mentioned, 'The M.H.A. [Mental Health Act, a law governing psychiatric patient management] allows people to be detained who may be dangerous to themselves or someone else, or who can not take care of themselves and may suffer impairment within weeks' (QSOS, 2002d). This is, indeed, how a prominent mental health lawyer, Michael Bay, explained the existing law to mental health professionals (2003).

Premier Mike Harris took up the cause to compel treatment as a part of his re-election platform in 1999 under Bill 68:

> 'The suffering of untreated mentally ill people is a real problem,' he told reporters after meeting with one man who told of hearing messages from aliens and with a woman whose schizophrenic husband shot their teenage son to death several years ago.
>
> 'For too long, we've given up on the mentally ill, some of whom do end up on our streets. We feel there sometimes is little we can do to help and we pretend that a problem doesn't exist.'
>
> At present, provincial laws require that a person be an immediate threat to themselves or others before they can be forced into treatment. The Tories would change the law to make it easier to institutionalize such people. (Ruimy, 1999)

Harris passed other tough love legislation like the Safe Streets Act, which meant to prevent 'aggressive' panhandling.

Several activists and I called for a town hall meeting 29 January 1999. Forty attendees signed up to help educate the public on Bill 68 changes, specifically Community Treatment Orders. We dubbed ourselves the 'No Force Coalition: Groups and Individuals Opposed to Force in Psychiatry.' The NFC's only position was to oppose the CTOs. This position was sponsored by eighty-eight member organizations drawn from Ontario and elsewhere, as well as by many individuals.

Many progressive workers and families were opposed and lobbied the government's Standing Committee on General Government. The Canadian Mental Health Association, Ontario branch (1998), described CTOs as coercive and contrary to therapeutic relationships in their policy position, and the Canadian Civil Liberties Association warned that CTOs could be applied arbitrarily (Ontario Legislative Assembly, 17 May 2000). The Ontario Medical Association, the Ontario Psychiatric Association, and the Coroner's Office, as well as at least two public campaigns (the Coalition of Psychiatrists and the Schizophrenia Society) were in favour. The Centre for Addictions and Mental Health took no public position and is now implementing CTOs.

In the mêlée, the one group that made the best impression on legislators, according to a leader of the New Democratic Party, was the Schizophrenia Society (Howard Hampton in conversation, 5 Oct. 2006). This Canadian non-profit organization's campaign to provide more access to treatment was informed by the National Alliance for the Mentally Ill and the Treatment Advocacy Centre in the United States (Torrey & Zdanowicz, 1999; Treatment Advocacy Centre, 2005). The Schizophrenia Society's Ontario chapter was well organized with financial assistance from drug manufacturers (Oaks, 2000). Their presenters knocked on legislature doors for a week, telling MPPs the dangers of mental illness and the benefits of treatment. This was icing on the cake for local news reports on madness, as local writer and journalist Scott Simmie explained to the Mental Health Commission of Canada recently:

> There was one other sort of near pushing, where a woman had been edged forward, and this woman was the wife of a columnist in a national newspaper. The columnist then proceeded to write a series of columns about the need for community treatment orders in Ontario that would force people to take their medication. What was interesting – because this had been a very hotly debated issue within the mental health field, and it was one that the Ontario Ministry of Health was struggling with vis-à-vis where it should go on this contentious issue. I had some contacts inside the ministry that I spoke with following these columns, which was when the province decided it would, indeed, proceed with community treatment orders. The individual told me that the province had been sitting on the fence, but when this series of columns came along it pushed them over to make the decision. So, even one person can have an inordinate amount of influence. (Canada, 2005)

Patients' stories of mandatory drugging and electroshock therapy, restraints and seclusion, iatrogenic impairment, and vacant lives generated little sympathy compared with not-so-common incidents of car accidents and stabbings. The following news story introduced the concerns of 'consumer/survivors'[6] through the Schizophrenia Society's spokesperson, Ted Fielding: 'The consumer/survivor people generally are people who have not suffered from schizophrenia and their concern is that they will somehow be swept up into this net,' he said of some people who have recovered from bouts of mental illness and feel their freedom will be at risk under the new laws. Stephen Connell of the Coalition of Ontario Psychiatrists said, 'it [the CTO] strikes the right balance for patients and the community' (Mallan, 2000).

But what of the council's objections, and those of the Canadian Mental Health Association (Ontario), the provincial Psychiatric Patient Advocate Office, and so many others? The government held hearings and promised that there would be protections to safeguard 'patient rights.' 'Some people who are mentally ill are not getting the help they need,' said [Minister of Health Elizabeth] Witmer. 'Our government will introduce changes to the law that will help families and health professionals make sure their loved ones and patients get care and treatment [. . .] We are taking responsible action to balance the needs of patients with public safety,' said [then Parliamentary Assistant to the Minister] Brad Clark' (Ontario Ministry of Health and Long-Term Care, 22 March 2000). Minister Witmer explained, 'We need to ensure that the rights of the seriously mentally ill patients are protected but we also need to ensure that public safety is protected as well' (Mallan, 2000).

Bill 68 passed on 21 June 2000, by a vote of 82 to 10. The law was proclaimed into force 1 December 2000. The No Force Coalition later disbanded. The Queen Street Patients Council was already being restructured by this time and would soon transform itself into the Queen Street Outreach Society and the Empowerment Council. The purpose of the society was to inform and educate the public from a patients' perspective. It never received funding for such a mission. The Empowerment Council still provides advocacy for clients, patients, and inmates at the Queen Street site and other sites of the amalgamated Centre for Addictions and Mental Health.

After finding other employment, in 2003 I applied to the Ontario Institute for Studies in Education to see if I might do a study on the effects of CTOs. I was accepted based on my prior academic work and

---

6 In Montreal, in 1989, Canadian survivors and consumers adopted a term 'consumer/ survivor' to work collectively towards common goals. The consumer/survivor initiatives that arose in the following decade in Ontario are not common throughout Canada.

my application. I soon found that rather than producing statistics or lab experiments, much of my work would consist of understanding social science research paradigms. Meanwhile, on the ground, no one seemed to know what was happening with Community Treatment Orders, and the government had not even started its legislated report.

I had wanted to study the material effects of CTOs. This would have required a scientifically countable set of descriptions of social effects, which really depend on what we are looking for. I decided I would ask a simple, exploratory question in my research. 'How do people experience Community Treatment Orders?' Soon after I started my studies I heard that the Ministry of Health and Long-Term Care had finally sent out a Request for Proposals for researchers to start the legislated review. I thought of my own research as a people's version of that review.

4 On the Ground

We have considered how experiences are constructed as 'mad' or 'ill,' as signs of potential violence caused by confusion, and how this has fuelled the call for compulsory care here and elsewhere. This book uses a local version of legally mandated treatment as a case study on chemical restraint and incarceration. This chapter presents empirical data from original qualitative research, state-conducted research, and a literature review related to coercive community treatment. It prepares the way for a discussion in the following chapters of historical, legal, and medical conditions that allow for compulsory treatment.

Ten mental health workers' perceptions of experiences with Community Treatment Orders in Ontario are considered here and in chapter 8 to connect everyday practices to literatures and texts. They also describe how rules and procedures play out in the field, not only by attending to clients' experiences but also how different state programs work and sometimes interfere with one another, how governments (do not) realize reform, and how clients suffer and wait for basic needs to be met. Later in this chapter I will compare these perceptions with the report of the Ontario Ministry of Health and Long-Term Care on CTO use (Dreezer & Dreezer, 2007). I will also present other ethnographic data, like the Canadian Broadcasting Corporation's public radio coverage of this subject in 2006, which highlights Rod Radford's story. Before I present what I learned in my interviews, I should explain how I did my research.

My ethnographic methodology allows for many ways of presenting my research, from using narrative inquiry to literature review to drawing from quantitative analysis by other researchers. When I first entered the Ontario Institute for Studies in Education (OISE) at the University of

Toronto in 2004, I was a bit overwhelmed by the many methodologies we were studying. Perhaps because of my subject, I was immediately drawn to something called Institutional Ethnography, an approach developed by a Canadian feminist sociologist, Dorothy E. Smith (1987, 1990a, 1990b, 2005). Aspects of other methodologies also impressed me, such as the democratic work of Participatory Action Research, and the communicative possibilities of Arts Informed Research. I was also exposed to interview techniques, university ethics review processes (I found out that psychiatric survivors were considered a 'vulnerable population' and if I wanted to interview 'them' it would take some time to pass the review process), and interview transcript analysis methods like Grounded Theory and thematic interpretation. I lost my interest in applying quantitative analysis.

Interviewing CTO subjects directly would have been a challenge not only because of the predominantly scientific orientation of the university ethics review process, but also because individuals under duress might not be in much of a position to report their perceptions candidly. Also, from personal experience, I knew that drug treatment could suppress patients' responses.[1] This relates to questions about how researchers, just like advocates, workers, and activists (my three other 'hats' besides being a psychiatric survivor and family member), relate to people being detained in facilities or forced into treatment. There is certainly a differential in power between a university-trained and -waged worker and a person who is so doped up his head falls forward every few minutes. Whatever my understanding of these dominant positions, I am also a body that is educated in English, that appears mostly white, male, and able-bodied, a winning combination in colonialist patriarchal capitalism. I could use this privilege to convincingly hide my psychiatrization, but I would rather use it to display psychiatry's functions.[2]

As a feminist and a materialist, Dorothy Smith is a staunch critic of how mainstream sociology turns its gaze onto women and disadvantaged groups. She is not interested in explaining social life using broadly conceived theories of cause and effect. Smith re-routes the analytical gaze by beginning from individual narratives of everyday

---

1 I want to describe a discussion I did not use in my research: an informant introduced me to a person under a CTO. He sat with us half-awake and drooling, trying his best to respond using only 'yes' or 'no' to answer simple questions.

2 My privilege means having time to think beyond survival. This brings a responsibility to inform others of what is happening.

life and directing the investigation outward onto social-institutional structures and practices. When she studied psychiatric work in 1975, in 'K Is Mentally Ill' (1990b), she found that women's narratives of their lives were reframed by psychiatric assessments. Any concerns outside the psychiatric nomenclature were excluded when considering how to help (e.g., K's spousal abuse went unacknowledged). Thus, psychiatrization could be seen to reduce social experience into a managerial language that is provided for women's 'treatment.' Checkbox assessments ensure that only some work gets done. Smith does not blame the worker, but the 'extralocal' rules that regulate and influence everyone's work.

I decided I would rely primarily on mental health workers' accounts to find out what was happening 'on the ground,' as Smith says. Building from there, I would connect these perceptions to institutional texts in order to define how practices of power were leading to the restrictions that workers and clients faced. For example, if housing workers were expected to find apartments for clients, yet were expected only to use certain kinds of housing, like government-subsidized units, while having leads on safe spaces elsewhere in the community, this would be a salient example of how the 'relations of ruling' shaped and constrained their work. To work around the rules, one might face consequences, and to work within the rules, one might only be able to help in ways that profited outside parties.

Connecting the personal and political, Smith reminds us that analysis does not have to distance us from what we learn in our 'everyday' lives. Conversely, our social location can be a rich resource for social research, qualitative or quantitative (or informal). She says, in *The Everyday World as Problematic*: 'Taking sides, beginning from some position with some concern, does not destroy the "scientific" character of the enterprise. Detachment is not a condition of science. Indeed, in sociology there is no possibility of detachment. We must begin from some position in the world. The method recommended here is one that frankly begins from somewhere. The specification of that somewhere and the explication of the relations to which it is articulated, including the ideological discourse, are the aim of this inquiry' (1987: 177).[3]

---

3 On the same page, Smith cites the work of Nancy Jackson, who supervised my research in the Adult Education and Community Development Program at OISE. She brought academic theory to life effortlessly in her classes and made sure her students did not lose a connection to the people and concerns that brought us to our research.

'Somewhere' seems quite simple, yet in conventional analytical research it is barely ever considered. By contrast, the tradition of Institutional Ethnography investigates real concerns of 'someone' beginning from their 'somewhere.'

Perceptions

To ask workers what they perceived of Community Treatment Orders, I wanted to welcome as many respondents as possible. I made a poster asking them to discuss recent changes to mental health legislation and e-mailed it to every agency related to mental health that I could find in the Toronto area (some 200 e-mails). I waited a month for the poster to be circulated and was surprised to find that very few people responded. Was everyone simply busy? I wondered if there were so few people on CTOs that no one knew them personally, or if CTO subjects were hidden from workers by medical 'privacy' rules as many coercive practices are. Was no one concerned?

Only three people, all of whom I knew, stepped forward at the beginning of my research. I assured them not to feel obliged to participate because they knew me, but they all wanted to take part in a 'focus group' because they wanted to know more about CTOs. Their discussion was frank and lively. Each of them had very different views and saw Brian's Law changes from different vantages. One was involved in legal representation, another with housing provision, and a third with peer advocacy. Nevertheless, the information they provided indicated that the uses of CTOs left a lot to be desired. They were hardly being applied in consistent ways, which made a 'causal' or experimental assessment of their effects impractical. This also made a rigorous application of Smith's Institutional Ethnographic methods, which depend on following standardized practices utilized by workers, rather difficult. But I did learn from these workers that in many cases workers were simply not filling out legal forms and following the rules, which opened up important new questions about how things actually work. We will look briefly at the rules before looking at workers' reports, and consider the rules in more detail in the next chapter. Note that procedures and rules can be analysed to discern how they invite misapplication by being overly broad or arbitrary or unmonitored. Furthermore, practices compared with regulations can show where workers try to get around the rules, leaving us to wonder why.

I realized also that if these associates knew people on CTOs, then quite likely so did most other workers. CTOs were, indeed, being used at an increasing rate, they said. As this was a preliminary stage in my research, I used a common method of analysis of my transcript, 'thematic analysis,' to consider what people were saying, what they agreed on, and how these perceptions could be pieced together into an image of what was happening. Themes allow for general simplification of hundreds of comments. I think of it like separating a group of stones by shape, colour, and size; each division may not neatly fit into other divisions, so the result is a kind of model, image, or narrative (see 'Focus Group Image' below).

Later in 2005, I started a subsequent interview process by sending another round of posters inviting any worker or activist to provide 'observations and opinions on psychiatric survivor experiences of CTOs.' This moved beyond preliminaries and presented a bit of the framework for my analysis. I was pleasantly surprised to find five more people to interview. I was surprised at the variety of their views. Few of them reported stories of Community Treatment Orders that were successful from the patient's perspective; many patients rejected them vociferously. Of course, these anecdotal reports are not generalizable findings, but they provide a source of 'intelligence' about what needs to be investigated. One of these respondents was a psychiatrist who used CTOs, and the interview with her was invaluable to me. It allowed me to analyse medical coercion in terms of everyday issues, intentions, and functions from a professional 'standpoint,' as Smith says (a standpoint, or sitpoint, is much like a social location: one's place in the social world as perceived by that person and others).

Three interviews involved people in two cities outside Toronto, and were conducted by telephone. Most participants knew one or two people on CTOs, though a couple knew more than ten (a small number of perceptions overall, in comparison with the government report). An additional two interviews were conducted by chance when I met people who knew CTO subjects, but these were not recorded and only general statements were transcribed in crib notes. Five of my interviewees had already met me through my work with the Queen Street Outreach Society, though I had seen only two of them in the past few years. During interviews I told those who did not know me that I was a former 'patient' (the poster had said I was known in the community in relation to CTOs). My effort was not meant to hide my identity so much as to let participants speak for themselves in an informal interview.

Most participants were former subjects of psychiatric intervention themselves, and of these all but one identified as psychiatric survivors.

Table 4.1
Research Participants' Fictionalized Names, Relative Positions, and Activities as
Psychiatric Professionals, Workers, and Activists, with Date of Discussion and Method
of Communication

Name	Relative Position and Activities	Date and Method of Communication
June	Legal clinic worker, activist	March 2005. Focus group
Tyler	Housing support worker	March 2005. Focus group
Rudy	Consumer/survivor agency worker, activist	Aug. 2005. Long-distance, semi-structured interview
Kim	Consumer/survivor advocacy worker, activist	March 2005. Focus group Aug. 2005. Semi-structured interview
Victor	Assertive Community Treatment team 'peer support' worker	Aug. 2005. Long-distance, semi-structured interview
Danielle	Assertive Community Treatment team psychiatrist	Aug. 2005. Long-distance, semi-structured interview
Carmen	Consumer/survivor agency worker, activist	Aug. 2005. Semi-structured interview
Emilia	Assertive Community Treatment team case worker	Sept. 2005. Casual interview
Fran	Rights Adviser with the provincial Psychiatric Patient Advocate Office	Sept. 2005. Casual interview
Phil	Assertive Community Treatment team training placement	2006. Email submission

The exception was one mental health consumer. (I have defined these terms in chapter 2; they are not discreet categories or the only categories of identity.)[4] Participants also occupied differing standpoints/sitpoints in terms of gender, race, class, sexual orientation, disability, and former psychiatric 'involuntary' or 'incapacity' status (i.e., being detained or force-treated, respectively).

I asked them all what CTOs looked like in the everyday lives of their clients. I planned to use questions like why were CTOs being implemented, and how did 'clients' feel about them. But usually the respondents intended to say something about CTO experiences, and I tried to use all their material in my analysis, from a broad representation of all comments to detailed descriptions. I never really knew then what

4 Common identifications are 'patient' and 'client,' the latter being more progressive to mental health workers. The term 'inmate' is rarely used anymore. Consumer, user, and survivor are used by people who identify as more than patients or clients, and prosumer (provider-consumer) is sometimes used for people who wear both hats. 'Mad person' is rarely used, and neither is 'thriver' or 'refuser,' as examples.

would be repeated and later highlighted as a theme of concern. But this narrative of their narratives tries to allow the most descriptive material to come forward, stepping from questions of what a CTO is and is supposed to do, to what it seems to be doing, to what helps in 'recovery.' Participants consider the internal contradiction of offering someone a coercive plan, the absurdity of people jumping the queue for resources by putting themselves on a CTO, and then major abuse situations (though this only touches on what comes in chapter 8). We then delve more into questions of identity and insight. The psychiatrist in this research speaks to positive examples of the use of CTOs, the purpose of CTOs, and how, for her, coercion is balanced against success. I analyse these cases in terms of the futility of refusing patient selfhood, and then I present an exceptional story of Rod Radford in his attempts to deal with CTOs.

Let me begin by describing CTOs, how they are supposed to be used, and yet are often abused, according to the Ontario Psychiatric Patient Advocate Office. I will begin by quoting someone I call 'Victor,' who is an Assertive Community Treatment (ACT) team peer worker. Victor describes CTOs from a ground view:

> Well they're being forced to take medication really, when you think about it. The CTO as I see it is basically a form of being hospitalized in the community. You're living in the community but at the same time you're being forced to take medication. So instead of having to take medication in the hospital you're having to take it in the community. Once you stop taking it in the community, once you fail to meet the [conditions of] a CTO, then the person would have to come into the hospital.
>
> For some people it's disempowering. It takes a lot of life out of them. And they complain about it. They don't like it. I personally think that it's hard to work with clients that are on CTOs because it totally takes away any kind of relationship you have with them. I find the focus of what happens with the ACT team's clients that we have, that are on CTOs, the focal point of the visit tends to be sometimes whether or not you know they're meeting the [stipulations] of the CTO, and it's hard to do other things. I don't think clients actually want much more to do with their workers either, because they're being forced to follow these guidelines.

Victor's description is in keeping with statutes. 'Eligibility' for a CTO in Ontario requires a person to be 'committable' under the Mental Health Act. That means being a danger to self or others due to an 'illness,' as evidenced in dangerous behaviour or lack of self-care (s. 15.1), or because of a 'mental illness' that can cause 'mental deterioration' and/ or other impairments that leave the individual 'incapable to consent' to a treatment that apparently has worked before (s. 15.1.1). So 'deterioration' (not just dangerousness) and/or incapacity to choose are grounds for medical incarceration, which lawyer Anita Szigeti says describes almost any mental illness and is therefore overly broad in legal terms (personal communication, January 2001).

According to law, a person must be committable within 72 hours of signing a CTO (appears at risk of 'deterioration' or incapable of 'insight'). The person is also supposed to have been in a psychiatric facility (even voluntarily) at least twice, or for 30 aggregated days or more, in the past three years. Note that these rules can easily be ignored in practice, perhaps because of a lack of oversight in the system.[5] 'Fran,' a Rights Adviser with the provincial Psychiatric Patient Advocate Office, complained of her caseload being far beyond her means, and yet most of her clients apparently had little interest in rights. Advocate Linda Carrey (personal communication, 28 Aug. 2007) reports that there is still minimal Mental Health Act rights oversight in general hospitals in Ontario (i.e., non-psychiatric hospitals). There is no CTO training or standards for psychiatric workers. She had heard of instances in which orders were imposed or offered to individuals who had not been hospitalized.

By law, the physician must be of the opinion that a patient could not live in the community without 'treatment' and would suffer 'mental deterioration' otherwise. The patient must also have been party to drawing up a 'treatment plan,' must be able to comply with it, and all the 'services' mentioned in the plan must be readily available (here the rules attempt to account for a general lack of resources in the community, as indicated by CTO opponents). A tribunal exists to hear challenges to CTOs and other impositions. However, as lawyer Suzan Fraser (personal communication, 13 June 2008) reports, the tribunal is

---

5 Gray and O'Reilly, Canada's medical authorities on 'mandatory outpatient treatment' ('MOT') openly say psychiatrists need not bend to the rules: 'While psychiatrists know that treatment would be quickly effective and relieve suffering, they can neither hospitalize nor treat. There is evidence in some jurisdictions, however, that physicians "bend" the law to help such patients. An Ontario study, for example, found that 93% of certificates did not meet the strict physical harm criterion' (2001: 20).

not keeping up with its caseload and has recently declared that it will not hear challenges dealing with constitutional matters, leaving patients to vie for expensive legal services or publicly appointed lawyers which are in great demand.

In Ontario, a person must sign a Community Treatment Order (a 'Form 45' under the Mental Health Act) for it to take effect. It expires in six months and is renewable (the tribunal was supposed to review each CTO upon a second renewal, but recent changes have dispensed with this oversight; CMHA, 15 April 2010). However, if the person is deemed 'incapable' by her psychiatrist, a close relative can sign for her, or even the state if no 'substitute decision maker' (SDM) is willing and available. Linda Carrey (personal communication, 28 Aug. 2007) reported that CTOs have been imposed by not one but many SDMs recently. The order (Form 45) comes with a 'community treatment plan' that is governed under the Health Care Consent Act (s. 2.1). Thus, an order becomes a treatment, which is defined in the latter act as 'anything that is done for a therapeutic, preventive, palliative, diagnostic, cosmetic or other health-related purpose' (s. 2.1).

According to Linda Carrey of the Psychiatric Patient Advocate Office, the following are but a few examples of CTO treatment plan requirements: routine pregnancy tests, frequent baths and laundries, taking non-psychiatric medication, and going off or on the 'Ontario Disability Support Program' (ODSP, government health insurance benefits), and abstinence from alcohol or drugs (without addiction counselling). In one CTO treatment plan, clinical observation included making sure that the client did not try to leave her boyfriend: if she did, it was a sign that she was 'decompensating,' or becoming 'ill' again. CTOs have also been attached to probation requirements (personal communication, 28 Aug. 2007). Linda Carrey also says that, on the whole, CTOs are simply not being used as they were intended to be used, on difficult, 'revolving door patients' who don't stay on treatments (personal communication, 29 June 2010).

According to statistics kept by the Ontario Psychiatric Patient Advocate Office, the number of people given rights advice for CTO issues in the province (with the minor exception of a few hospitals and lack of data on private practitioner use of CTOs) has been rising steadily all decade, from 108 in 2001 to 845 in 2004 to 1,786 in 2008 (PPAO, 2009): 'There are not only more individuals on CTOs, but a greater proportion of these individuals were found incapable of consenting to the issuance or renewal of a CTO. Accordingly, a greater percentage of issuances and renewals were consented to by SDMs (usually family members appointed to make medical decisions), with an overall rise in rights advice given to SDMs from 57.6 per cent in 2005 to 65.5 per cent in 2008' (ibid.: 12).

Experiences

Like in Victor's account, one person who worked on a mobile psychiatric unit, called an Assertive Community Treatment or ACT team, said her work consisted of nothing more than going from rooming house to rooming house and making sure CTO subjects were taking their meds. 'Emilia,' an ACT team case worker, said their lives were an endless succession of days smoking in their rooms, languidly bobbing back and forth under the 'side effects,' sitting in front of televisions, barely ever going out. They reminded her of people in old photographs tied up in chains, dejected, forgotten. She said the hospital out of which the team worked released most of its patients under CTOs. She asked in exasperation whether her treatment team was doing to people what she saw in those historical images.

Someone I came into contact with more recently trained for a month with an ACT team – which usually employs a doctor, nurse, social worker, occupational therapist, and sometimes a 'peer' worker. ACT teams bring mental health services to people in their homes or anywhere else such as when they are homeless. In an e-mail 'Phil,' an ACT team training placement trainee, gave a detailed description of what he had encountered, which I quote at length for its rich description:

> Basically, just about half of the eighty-some patients at this clinic were on CTOs. During the daily morning rounds, the biggest topic was keeping them 'compliant' with their medication regimen, CTO or not. The second biggest concern was the patients' 'state of mind' and keeping them out of hospital; and the third was keeping them out of trouble with the law (as many of the patients have records for petty crime, such as stealing a chocolate bar or being a 'public nuisance,' etc.).
>
> When patients weren't compliant with meds, they usually sent a team of workers to their house to 'convince' them of the 'appropriateness' of continuing their meds – and even when there were clear debilitating side effects (e.g., diabetes, massive weight gain, etc.) the workers' rationalization was invariably 'well, yeah, but what's the alternative?'
>
> If, however, the patients refused them entry, which was often the case (although it also depended on their personality), the workers would enter

with the office key, which is often the 'agreement' they make with the patient as a condition of their release from hospital, again more coercion. If the patient remained 'belligerent,' they'd come back with the police, and then have them committed. If they didn't have a key, they could get a super to open the door, and then if the patient ended up in hospital, they were likely to make their release contingent on allowing 24-hour access to their property or even signing a CTO, for those already not on one.

Some patients 'agreed to' giving up a copy of their key on condition that the workers only entered their premises if no one answered the door (the idea being that the patients may have harmed themselves). Although naturally if the patient didn't want to answer the door, the workers could open the door anyway, which is really simply more of the farcical make-believe game of the team pretending as if their patients have a legitimate say in 'treatment.'

One can see from this account, which is supported in others' perceptions and even the government report at times, that mental health workers are not so much being constrained by legislation (which presumably tries to ensure rights are addressed) but are freed to follow competing interests in the absence of systemic oversight. Phil continued:

Again, though, the issue of whether or not to 'execute' the CTO on the patient had little to do with the patient's state of mind, and entirely to do with whether or not they were compliant with meds. For example, there was a guy I saw a few times with severe Dystonia [muscular contortions]. This was from taking medications. He was very bright and aware of his surroundings, but at the same time extremely paranoid, and I imagine this was partly from a lot of the stuff he'd experienced throughout his life, including with psychiatry. This included very severe trauma, which I won't discuss in detail here [. . .]

This patient would often refuse to take 'his' meds because of the horrible side effects [. . .] When he refused taking 'his' medications – which he had good reason to do – they basically devised a plan of 'tricking him' into coming to the office, through ulterior reasons unrelated to the meds, and then once in the office, they would somehow convince him to take the needle. The 'benefit' of needles [. . .] is that the drugs stay in the system for much longer, although it's only certain drugs that you can take with needles. All I can remember is two workers with him in the office and him shouting as the nurse gave the needle, although in this instance he had 'consented' to the procedure – thus I suppose it was more than the needle that was making him uncomfortable.

If this is not outright force (which is disallowed off hospital grounds by law) what led to this form of 'coercion'? To me it indicates a prior arrangement that can be resisted vocally but not physically, an 'infantilized' response under forced treatment.

I should note that this informant has, as a result of working in a facility with psychiatric patients in extreme distress, started to question whether coercion is not altogether arbitrary or unreasonable. The stories he has been told by clinicians, of extreme hallucinations and terrifying attacks on a locked ward, suggest to him that forced treatment is sometimes necessary after all. Fear and violence, wherever it starts, can impel the status quo. We will return to the apparent necessity of tackling patients with needle in hand, but I want to zoom out to the larger image that my focus group provided as a way of considering the social relations at work in forced treatment arrangements.

Focus group question: what is happening to people under CTOs?

To give an overview of what was said to me at the early stages of research, I will put comments together in ways that describe a scene. To find emphasis I will show how much agreement there was for certain commentaries using the number of such statements made and who made them. In this narrative, J is 'June,' a legal clinical worker and activist; K is 'Kim,' a consumer/survivor advocacy worker and activist; T is 'Tyler,' a housing support worker; and E is me, Erick. Note that the number of times something is said is not related to its relative importance.

Psychiatry is steadily moving into the community. (18 comments / J and K made them)

CTOs are only a part of an old phenomenon of coercion. (one / T)

CTOs obscure coercion, psychiatric oppression, even further. (5 / J,K,T)

Few patients are on CTOs, but more are getting on them yearly. (5 / K,T)

Few clinicians know enough about the law to put someone on a CTO. (3 / J,K,T)

No one seems to know who is on CTOs. (2 / K,T)

No one asks clients, out of respect or convenience. (2 / K,T)

Not even clients know if they're on a CTO sometimes. (4 / J,K,T)

Poor people get less social support from professionals. (8 / J,T)

Staff sometimes tell patients they have no other choice but to accept a CTO. (one / K)

When CTOs fail, clinicians that signed on don't sign on again. (one / J)

Patients' wishes are seldom heard by professionals. (10/J,K)

Capable patients who volunteer to receive services are turned away (until they're in extreme crisis). (3/J)

People elect CTOs just to find services they need. (4/J,K)

CTOs do not ensure people get the services listed in a treatment plan. (5/ J,K)

Only people with personal supports are put on CTOs to prevent failed CTOs. (4/J,T)

The system has no real personal counselling supports. (12/J,K,T)

Emotional crisis and life problems limit people's ability to navigate the system. (2/J)

People in distress avoid the mental health system and this is understood as part of their mental illness. (2/J)

Trauma can escalate into delusion and hallucination, and only then do workers get involved. (one/J)

Medication and lock up is additionally traumatizing. (one/J)

Overdrugging prevents patients from protecting their own interests and rights. (9/J,K)

Patients are not informed about the legislation or their rights. They often depend on word of mouth, such as when speaking to peers (12/J,K)

'Legalese' prevents people from understanding patients' rights. (2/J,K)

Legal rights advice is not sufficiently provided. (5/E,J,K)

Professional rights advocates are too few and often defer to medical paternalism. (7/J,K)

Decisions over CTOs can be complicated by family or others with their own agendas. (5/J,K)

Drug compliance is the only way to obtain social standing and is almost always seen as being in the best interests of the patient. (9/J,K,T)

CTOs are used to force people to accept services they don't want. (12/K)

CTOs are designed without clients. (one/J)

CTOs are signed by patients while they are still incapacitated. (3/J)

Psychiatric identities are formed early in the process of institutionalization. (3/J,T)

Patients fear professionals and avoid confrontation over their own wishes. (16/J,K,T)

Survivors can resist CTOs when they understand them. (2/K)

Survivors approach other survivors about their rights by building relationships. (6/K)

CTO enforcement has been well funded. (6/J,K,T)

Once CTOs were passed, professionals originally opposed to them started enforcing them. (3/E,J,K,T)

CTOs have polarized the mental health service provider community. (2/K,T)

Professionals avoided this research project. (12/E,J,K,T)

The CTO review (being conducted at that time) is being rushed without much communication. (one/K)

The CTO review is being done by professionals in a conflict of interest. (3/J,K)

The greatest number of Toronto CTOs are imposed by a CTO lobbyist doctor who practises at a local general hospital. (2/K)

These are only perceptions, not experimental data. They can be taken as an informed perception of what is happening that could be followed up with quantitative fact-finding.[6] I think workers would want to be honest in research, not only to be concerned and involved with people in pain, but also to abide by practitioner ethics and standards of care that claim to be 'client-centred.' What emerges is not only a picture of forced treatment (under a therapeutic guise), but of an industry that is radically disoriented in assisting people.

Contradictions

I want to look at an example of a Community Treatment Order that works. Here is one that appears to curb 'symptoms,' albeit with some level of coercion. The information is from Victor, a peer worker on an ACT team:

Another woman we work with has schizophrenia as well. She's on a CTO and part of her requirements are that we see her almost every day and give her medication. I'm not a big fan of that kind of idea, seeing the client every day. I think it's disempowering, and for this person, we see her every day, and she still has pretty fixed delusions [strange beliefs], and she has

---

6 I have told allies to call for record keeping regarding restraints and treatments simply to foster basic accountability, though this is but one institutional responsibility, and it may certainly be formalized in a way to make restraints seem to disappear, as Fennell reminds us (1996).

problems with her illness sometimes, but generally she tends to function fairly well. She has her own finances, her own apartment. She's been out of hospital for a few years now. So in some ways, she's someone that the CTO has helped; she's been able to stay out of hospital, but I ask, how long would you keep renewing the CTO?

While the medication does not seem to be doing much for this woman, or her 'positive symptoms of schizophrenia' (i.e., hallucination rather than 'negative symptoms' like apathy), as clinicians say, it has kept her out of hospital. As long as the team is supervising her closely, she is able to maintain herself much as she would on the ward (though Victor goes on to say she will have nothing to do with the ACT team otherwise). In a sense, this might be considered a success because the patient is not expected to recover, and she has the freedom to live in the community as she would on the ward. But Victor thinks she could benefit from more agency in her care. He says:

> I think [we should be] giving her more responsibility for her own medica-tion, taking her medication on her own. Maybe even just seeing her three times a week [not more], at least try it. I think there's this problem with CTOs and in general with mental health care providers that they need to coddle everybody and make sure they're okay, and that they're not just faking [being 'ok']. Everyone's worried about risks, and to me it's not all about risks. People need to be able to take chances and to fail and to do their own thing. I think on a CTO the person tends not to have a lot of say on what their treatment is about. If you're not in control of your own treat-ment it's hard to move past that.

Victor's account shows that workers and the public normally con-sider people 'unmanageable' or 'incurable' while former patients think they have more possibilities, based on having had similar experiences. If this is just bias, remember that without it those patients would not have 'recovered,' given the usual prognosis of chronic illness and care they received. The supposedly well-researched theories biased against our very survival makes our self-appellation a matter of empirical fact more than perspective. But Victor says managing legal or medical risk is more important to psychiatric workers than 'recovery,' a move he calls 'coddling.' He feels people need to make their own decisions, take risks towards social 'recovery' or 'integration.' 'Recovery' is often defined in the mental health literature as a remission of most or all symptoms, the

attainment of independent income and/or housing, and the formation
of significant relationships (see Jacobson, 2004; Harding, 1987), yet it is
also defined as a personal process in which we are all a part and forever
will be (Deegan, 1988; Ahern & Fisher, 2001).

While 'recovery' seems to demand that everyone be (or act) 'normal,'
it debunks prior psychiatric textbook theories that say only some 5 per
cent of people with 'schizophrenia' could become independent based
on Bleuler's hundred-year-old observations, which are still influential
today. Recovery is a rather new, and sometimes still controversial idea
in psychiatry. Its roots go back to moral therapy (which Foucault critiqued as the imposition of 'morality' through what modern workers
would call 'normalization,' which is basically to make a person appear
and act like 'normal' others as much as possible). In any case, an alternative to biological normalization is shown to be possible in many
studies that say half to two-thirds of supposedly 'serious' or 'chronic
patients' find jobs and relationships and report no 'symptoms' after
many years (Jacobson, 2004; Deegan, 1997; Harding, 1987). Like Scull's
work (1984), Harding (1987) shows that drugging actually *reduces* the
chance of 'recovery.'

Workers are managing risk with chemical restraint, perhaps due to
industrial or commercial structures. This study's participants describe
the kinds of clinical descriptions used to authorize CTOs, such as 'lacking insight,' 'non-compliance,' 'mentally deteriorating,' and 'repeated
hospitalizations.' Victor reports:

> Well, for example, I might work with people on a CTO who aren't taking
> their medication. Usually it ends up that they need to be brought into
> hospital if it comes to the point where their lives are disturbed, or they're
> having a problem with living, [or] if they choose not to get on medication.
> Sometimes, I think a lot of it comes down to people having a hard time
> with their insight into their illness.

People who no longer take 'medication' or who are too 'disturbed'
are CTO candidates in Victor's view. The stated purpose of a CTO is
to reduce hospitalizations: 'The purpose of a Community Treatment
Order is to provide a person who suffers from a serious mental disorder with a comprehensive plan of community-based treatment or care
and supervision that is less restrictive than being detained in a psychiatric facility' (Mental Health Act, s. 33.1.3). A CBC news article explains
the contradiction that while CTOs attempt to prevent rehospitalizations

by imposing compliance with 'meds,' the patient ultimately decides whether to comply: 'In plain language, Community Treatment Orders mean "Take drugs to control your illness or you'll go back to hospital." But [then MPP Brad] Clark says, as a consent-based system, if they say "No" then "they go back to hospital"' (CBC News, 2000).

Another contradictory phenomenon related to CTOs is that they were often chosen by some patients in order to get housing or other services in spite of their coercive function. This was surprising to me at first. But if services dried up, the CTO could not really create new services. (By law, a CTO should not be implemented if services cannot be arranged).

'CARMEN,' A PEER WORKER: what initiated him being put on a CTO [. . .] was that he lost his housing. The other thing was that he got arrested. You know there was a number of things that happened in his life, but in terms of the services that he got as a result of the CTO, I didn't see any differences in the services. We were the ones [peers] – and we're not part of his order, we're not named in the order – we were the ones that had to secure him housing and arrange for his money to move.
ERICK: So his treatment plan didn't do that?
CARMEN: The treatment team? No, no.

Some participants said that people who already had family looking after them would try to get services through CTOs, indicating an imbalance in how services are distributed. Perhaps some CTOs are used to constrain people in the community by threat of rehospitalization, while others are being used to provide services for presumably middle-class consumers. June, a legal worker, states:

I'm finding that the group that is less likely in the neighbourhood to be put on a CTO is somebody who's transient, or homeless, and has no supports in their life. I'm suspecting that's because of the complex issues that somebody has when they're living on the streets and they're poor and homeless. They're a little more difficult to serve in mainstream organizations because they don't fit the criteria that get service, like [having] 'catchment area addresses.' And, because they don't have family contacts, nobody wants to assume responsibility, and doctors and nurses and social workers won't assume responsibility if there's not somebody else to ensure the CTO is followed through in the community, which is going to be a family member.

However, middle-class consumers had problems of their own. CTOs were perceived to help some families keep their loved ones under surveillance while on medications. 'Rudy' is a consumer/survivor agency worker and activist.

RUDY: [In terms of homelessness] I don't think the changes in Bill 68 made a lot of difference [. . .] Some agencies are making some attempts to help people on the streets. It's not that they're being totally ignored. I'm just saying that Bill 68 didn't make any difference to that population, no significant difference.

It was a political bill, in response to the Schizophrenia Society of Ontario [a family group lobbying for more medical interventions and research]. [. . .] [A]ll of a sudden we've got a law that many people labelled 'draconian,' a step backwards, not a step forward for any kind of enlightened care of people in our community [. . .]

RUDY: [. . .] following the statistics, you will find the vast majority of people who are served by [workers who impose CTOs], in fact, have a diagnosis of schizophrenia, and that's interesting to me.
ERICK: What does that suggest to you?
RUDY: I'm curious as to why it happens to be one diagnosis. All it suggests to me is the influence of the Schizophrenia Society of Ontario, and the parents of people who experience schizophrenia lobbying strongly, and the government putting a lot of money behind it. They talk about ten percent of people with schizophrenia committing suicide. [But] I'm saying look at the people who are depressed; huge numbers of people who are depressed commit suicide.

This commentary takes us away from reports of CTO experiences on the ground, but it shows how politics and policy determine aspects of treatment, including how diagnosis and social class influence worker decisions. While CTO programming does not constitute a sizable segment of mental health funding, which is small in comparison with Ontario's health care expenses in general, it is certainly more expensive than 'alternative projects.' This does not mean that people who are 'homeless' are not being forcibly treated at a significant cost. 'Danielle,' a psychiatrist on an Assertive Community Treatment team, points out:

The only person I demanded a CTO [for] upon discharge. That's a complicated story. The guy was very, very high risk according to others and did not have the cognitive capacity to stay on treatment by himself [he was labelled 'developmentally handicapped']. There's just no way that he could be managed without a CTO. So, he's one of those people who's kind of beyond ACT anyway. Not that we're in the business of protecting the public, but for people who have a high risk directly related to their untreated state, the CTO becomes more of an option because that's the only way you can get them out of an institution.

As we gather comments and find structures at work in forced treatment, we find some of the rationales taken up in dispensing coercive care. While people who would need direct support for some time are imposed upon with tranquilizers, many psychiatrists believe CTOs are ineffective in ensuring 'treatment compliance,' according to the provincial CTO review. Despite the legal definitions of constraint that define such orders, many psychiatrists refuse to believe they impinge on patient rights at all (CAMH/CMHA, 2005). This may be because many clinicians think in terms of a 'treatment rights' approach, which says treatment allows a disordered body to think clearly enough to practise its civil rights. Nevertheless, a Canadian Mental Health Association study (2005) found that more CTO subjects than non-CTO subjects felt coerced, though all felt significant levels of coercion.

Danielle believes that coercion may be useful but only as a last resort, and then only if treatment seems to work (from her perspective). When she was asked, 'What sort of factors might lead to you putting clients on CTOs?' Danielle described who she believed should be on a CTO:

Well, that's always changing over time. I must say that philosophically I've never been very – I didn't lean towards CTOs. But given the job that I'm in and certain social mandates that come with it, I do have to think about it. But I guess what I've selected over time in terms of benchmarks or guiding principles for me has been the gradient between the untreated person (so the person with no medication, how they function), what their life is like, and how they are when they're medicated. That gradient has to be extremely large. And what I mean by gradient is the perceived change in their life, in their eye, even though – throughout all of my patients – they wouldn't attribute that change to medication or the CTO. So, if that gradient is not large, I will not put them on a CTO. It's not worth it. In fact, the larger that gradient is the more I will consider it [. . .] I don't issue CTOs unless the person's deemed 'incapable' to make treatment decisions.

Thus, for Danielle, CTO efficacy is achieved if drug treatments improve the ability of the individual to function in society even when that person believes medicine is not causing the improvement. Danielle elaborates:

> So when he's untreated, okay I've told you what he's like, but when he's treated, when we did keep him for a year on a CTO, from the outside it looks good. He maintained housing for a year.

Generally, psychiatric workers and patients will agree that having a job and housing are good things. But do people become 'functional' because of the treatment, or do doors open for them once they are 'compliant' and 'calmed'? Dennis and Monahan's work (1996) suggests that people are given supports and do well only because they are perceived to be taking their 'meds.' My informants explained that landlords demand that their tenants be on 'medication' before accepting them. The relationship between treatment success and 'adherence' needs to be critically examined. This puts into question Danielle's and most psychiatric workers' belief that a patient who does not notice the benefits of medication should sometimes be imposed upon for her own good.

The issues raised in a few comments already provide for a number of structural problematics, beginning with theory ('recovery' bearing fledgling status as an idea in Kraepelinian psychiatry), moving to practice ('compliance' as a mode of ensuring treatment 'happens,' the hidden restraint), and organization (the manipulation of a population through TAC, NAMI and SSO players, agencies well-stocked by corporate interests) a sketch emerges of a system that is borne to draw on more and more markets, and this contention, some would say observation, has not slowed the companies. One of the reasons I wanted to write about imposing drugs is that they really do a lot to the body, the brain, the person, and the social politic. Politically and economically, drugging prevents a voice from crying out. I was too dazed for advocacy as an in-patient, but to say that brings accusations that I'm not taking responsibility for an illness, or that I was therefore incapable anyway. My prior wishes might not be respected the moment I am deemed incapable.

Abuses

Racial division imposed by European colonial powers informs and sustains psychiatric oppression, and vice versa. Refugees from other countries come out of horrifying violence to safety on Canadian soil, only to find themselves in psychiatric care. I have heard from three separate sources indicating that refugees are being put under CTOs. This can work as a legal tool, as June, a legal worker, reports:

> I've had [a few] people [I know] on CTOs. Some are immigration related. The CTO has prevented them from being able to leave the country. They want to be deported, because they've been in the mental health system (I'm not sure if you see that a lot) but people that are held against their will in the mental health system who are on a refugee application want to leave. So part of what I do is [start by] trying to talk to refugee applicants about what's going on with them, 'cause most of them are experiencing – and I have a case this week – 'post traumatic stress.' His father died horrifically in March. They've just diagnosed him as 'schizophrenic.' The problem with that is that it might make him 'medically inadmissible' [to Canada]. So I was talking to him about like his options, and he thought going to the hospital might be a good option. And I'm like, 'If you're really concerned about your freedom, and if you're concerned about this thing that they call "schizophrenia," what you're going to read in a book is that it's permanent and it's not curable unless you take medication.' And I said, 'But the reality is, your dad died, you know?'

A CTO imposed on racialized bodies acts to prevent them from escaping a country that promised freedom from oppression and injustice. June continues:

> So if there is something going on like depression, grief, trauma, it escalates, and gets worse and worse and worse 'til they're put in the system against their will. At that point, they're probably feeling most like delusional stuff from the trauma they come from – this country is pretty like delusional itself – language issues, all these things. And then you're being told by this doctor, you're going to get hit up with this drug, which is going to give you serious side effects, and you cannot leave the hospital. So then you tell the doctor, 'I want to leave the country, call my lawyer.' They're like, 'we can't deport you 'cause you're being held here against your will.' Somebody in prison, they can make arrangements to deport them after their term or to just return them to the country. We're finding that many of the refugee claimants [under CTOs] are not being given that option. And I don't really know how to help in that situation [. . .]

So, they [refugees] can't do anything, but then they don't have any money to leave, right? But the thing that concerns me the most is that you've come from a god-awful situation and you've come here, and you want to leave this god-awful situation for the one which, politically and economically and violence-wise, is probably worse. But the fact that people are perceiving our mental health system as a form of torture that's worse than the one they escaped should concern people.

The issue of torture has been taken up at the United Nations by Tina Minkowitz and other disability activists. How treatment could possibly be considered torture is indicated in Danielle's observations about some of her patients' selves being in straitjackets, and Tyler's question of whether compliance impedes personal growth.

DANIELLE, A PSYCHIATRIST: [. . .] they can't stand the mental straitjacket. They just can't take it anymore. And it becomes a whole issue of 'what is self'? Like what is your experience of your self? And if you have no sense of your emotions, what is that? I don't know.

TYLER, A HOUSING WORKER: Well, just in how, we were saying that, it's all about compliance with taking medication. So where does that leave, you know, discovery, or trying things differently, you know?

Dreams of escaping Canadian mental health imposition were not only reflected in refugee narratives, but also in stories of people who had been in the system for many years, as Rudy described. A peer worker, Rudy spoke of a middle-aged white male CTO subject who felt he was better off in a psychiatric facility than in his apartment under a CTO:

Well actually he's back in the community because of a Community Treatment Order. This was a gentleman who had an experience that they labelled psychosis, and he was hospitalized for a fairly lengthy period of time. He was satisfied with that. He was able to take a medication in the hospital orally. That was the medication that was prescribed.

The hospital decided they didn't want him in the hospital, that they wanted him to be in the community, and they wanted him to take the medication by injection, because they did not trust that he would take the medication orally. He did not wish to have the medication by injection. He did not want that at all.

They made the decision to apply for a Substitute Decision Maker, the [Public] Guardian [and Trustee] of Ontario [see chapter 5], who was appointed [and] agreed with the hospital that he would be put in the community and given his injections. He was put back in the community into his own apartment, and this was an apartment he'd had for a period of time, and he did not wish to have the injections, so they had the police come, take him to the hospital, which was a forty-five-minute drive, inject him, and the police returned him to his home, and this has happened on a number of occasions since his release from hospital.

The CTO requires that Rudy's friend adjust his lifestyle to enable police to enforce workers' injection appointments. He would rather flee Canada than live under a CTO. Rudy continues:

He's bothered in his life now because of the CTO. Recently he talked to me about wanting to leave this country. He felt that strongly about it!

He said, 'I'm not safe here. This is what they do to me. They come – the police take me away when they choose to take me away and do this to me – inject me when I don't wish to be injected.' You know? It was a sadness in him, and some fear, a loss of control in his life, which disturbed him very deeply.

And again, he's talked a number of times, 'How can I get out of this country?' In practical, real terms, I think it would be extremely hard for him to leave the country, first of all financially. And then, what border can he cross given that he is on a CTO and there is a Substitute Decision Maker for his affairs?

Yeah, there's a sadness. I have a sense of sadness around it as well. Here is a person that is being hurt. I don't know what the word is; I was thinking of the word 'coerced' – it's a stronger word than what should probably be used to describe that. It's 'oppressed.' He's being oppressed, and that's the reality of his life.

There's a sadness about it because he also just accepts that this is his fate in some way. It's like, 'Okay, I'm not going to make too much trouble. I don't really want to be doing this. I don't see that I have much way out of this. There doesn't appear to be. The "authorities" are saying that this is what they're going to do, this is best for me. They're making that decision. I don't really have any protection. I don't really have any way of stopping that.'

I mean, at some level I think he's right. You know you have psychiatrists who have in their expert opinion said that this is what he requires.

That's reality, you know, and I think that's life in this province under CTOs. Absolutely. I've seen that happen in other situations not to do with CTOs as well, in terms of Consent and Capacity [see chapter 5] and that's what happens.

The patient has already caused trouble simply by requesting no injection. His identity, self-esteem, and 'community' freedom are eclipsed by his status as a CTO subject. Rudy's friend feels the Canadian Charter of Rights and Freedoms cannot protect him and he longs for escape. This theme of escaping CTOs links to questions of identity insofar as our self-concept is bound up in our story of self. But let's remember that stories provide us ways of exchanging ideas, and transcending them. A 'self' can be described in so many ways. So the identity of Mad or patient status, different as they are, cannot encompass all that we are becoming.

Identity as Lack of Insight

The idea of the 'incapable' patient who is unable to recognize his or her need for medical treatment relates back to my chapter on Mad identity. States Danielle, a psychiatrist:

> So an example would be a person, and this is a true example of a young – well not a young man actually, he's late-forties – with thirty years of illness, and when untreated went off meds. In treatment he responds to small doses of antipsychotics, and when off meds he is unable to stay out of an institution. He's catatonic in the middle of a street. He cannot escape an institution because that's just the way our society works – you don't want someone like that out on the street. So he ends up being picked up by police and brought into hospital every time, and every time it's 100 per cent predictable: when out of hospital he will not use medication because he doesn't think he has an illness.

Again we see medicine freeing the patient from the institution in this narrative, but the patient disagrees that he is 'ill.' This seems utterly absurd to anyone trained to recognize and classify 'disordered' behaviour. Only if we consider 'improvement' to be socially mediated might we consider the patient's identity to be at stake.

DANIELLE: And when on small doses of medication on a CTO he is able to maintain independent living, attend college, register for a medical technician's course, and continue with that. The gradient [of improvement] is incredibly huge. But even when treated there is no connection in his mind between his state of studying and living independently, and the Community Treatment Order and the medication. There is no connection in his mind.

ERICK: What does he attribute the improvement to?

DANIELLE: Oh, he just won't answer the question, or circumstances, or his efforts. Usually the question is debated. So it's a high, high level of what we would call 'denial.' They just do not at all integrate a psychiatric formulation of their life situation. But a person like that, you could ask him, is his life – does he prefer going to college and living independently to being in a hospital? And absolutely that's very important to him. But the more that the importance – that's what I mean by the perceived quality of life: the difference in treated state is very great and is very *important* to them – for me it's worth the emotional and the resource investment in implementing a CTO. But it's also worth the moral or ethical dilemma that it puts you in.

As we see, while some patients may agree that their lives have changed for the better on coerced treatment, they may disagree that their medication has caused that change, or at least that their rights should be withheld to that end. Danielle believes her 'client' is doing better because of treatment. She is beholden to psychiatric understandings that her client refuses to accept. Even if this demonstrates her client's utter denial of reality, it seems useless to demand that he pretend otherwise, or to say that his efforts had nothing to do with attending school and other 'improvements.' Mad relation suggests that if a psychiatrist refuses to believe that a patient's self-concept affects her relationships and therefore her 'recovery,' the patient could only be seen to 'present' a socialized, ersatz 'self.' This relates to the madness-as-zombie trope. As to whether any of us have selves, I am speaking in relative terms rather than essential ones.

To underscore the futility of psychiatric refusal of self-narrative (whether or not we accept the industry's psychopharmacological claims), note that inmates may ascribe success to anything but 'treatment.' For example, an electroshock treatment survivor of the 1940s said that the reason that multiple treatments (without anaesthesia and muscle relaxant in that era) 'worked' for him was, 'there existed a "love relationship," a relationship similar to that between father and son, between myself and Mac [the attendant who held him down for this procedure], a relationship such as is established between psychiatrist and patient in narcosynthesis [emotional "catharsis" through drugging, in the institutional language of that era]. I believe this lucky accident proved to be the focal point of the entire treatment' (Alper, 1948). If I can borrow from psychological discourses for a moment, it seems as though the survivor would rather pin perceived success on the torturer's touch than the torturer's tools. This is a clear denial of instrumentation and a seemingly absurd validation of the machinist's contorted empathy.

Mad identity is construed in very nuanced ways. Rod Radford is an example of a person who speaks publicly about his 'schizophrenic' experiences as 'dreams.' He gave an interview and shared parts of his medical file courageously for a CBC radio program called *The Current*. Radford, who I have met briefly since the interview, contested his workers' intentions to put him on a CTO. He argued that he should not be put on an order because he was in control of himself and had sufficient supports to prevent a psychiatric 'crisis.' He tries to explain his 'symptoms' to his audience: 'My dreams are never violent. Like I'm never killing people or being oppressed by anybody. My dreams are more dreams of grandeur, just dreams of grandeur I guess, thinking I'm king of the world, I'm the genius, and I have powers of some sort. I don't get messages from the TV saying go out and kill somebody to free them or something like that' (Quinn, 2006).

Radford's experience, which others attribute to 'paranoia' or 'grandiose delusions,' is his own experience, albeit mediated by many forms of knowledge and terminologies. Even if we say his experience is not correctly represented by his terms, we must admit that his narrative implies an audience of people who understand the medical world he lives in. From a therapeutic lens, it should not be assumed that others' refusals of his narrative weaken his own self-narrative. Workers may pretend not to attend to 'delusional content,' yet they cite 'lack of insight' as central to their cause for intervention, tacitly demanding that Radford abandon his 'strongly held' beliefs. Radford also explicitly claims that his 'madness' is not violent. Implicitly he is saying 'delusion' is not necessarily causing (his) violence or anger. While progressive workers may agree, Radford is still forced to negotiate his rights using the medical nomenclature, psychiatric terms given to him during his many detentions. To a critical but privileged outsider, his negotiation may appear an acquiescence. His life narrative may seem marred by words that deny his experience (Quinn, 2006):

I can't speak for other schizophrenics but I know for myself I've been lonely. See you can't go out and make friends with normal people 'cause they always suspect you of something. I mean conversation-wise, they're always turned off. You know, I'm tripping the light fantastic[7] and they're talking about sports. I suspect other schizophrenics are lonely too. I mean I've got family, friends, but, uh, no lover. Who would choose schizophrenia? Nobody.

I doubt that there's a soul in the world who wants to be a schizophrenic.

Radford seems to be choosing schizophrenia when he says he prefers 'tripping,' but the label 'schizophrenia' does not entice in the end. Rather, his desire is somewhere else. His father takes a very different view of his dance. He underlines the need for control. Note the way in which Radford's questionably 'paranoid' objection is plotted between his father's moving emotional appeals in the audio documentary:

RADFORD'S FATHER: As a parent, you know, it's your child. Always wondering. Always thinking. Will he be on the street homeless? Will somebody take advantage of the opportunity? It's like that. Maybe he'll get hurt physically. It's a pain that you can't describe it. Point is . . . what will happen? When he becomes so bad that he'll be on the street and do something to somebody, and he goes to prison or jail, because most people don't understand what a schizophrenic is like?

RADFORD: [faded in] And that's what they use. A definition of a schizophrenic. I think they fear me. That's what I think. They all fear me.

RADFORD'S FATHER: Sometimes you wish that (um, I shouldn't say that) that he'll be calmed down. That is a person you can't completely control, you know? Someone that, um, is totally not capable of doing anything, just like a zombie, you can control him if you know him a lot, his words. So you can take care of him.

Radford's father sees him as a 'zombie' when he is feeling 'fantastic.' But he only wants him to be safe, to have a place to live. I believe Radford's father does not truly wish for complete control over Rod, but simply to provide a helper at the ready who understands his ways and might take the edges off at times, perhaps divert him from a dangerous

---

7 'Tripping the light fantastic' refers to an old English usage meaning to dance.

mission and remind him of simple self-care. This is not unlike mutual aid ideals espoused by survivors and radicalized psychiatric workers who do not depend on the needle.

Reviewing Orders

Treatment orders were so hotly debated in 2000 that Brian's Law was modified to call for ongoing public reviews of CTO use (to conceive 'improvements'). This was to be initiated sometime after three years, and when completed it would have to be completed every five years thereafter. I started my research to find out what was happening to people under CTOs, something few concerned people seemed to know.

The Ontario government hired Dreezer and associates to conduct the legislated review. A few researchers withdrew because of a perceived conflict of interest in November 2004 (conducting paid research on CTO use while paid to use CTOs). The remaining team members produced the report in December 2005, as I completed my own. They heard from their research participants, as I did from mine, that legislation was being distorted in practice, and rights were not generally respected:

> Notwithstanding the obvious success stories that we encountered, it became clear that CTOs are sometimes put in place and maintained in ways that appear to be calculated to circumvent the legal and procedural protections in the legislation. We note that while the protections appear to have been designed to ensure compliance with fundamental legal and Charter principles and internationally recognized standards to which Canada subscribes, the result is often different.
>
> We met clients whose lives have emerged from darkness to light as the result of a CTO. But we met others who told us that they felt a tremendous sense of violation and lack of respect as the result of the way that they have been treated under their CTOs. (Dreezer & Dreezer, 2007: 124)

It took some time for the ministry to provide the Dreezer report to the public. The former Minister of Health and Long-Term Care George Smitherman approved it in the summer of 2006. Then the ministry sat on it while several of us asked after it. Finally, only three days after receipt of a Freedom of Information Act request from activist Ms. Lucy Costa, the ministry made the report available on its website, on 10 May 2007.

The report admits that 'clients' may be led into abusive situations as a result of using CTOs:

> Unlike other treatments, a CTO exerts ongoing control, potentially over numerous facets of the client's life, many of which are outside of the areas that we would normally think of as being components of treatment.
> [. . . .]
> We met a long-standing CTO client whose spouse is her substitute decision-maker [legally agrees to enact a CTO when she is deemed 'incapable']. She told us that an already difficult and somewhat abusive relationship had become considerably more difficult and, from the client's point of view, frightening, since the spouse was given power under the CTO to control even more aspects of her life and further solidify an already troubling power imbalance. (Dreezer & Dreezer, 2007: 92)

How such a situation came to be indicates much about the lack of feminist principles in psychiatric practices. Ignoring the responsibilities of state-sanctioned use of force in reports of such abuse, these are set alongside anecdotes of positive outcomes attributed to the Community Treatment Order, without explanation. There is also little description of how the CTO 'client' improved in her life. There is no accounting for how legal coercion improves or does not improve treatment. At least the report questions whether legally coercive elements of CTOs are necessary for their supposed success, though informal coercion is never questioned as such.

In fact, the report provides quantitative evidence in its literature review (which I will take up below) showing legal coercions do no better than outpatient services provided in the 'community.' Despite this the CTO is seen to have positive effects. This is, indeed, the mainstay of the report, that CTOs are 'useful.' The report thus recommends hiring more 'CTO coordinators,' planting the CTO scheme deeper into the public purse. As for legalized coercion, more research is called for in the report. There is no indication that the CTO program, which was propounded as necessary legalized coercion, should be stopped before such research on legal coercion is conducted. But this lack of transparency began with 'public consultations' in 2000.

As for the rhetoric about CTOs preventing mad violence, the report says 'a negligible number of CTO clients have any criminal involvement with the legal system,' and that CTOs are used for allowing patients to live in the community (2007: 130). The ministry found that CTOs were used by fiat in some locations, such as in North York and Sudbury, yet not at all in the city of Chatham and hardly ever in St Catharines and Sault Ste Marie. However, I have heard from workers in these cities that CTOs are certainly in use there now. The researchers attributed an absence of CTO use to 'well-integrated services,' and any egregious use on lack of 'service coordination.'

While the review was in part meant to appease critics of CTOs, it was set in motion to 'improve' rather than evaluate the CTO program:

> We [the researchers] have been asked to answer five questions and to make recommendations that are clearly linked to our key findings and to iden-tify opportunities to improve both CTOs and the next legislated program review. Two of the questions relate to the reasons that CTOs were used or not used and the effectiveness of CTOs. The answers to those questions are key to formulating our recommendations with regards to improve-ments to both the next review and CTOs themselves.
>
> As we travelled the province we heard repeatedly that Community Treatment Orders have profoundly changed many lives and even saved lives. However, it is less than totally clear which factors, or combination of factors, have led to this apparent success. It is difficult to know whether the key is the order itself and the legal control over the patient that it con-veys, the services and the treatment team that is frequently assembled to support the patient, or some combination of these factors. (Dreezer & Dreezer, 2007: 124)

The raw data available to researchers on CTOs used from 2000 to 2004 were taken from separate and incommensurable reporting sys-tems, something the team could be critical of in their consultation process. This problem and several others are said to be correctable by administrative changes, especially by increasing resources to the CTO bureaucracy of 'coordinators.' Minor changes to legislation are recom-mended, such as clarifying whether or not a CTO is voided when a patient is recalled to her psychiatrist by use of a Form 47 (new legisla-tion allows for a continuation of the CTO; CMHA, 15 April 2010). But generally, the CTO is said to have succeeded in a number of contexts, and it is recommended for expansion even into First Nations and rural communities.

Perhaps more important to a qualitative researcher is the use of other data, the comments and queries submitted to reviewers by hundreds of workers and 'consumers.' Thankfully, the report does not try to hide the ambivalence of a large number of clinicians regarding CTOs, nor the resistance of mental health consumers. In rhetorical terms, these groups are presented quite differently in the text. While professionals bear grand objections to coercion, clients desperately seek medical help:

> Many CTO clients expressed support for the CTO concept and for their own CTO. We heard from clients who believe that the CTO has turned their life around or kept them out of hospital. We met consumers who told us that they wish that they had been on a CTO in years past instead of spending so many years suffering until they gained the insight necessary to turn their lives around. Several clients told us that they liked their CTO because it allowed them access to case management or other services that they needed. Many CTO clients told us that they felt that they were a true part of the CTO team and that they had been consulted fully during all stages. Some clients and former clients told us that the enforcement provisions of the act did not trouble them, as they were not needed in their case. Others told us that their awareness of the enforcement provisions had encouraged them to comply with their treatment during periods when their insight was less than ideal.

In these 'pro' CTO narratives, the 'client' is depicted as a fully free individual who would choose compulsory treatment like any other treatment. Compulsoriness is credited for success, in the patient's own words, whereas elsewhere in the report increased services, not compulsoriness, is considered the instrument of success.

In the above narrative, we move from 'client' acceptance of CTOs, to a stop in rehospitalizations, to an end of suffering and insight regained (all achieved by medicine). This leads to services accepted, then to involvement in therapy (the client is 'part of the CTO team,' unless he or she loses insight), to acceptance of 'enforcement provisions' thereafter. There are no caveats before we move to the naysayers. This narrative simply works for CTO 'clients' who seem to have recovered.

The story could be reversed. It might better reflect what the rest of the report admits. The client has an insight that enforcement provisions should be accepted in order to join the therapeutic team in finding services that will finally end suffering after years of waiting and rehospitalization.

The 'con' narratives are jumbled. Mixed in with sheer terror at force-ful interventions are complaints that serve the CTO program, like get-ting rid of cumbersome oversights:

> Some CTO clients and former clients told us that they had only consented to the CTO as a way to secure an early discharge from hospital but that they now felt that it had been very beneficial for them. Others informed us that they had consented to the CTO under this sort of pressure, that it had been of no benefit to them and they felt that the pressure that they had been subjected to compromised their basic human rights.
>
> Other clients and former clients had told us of their discomfort with the mandatory hearings and their belief that it was not necessary in the case of a voluntary CTO. Others felt that it would have been sufficient if a rights adviser had met with them and confirmed that they did not wish the annual hearing. Some clients felt that rights advice as well as optional and mandatory hearings are necessary safeguards for their rights.

The language researchers used to characterize resistance to CTOs is quite emotional:

> Some CTO clients and former clients took a much less charitable view towards CTOs than those referred to above. Some informed us rather vehemently that they saw the CTO as an affront to their dignity and autonomy and that it had not assisted them in any way. Some consumers told us that the spectre of a CTO was regularly used as a threat in their region in order to ensure compliance among consumers in the commu-nity. We also heard that some consumers who are not on CTOs are led to believe that they are in order to ensure compliance [. . .]
>
> It should also be noted that it was forcefully brought home to us that a sector of the consumer survivor community remains adamantly opposed to CTO on principle; a position, it would appear, rooted primarily in the adher-ents' original philosophical opposition to the scheme rather than experience since the inception of the program. (Dreezer & Dreezer, 2007: 84–5, 86)

The researchers' are open to experiences, just not the ones that cri-tique CTOs, we who circle in outdated 'philosophical' posturing. So, the 'con' side, painted as 'less charitable,' 'vehement,' 'affronted,' haunted by 'spectres,' and 'adamant,' has said very little about problems with CTOs that might be validated by empirical research or used to push levers of power. They seem to make little sense, shooting down rights while demanding rights.

Of course, the review was not meant to critique CTOs, and one cannot expect researchers beholden to the medical model (and lifelong careers in the industry) to come up with a balanced view of the group they impose upon. But Dreezer and associates are careful to insist on 'least restriction' and 'best practices' for all. Their report admits that these will not be found until 'CTO co-ordinators' are hired to iron out the wrinkles in CTO delivery. And as for the philosophical issues:

> Given the provisions of the Canadian Charter of Rights and Freedoms and the internationally recognized standards to which Canada subscribes, it is difficult to justify the diminution of patient autonomy inherent in a CTO without a clear understanding of the role that legal restrictions play in the success of a CTO.
>
> Our literature review failed to identify any compelling body of research in this regard (see section 3.3 Clinical Trial Evidence), and there appears to be a general consensus that more specific research needs to be undertaken. Therefore, it is critical to know whether there is significant added value to justify the legally intrusive nature of CTOs, and also for which patients they are likely to be efficacious. In our view, there is no justification to continue the program in its current form in the long term without this information. Therefore, we recommend the following:
>
> Recommendation 20:
>
> The MOHLTC should monitor national and international research findings and commission scientifically rigorous Ontario-based research into:
>
> - the importance or lack thereof of the legal component of CTOs
> - defining the profile of individuals likely to benefit or not benefit from the legal component of CTOs. (2007: 130)

The authors' conclusions seem almost strident. But it will be difficult to find no benefits to legal coercion when informal coercions are assumed necessary. If there are no differences between the two, then why get rid of a program that seems to be working for some people? The researchers have utterly failed to grasp other CTO research from quantitative orientations that indicate an insoluble problem occurs in designing a kind of clinical trial for mandatory treatments. What should they be compared with, for example? What sample of the population would be used as the guinea pigs?

The qualitative problematics of defining a pool of participants who might benefit not just from coercion but legalized coercion is beyond

Dreezer's team, and the ministry will likely not consider it. To those who implement the relations of ruling, research is not a matter of relating to the data, as the above narration of 'consumer input' suggests, but of relaying data. This deployment sustains technical purposes by ignoring the 'philosophical' issues (i.e., many relational and interpersonal issues). Its industrial purpose assumes positivistic grounding only through the enumeration of its subject.

The second legislated review, which was due in 2008, or 2010 if we accept the submission date, or 2012 if we go by the actual publication date, will be a familiar operation of explication, one of the practices of power in which survivors are described and silenced, consumers are described as supplicants, and in which professionals are at pains to show coercion is their last resort.

Literature on Community Treatment Orders

Ontario's Ministry of Health and Long-Term Care in its review found that research on CTOs, most of it originating in the United States and elsewhere outside Canada, did not support the use of compulsory community treatment (Dreezer & Dreezer, 2007). Community Treatment Orders and Involuntary Outpatient Committals (IOCs) in the United States are part of a broad set of mechanisms, including leave agreements, that are called 'mandatory outpatient treatment,' 'coercive' or 'supervised community treatment' (CCT and SCT), and 'assisted outpatient treatment' (AOT), among other usages. They are evaluated in qualitative and quantitative research with mixed results as to whether such implements 'work,' whether they will help or hinder. Rarely is the question a matter of whom it might help or hinder, and by this I do not mean which kind of patient but what person or social group in context. Much of the literature also says that because mandatory treatment seems helpful to some, it should be considered potentially useful generally (a good example is Churchill et al., 2007). This literature rarely moves beyond a therapeutic framework, and I will not provide an extensive review of it here, but I invite readers to look at such documents as the Churchill review (retrievable online), or even the Ontario CTO report.

Since this research got under way, professionals' have shown ambivalence in imposing community treatment (Geller, 1986; Levy, 1994; Dawson, Romans, Gibbs, & Ratter, 2003). Professionals started considering community coercions in the United States in the 1970s as the project of 'deinstitutionalization' continued to flounder, as Scull showed

(1984). Some raised the issue of whether mandatory treatment in the community truly constituted the 'least restrictive alternative' to physical institutionalization (Switzky & Miller, 1978; Miller, 1982). In the 1990s, when involuntary outpatient committal laws became more popular in the United States, with a good push from the pharmaceutical lobby, issues of 'reciprocity,' that is, 'availability of services,' took the fore (e.g., Eastman, 1994). The age-old question of whether coercion despoiled 'therapeutic relationships' was raised (e.g., Dennis & Monahan, 1996).

It is from such doubts about IOCs (in U.S.-based research) that researchers began attempting to evaluate their effects. The literature on the 'effectiveness' of coercive community psychiatric work is somewhat unsatisfying for both proponents and opponents because definitions of success provide much ground for disagreement. The literature seeks 'improvements' such as the following: decreased rehospitalization, increased drug compliance, 'quality of life' (usually the obtaining of housing and/or employment), and decreased arrests or violence reports (e.g., in Canada: O'Brien & Farrell, 2005). Such seemly improvements may be the result of the industry's rewarding 'compliance' rather than reducing 'symptoms,' as the coercion and restraints literature suggests (e.g., Dennis & Monahan, 1996). Some studies also address 'symptom management' or mere 'perception of coercion' (Steadman et al., 2001; Swartz et al., 2004). As with restraints literature, relational issues are missed. The relationship between worker and patient is assumed to be equal in many respects.

Often cited in newer reviews are two major scholarly reviews of the literature, the RAND evidentiary study (Ridgely et al., 2001) and the Cochrane Collaboration review (Kisely et al., 2004). Both of these found that only two field studies used randomized trials to study involuntary outpatient committals, one in New York and one in North Carolina. Thus, other studies, especially those conducted before the 1990s, had several methodological problems, and their results could be attributed to factors not considered in their research design.

The RAND study cites four problems with studying compulsoriness statistically: unclear target population (how do we enumerate the 'revolving door patient' or the 'violent mental patient'?), differential operationalization of outpatient commitment (methods of delivering IOCs and CTOs vary widely), selection bias (people who resist institutionalization may not represent a proper sample, and may 'respond' to a variety of interventions), and unmeasured variability in forms of treatment (each 'treatment plan,' even within a jurisdiction, is different). The RAND review claims that the alternatives to coercive community treatment include community interventions and housing, but this is not an answer to the question of whether legal coercion 'works.' Housing is a basic rallying cry by professionals and survivors alike.

A good example of quantitative evidence that supports mandatory drugging, but which lacks methodological rigour, is the New York State review, which appraised the effects of Kendra's Law and IOCs after five years. This study asserts that 'involuntary outpatient committal' increased compliance with chemical treatments and use of psychiatric programs; there was also a reduction in aggression and 'hospitalization.' A predictable pattern of psychiatric racialization in the inner city (Metzl, 2009), which was not seen in upper state New York, is that non-Hispanic blacks were disproportionately represented in the data. Though hailed as a breakthrough success by the Treatment Advocacy Center (2005), Paul Appelbaum (2005) cautioned that 'improvement' ratings were made by 'case managers,' who may be biased. He said a longitudinal study needs to be done to confirm long-term 'improvement' and that the study had no control group.

By contrast, the two studies cited by RAND and the Cochrane reviews were at least randomized. North Carolina's 'Duke' study, like the New York 'Bellevue' study, found that IOCs did not work unless 'services' were well-provided, which questions whether legal compulsion has any treatment value (or intent). However, the North Carolina study did find that coercion over a longer period (after 180 days) of time did result in the sort of successes that legislators are interested in. The RAND study is quoted in Ontario's CTO review: 'In contrast to the New York [Bellevue] study, the Duke [University, North Carolina] study, which is the better of the two, suggests that a sustained outpatient commitment order (180 or more days), when combined with intensive mental health services, may increase treatment adherence and reduce the risk of negative outcomes such as relapse, violent behaviour, victimization, and arrest' (Dreezer & Dreezer, 2007: 40).

Medication is assumed to be the necessary element in positive outcomes for patients, not others' expectation of compliance, for example, or the increased docility of tranquilized patients over time. Like the RAND review, Cochrane's authors concluded that there was not enough reason to believe compulsion was necessary to successful care: 'It appears that compulsory community treatment results in no significant difference in service use, social functioning or quality of life compared with standard care. There is currently no evidence of cost effectiveness. People receiving compulsory community treatment were, however, less likely to be victims of violent or non-violent crime. It is, nevertheless, difficult to conceive of another group in society that would be subject to measures that curtail the freedom of 85 people to avoid one admission to hospital or of 238 to avoid one arrest' (quoted in Dreezer & Dreezer, 2007: 41).

This only confirms what was written in prior work with regard to efficacy. That is, coercion doesn't work, and doesn't have to be relied upon if other supports are in place.

5 Authorization: Psychiatric History and Law

In chapter 2, I introduced psychiatric survivor experience as a starting point for researching psychiatric restraints, using a methodology based on critical modes of ethnography including Smith's Institutional Ethnography. This methodology allows me to move in this chapter from personal story to testimonial narratives to institutional texts that authorize treatment. How pre-emptive forced treatment is authorized encourages procedures and practices that are coercive, complex, and sometimes contradictory. However, texts allow us to perceive the goals of the industries and institutions that are generated from our affiliations and work.

The mental industries embody institutional texts that authorize psychiatric professionals to enact state powers largely at their discretion, as I will argue here. In this chapter, specific legal texts that inform and enable practitioners include case law, mental health legislation, and the very procedural forms that enact the powers of juridical texts. Smithian methodology leads me to 'mental health forms' and their use, as provided by the Ministry of Health and Long-Term Care in Ontario. At an interactive level they set out the conditions by which force may be enacted. It has implications for the family and other social institutions. Juridical texts arise from historical conditions that I will briefly introduce here for the purpose of understanding restraints use. Andrew Scull's work and others' can be useful for a more detailed look, though all histories bear important perspectives.

Europe-centred histories of 'madness' such as Foucault's ([1961] 1965) and Porter's (2002) suggest that before the advent of rigid social structures, people who could be labelled as psychotic might have been less distinguishable from others. The hackneyed Western image of the mad person as shaman arises from our distance from shamanism as it is practised today. In agrarian and metallurgical societies, those who saw or believed the impossible may have connected with others and with the cosmic beyond, but they may also have been excluded accordingly. In ancient Greece, Hippocrates interpreted mad experiences as malady, as an imbalance in the 'humours' of the body. We have few records of how 'mad' people were treated in antiquity but they were probably both cherished and detested in various milieu – and chained, beaten, exiled, or killed as they still are today in any society (Facchi, Majoli, & Constantino, 2004).

Social relations take a turn for commercial profit in the modern bourgeois era. Throughout modern Europe the well-off could send their 'mad' family members to be entertained or chained in a madhouse run by ordinary folk. Even then 'physic' (i.e., 'medicine') was force-fed to people using a 'bulluck's horn' (an ox horn; Belcher, 1997: 131). The madness trade expanded and asylums were created, again welcoming or horrifying places depending on the interests of family patrons and owners. Meanwhile, the state detained less fortunate lunatics, paupers, delinquents, and disabled others in almshouses and workhouses, unless they were simply pushed out of town. Two important rival factions grew out of this polyglot market in the 1700s: the Quakers' 'moral therapy' movement, which called for kindness and acceptance towards the distressed (critiqued for its religious roots by Foucault and others), and 'alienists,' who called for objective medical study of the ill body.

By the early 1800s psychiatric history began in earnest with the profession vying for medical status. It bumped moral therapy out of the therapeutic race, partly by fudging its numbers on how well it did to help people 'recover.' By the mid-nineteenth century psychiatry was overrun by masses in need, and it built more large institutions on the edges of cities (including the Provincial Lunatics Asylum in Toronto). Psychiatry went through numerous reforms that sought to end the beatings, dunkings, doping, chaining, and other tortures seen as treatments. Noted among asylum inmates-turned-reformers are John Perceval (see Bateson, 1974; Hervey, 1986) and his Alleged Lunatics' Friend Society in the United Kingdom, Elizabeth Packard and the Anti-Insane Asylum Society, and Clifford Beers ([1908] 1953), who started the National Committee for Mental Hygiene.

Beers is a somewhat controversial figure because his movement eventually embraced eugenics, which called for the sterilization of people considered genetically inferior. Eugenics militated into the T4 program in Nazi Germany, which killed thousands of mentally and physically disabled people in preparation for the Holocaust. Meanwhile biological cause theories for madness had gained ground with Emil Kraepelin's theorization of 'the psychoses,' illnesses thought to belie untreatable people in his asylums. Freud said his psychoanalysis would never work for them, only for people with 'neuroses.'

As discussed in chapter 2, practices moved from brute implements and drugs to brain-targeting treatments in the twentieth century, including electric shock, insulin-induced coma shock, and lobotomy/leucotomy. This move was meant to show that psychiatry was, indeed, a medical specialty, making strides in understanding the brain. When phenothiazine drugs came on the scene in 1950, they were rejected as less advanced than lobotomy. However, when drug therapy was soon exploited, the procedure was proudly hailed a 'chemical lobotomy' by psychiatrists.

At about this time, a new wave of reform occurred. Critics like sociologists Erving Goffman (1961) and Thomas Scheff (1967), historian and scholar Michel Foucault (1961), psychiatrists Thomas Szasz (1960) in the United States, Ronald Laing (1961) in the United Kingdom, and Franco Basaglia (1968) in Italy, among others, each wrote scathing indictments of psychiatric institutionalization (a critique that goes back to the nineteenth-century reformers, as Scull notes). As mentioned before, 'deinstitutionalization' began well before these critics got started (though they were later credited with the moral push to reintroduce 'the mentally ill' into society). The drug industry called phenothiazines 'antipsychotics' by the end of the 1960s (Whitaker, 2001).

By the 1970s, the Mental Patients Liberation Movement got under way (beginning with the group We Shall Overcome, in Norway in 1968; see http://www.wso.no). Asylums and hospital spaces were closed without much community planning and assistance, as Burris shows (2004). The expanding sale of 'antipsychotic' (major tranquilizers), 'antianxietant' (minor tranquilizers), and 'antidepressant' drugs rose along with community psychiatry, homelessness, and managed care systems in the United States (see Simmons, 1990; Bachrach, Goering, & Wasylenki, 1994; McCubbin, 1998).

In the 1970s 'community psychiatry' started to bring practices out of the ward into public settings, such as by monitoring behaviour and drug dispensing. The Program of Assertive Community Treatment (PACT), which was progressive in its inception in attending to people's basic needs (the 'Madison model'; Jacobsen, 2004) expanded across

North America, and it is now commonly called ACT, that is, Assisted or Assertive Community Treatment. Its mainstay in the contemporary moment is the assurance of patients' medication 'compliance.' Critics of ACT cite the expense of such 'million dollar' teams working with only 'about 80 clients,' as one participant said. Some peer support workers on ACT teams attempt to turn ACT professionals to 'alternatives.'

Social conservatives blamed 'deinstitutionalization' for its own failure. Especially in American cities, the general population was becoming unnerved by released mental patients in their midst. By the late 1970s, legally mandatory treatment was being considered as a means to curb 'crazy' aggression and violence outside the hospital. As institutions would not be reopened, 'outpatient committal' was considered by some to be the 'least restrictive alternative' to incarceration (Switzky & Miller, 1978; Miller, 1982, 1987; Hiday & Goodman, 1982; Mulvey et al., 1987).

Meanwhile the mental patients liberation movement had started to call itself the psychiatric survivor movement to remind a largely disinterested public about our oppression under eugenic and biopsychiatric interventions in the twentieth century. In Toronto, agitators like Don Weitz, Carla McCague, Pat Capponi, David Reville, Mel Starkman, and so many others, set the stage for the creation of *Phoenix Rising: The Voice of the Psychiatrized* (1980–88), not without help from allies like Dr. Bonnie Burstow. *Phoenix* is now available online from the Psychiatric Survivor Archives, in Toronto. In the 1980s, a less radical movement of mental health consumers sought partnerships and reform with progressive mental health workers (see Church, 1996). In the late 1980s, legal compulsion schemes were being adopted by several U.S. states. One community intervention was legally challenged by the New York Civil Liberties Association (Failer, 2002).

This sets the stage for what happened in the 1990s. In Toronto, Randy Pritchard and Irit Shimrat led the Ontario Psychiatric Survivor Alliance until its dissolution in 1991. The Consumer/Survivor Development Initiative started satellite agencies across the province at about the same time, and provincial psychiatric hospitals were made to develop patients' councils. I joined the psychiatric survivor movement in the summer of 1993, which I describe in chapter 3.

But it was the furor over 'deinstitutionalization' in the United States that led to a surge in 'outpatient committal' laws. Involuntary outpatient committal laws have been adopted in forty-four U.S. states since the 1970s, most fervently during the 1990s. They surfaced in

Canada in 1993. Saskatchewan's New Democrat government passed Community Treatment Orders. Ontario's Conservative government passed CTO legislation in 2000. Nova Scotia's Liberal government followed suit on 31 October 2005, then Newfoundland and Labrador in 2007, and Alberta in 2008. All other Canadian jurisdictions have 'extended leave' provisions that can be used like a CTO (Gray & O'Reilly, 2001). Australia's provinces and New Zealand use CTOs, as well as Israel, Romania, Scotland, and a few other countries. England and Wales, after extensive debate, introduced CTOs in 2007.

These laws were promoted by E.F. Torrey in the United States (his Treatment Advocacy Centre (2005) was well endowed with drug company funds), the National Alliance for the Mentally Ill in the United States, and the Schizophrenia Society of Canada (formerly Friends of Schizophrenics) with its robust provincial branches. These supposedly grassroots organizations encouraged families to publicize anecdotes of violence and get authorities to legislate imposed psychiatric treatment. D.J. Jaffe in the United States said: 'Laws change for a single reason, in reaction to highly publicized incidents of violence. People care about public safety. I am not saying it is right, I am saying this is the reality . . . So if you're changing your laws in your state, you have to understand that . . . It means that you have to take the debate out of the mental health arena and put it in the criminal justice/public safety arena' (cited in Monahan et al., 2001).

Progressive clinicians argued that legal constraints should only be imposed if 'reciprocity' is guaranteed, that is, services and basic supports (Eastman, 1994). Critics also claimed that legal coercion threatened therapeutic relationships (Dennis & Monahan, 1996). In the 1990s, researchers evaluated the effects of legal coercion in terms of 'quality of life' and 'client satisfaction,' finding no major differences in outcomes between mandatory and ordinary programs (RAND, 1998). Such research was and still is oriented towards therapeutic 'efficacy.'

The Canadian Mental Health Association, well-resourced in the 'mental health sector' and touted as a defender of psychiatric patients' rights (though it was once a part of the eugenic 'mental hygiene movement' in Canada), hedged their anti-CTO position (compare CMHA, 1998, and Everett, 2001), and some local branches took funding to 'coordinate' CTOs (also compare CMHA Metro Toronto, 17 May 2000, and Centre for Addictions and Mental Health/CMHA, 2005). However, it is Community Treatment Order coordinators who stand to gain the most from Ontario's CTO review recommendations, and the program awaits expansion.

Often, in the United States coercive community treatment is associated with Assertive Community Treatment teams (Ridgely et al., 2001; Dennis & Monahan, 1996), as it is in Canada, though CTOs are often imposed without mobile 'crisis support.' ACT is not homogeneous in application, however. In two community mental health centres in the South Bronx area of New York City, neither ACT team performed better than 'outpatient' hospital clinics ('day programs') in attending to primary needs for 'outpatients,' such as housing and employment (Nieves, 2002). Despite the heterogeneity of practices, ACT teams are commonly associated with involuntary outpatient committal laws in the United States and Community Treatment Orders in Canada.

Legal Capacity

A legal suit by Steven Mullins can be used to frame case law related to chemical restraint, because he was deemed of 'sound mind' rather than ill. Mullins' suit is also used here to provide a comparison with my own narrative of incarceration. In August 2005, Mullins won his suit against the Vancouver General Hospital (VGH), the same facility where I was detained.

Suffering anxiety from grieving two deaths in his family, Mullins sought help voluntarily. Shortly after being seen by a psychiatrist, who was prepared to release him, he ventured to leave his room. Guards blocked his way and ordered him to stay, so he tried to push through. They overpowered him, dragged him to an isolation room, and cut away his clothing. Clinicians administered an intramuscular injection of the major tranquilizer haldoperidol. Mullins was held for five days and only released after he agreed to continue 'treatment' and 'supervision' as an 'outpatient' (*Mullins v. Levy*, 2005, BCSC 1217). Such events are rarely discussed openly, far less argued in court. Attendants' methods at the VGH that I experienced in 1993 continue, provoking 'behaviour' that feeds the use of drug restraints.

Mullins was far more fortunate than most. Within hours, while still unconscious, a lawyer arrived (his father) and began scrupulously documenting clinicians' activities, noting their use of legal forms. Despite a number of problems in procedure, some of them substantive, the staff members were generously protected by British Columbia's Mental Health Act (s. 16). In court, they argued that they performed their functions without malice, complying with established protocols based in medical knowledge and ethics.

To save an unconscious patient who is unable to consent to treatment, physicians should be able to treat her. In the *Mullins* case, clinicians argued that a 'delusional' person who is 'agitated' (meaning excited or abusive) might reject her 'diagnosis' and 'treatment.' The 'illness' is said to rob her of the ability to think correctly, to 'understand and appreciate' the treatments being proposed to her. Such a person must be seized to deliver life-saving remedies. One doctor boasted that he subdued several 'psychotic' patients in this manner daily, seeing it as a fine and necessary technique (S. Mullins, personal communication, 12 Sept. 2005). In fact, some clinicians unofficially call haldoperidol 'Vitamin H' (not to be confused with biotin), even providing jocular instructions on subduing 'patients' online (Rosenberg, 2002; Forrest & Forrest, n.d.).

In *Mullins*, Justice Holmes ruled that clinicians were, indeed, acting in good faith, and that the attendants did not 'punish [Mullins] and the intention was clearly to aid him' (*Mullins v. Levy*, at para. 224). His Section 7 Charter right to 'life, liberty and security of the person and the right not to be deprived thereof except in accordance with the principles of fundamental justice' (Canadian Charter of Rights and Freedoms, 1982) had not been violated. Mullins had no authority to question the constitutionality of such aid, not because he was deluded and would not understand its benefits, but in this case because he did 'not claim to be mentally ill' (*Mullins v. Levy*, at para. 226).

The 'right to treatment' logic is at play here: the mad body has a fundamental right to therapy that exceeds all other rights in a crisis situation, and a sane person has a right not to be attacked with needles, but cannot claim the attack was discriminatory because treatment was simply provided in error, to a sound mind. The judge found the attendants breached the Mental Health Act because they lacked the authority to 'aid' Mullins when they blocked him (because he was not 'mad'). Their assistance was thus negligent, indeed, 'violent,' and inappropriate for a 'normal' person, which Mullins was, as the judge said. After such brutalization, and seven costly years in court, Mullins was awarded $15,000 (far less than some people are awarded for improper police seizures).

While the *Mullins* case does not deal with coercion outside of hospitals, it provides a view to how people become involved with the psychiatric system through *pre-emptive* force practices in many cases. It is important that no one dares ask the random consumer whether she would ever accept a restraining intervention (e.g., if she might suffer 'mental deterioration' in the future). It also shows how difficult it is to obtain legal help or oversight of custodial practices that are understood merely as 'therapeutic.' Even when an experienced lawyer is on hand to record injustices, a court is not likely to rule that the medical establishment is violating a person's constitutional rights. Most importantly, it shows the mentalist standard of what kind of treatment can be dished out for the disabled body-mind. Our constitutional right to bodily safety, especially in conflicts and crises, is predicated largely on sanist ideals of reasonableness, responsibility, and self-representation.

Informed Consent

I will turn now to Canada's famous *Starson* case in the jurisdiction of Ontario to compare Mullins with someone who suffers the 'psychotic' diagnosis. In British Columbia, treatment can be imposed without consent whether the person's official status is voluntary or involuntary (the legal concept of 'consent' is denied to psychiatric patients in British Columbia, as I found). However, mental health legislation in Ontario was changed in 1967 to include the right to choose or refuse treatment, regardless of whether a person is detained against his or her will. Despite this radical change to Ontario's law, physicians were surprised when they discovered the shift twelve years later, during another governmental redrafting of the Ontario Mental Health Act, and they lobbied vociferously to have these provisions revoked (Simmons, 1990).

In theory, an Ontario physician must inform a psychiatric patient or her 'substitute decision maker' of: the nature and reason for a proposed treatment, its risks and benefits, and any alternatives possible. Rights are monitored, not enforced, by the Psychiatric Patient Advocate Office, which was funded 'at arm's length' from the Ministry of Health in 1983. This body came into existence soon after the Aldo Alviani inquest, in which a 19-year-old man's death due to 'overdrugging' at the Queen Street Mental Health Centre in Toronto was declared by a provincial coroner to be a 'therapeutic misadventure' (Simmons, 1990). Though British Columbia's psychiatric laws do not provide for consent, Ontario's consent rules are not systematically enforced. As workers reports in chapter 4 show, 'rights advice' and other provisions in the Ontario Mental Health Act are often not delivered due to resource and programming barriers.

The Schizophrenia Society of British Columbia was allowed to act as 'intervenor' in the *Mullins* case, that is, as a third party with pertinent additional information. The Schizophrenia Society, thanks to drug manufacturers' financial assistance, has local, provincial, and national extensions to intervene in many cases across Canada, often as the lone voice of the 'community' behind those of psychiatrists, workers, hospital administrators, and as in *Mullins*, the provincial government. They are seen as the voice of families and the 'mentally ill' (it should be pointed out that many families oppose coercion).

Schizophrenia Societies advocate for more chemical treatment, pharmaceutical research, and stronger legal mechanisms to enforce treatments (they also promote 'destigmatization'[1] and social support like almost any organization, though these were hard-won concepts for consumer activists during the 1980s). They argue that interventions save lives and should not be restricted to situations in which the person is outwardly 'dangerous.' Committal criteria should be expanded so that individuals can receive treatment when they begin to 'mentally deteriorate.' The law should not tie the hands of the psychiatrist until the person has become a threat. Such restriction is considered to be a denial of predictable and repeated patterns, just for the sake of a dry ideal of autonomy, a civic right that an unconscious person cannot exercise. 'Libertarian' idealism of the 1960s and 1970s is blamed for preventing treatment, though psychiatrists have had a great degree of discretion in these determinations, and they may refuse to impose treatment for various reasons.

According to Schizophrenia Society advocates, 'mentally ill' violence in the family dwelling is a common occurrence; during such emergencies, it is difficult to prove to authorities that their loved one has become dangerous. In response to these sorts of concerns, Brian's Law made it unnecessary for police to witness destructive behaviour before apprehending someone under the Mental Health Act.

In the landmark case *Starson v. Swayze* (1 S.C.R. 722, 2003 SCC 32), in which the Schizophrenia Society was not the only intervenor, the Supreme Court of Canada ruled that Professor Scott Starson had the right to refuse treatment. Starson is a physicist who 'became psychotic,' was incarcerated and later transferred to Penetanguishene Mental Health Centre's maximum-security Oak Ridge facility for uttering death threats to a doctor and fellow tenants. Accordingly, he went from the civil psychiatric system to the 'forensic' psychiatric system after he was

---

1 Stigma was theorized by Erving Goffman as a shame imposed by a group onto an individual for some distinguishing characteristic. Destigmatization attempts to change the group's attitude, such as by calling madness 'mental illness.' This would make what seems like a moral failure a mere medical condition.

found 'not criminally responsible,' yet the legal rules regarding forced treatment in that system are essentially the same.

Despite his exceptionally difficult situation, Starson represented himself in the proceedings, lending to the credibility of his claim that he refuses medication competently. He was supported by Toronto lawyer Anita Szigeti, who is the co-author of *A Guide to Consent and Capacity Law in Canada* (Hiltz & Szigeti, 2005). The case brought to light the seeming ease with which psychiatrists could impose treatment based on a patient's refusal to comply. It also provides an excellent view on psychiatric law in Canada and the legal notion of 'capacity.'

In the judgment, three competing values were identified regarding forcible treatment: the patient's autonomy, everyone's 'right to treatment,' and an overarching duty to protect 'public safety.' This medicolegal constellation assumes the biological explanation that some behaviour is caused by 'illness' requiring 'treatment.' A person may not be chemically treated against her will (which is legally considered assault) unless the state deems that person to be a threat to society, or the self. I will leave aside the questionable right of the state to incarcerate people who want to commit suicide;[2] in the *Starson* case the court recognized that the patient-inmate was no longer a risk to others or himself when he was drugged. However, Ontario law explicitly provides for forced treatment even when there is no dangerousness (if the person would suffer deterioration without 'treatment').

What would be an assault for 'normal' people is acceptable for the sick.

The purported responsibility of the state to protect its 'mentally ill' citizens (through *parens patrie* law or paternal law) is used to sustain this argument, and crystallized in what is called 'therapeutic jurisprudence/justice' (Caulfield et al., 2002). Under this view, constitutional rights are actually conferred through treatment (O'Reilly, 1998). This 'right to treatment' argument counters 'autonomy rights' reinforced during the 1970s (Perlin, 2000; Caulfield, Downie, & Flood, 2002). In this legal theory, the 'seriously and persistently mentally ill' should, by chemical management of their symptoms, recover their reason and exercise their rights within society. Responsibility confers rights. The 'ill' may recover full participation in society, but failing that, the Court

---

2 The right to die needs to be considered in this regard (Odette, 1995), in terms of euthanasia and eugenics, as well as drug-induced 'suicidality' (Breggin, 2003/04).

generally assumes treatment 'can [at least] improve functioning and alleviate suffering' (*Starson v. Swayze*, at para. 9).

Thus, the state intervenes in our lives not based on safety issues alone, but on our supposed 'illness' and 'need for treatment,' with confidence that medical questions have already been sorted out. As mental illness is said to come with the threat of dangerousness, psychotherapy may be preferred by a patient, but seems useless to the state as an immediate response at least.

In *Starson*, the Court authorizes drugging to remedy unwanted behaviours to balance autonomy rights, despite the availability of less physically damaging 'treatments.' This authorization is enacted when a psychiatrist deems a patient legally incapable to make treatment decisions. To do so, the psychiatrist must inform the patient under assessment of the following: the 'diagnosis,' the 'treatment,' its associated 'risks and benefits,' and whatever 'alternatives' are available. Then, acting with the authority of Ontario's Health Care Consent Act (1996), the psychiatrist tests for capacity by deciding if an inmate shows the ability to 'understand' her own symptoms and the 'treatment' suggested, as well as her ability to 'appreciate' the consequences of deciding or not deciding to use such treatment. The test is not whether the person can repeat specific terms or agree with the psychiatrist's terminology or specific 'diagnosis,' as the *Starson* decision now provides. The Court says a psychiatrist must decide whether the person recognizes that some 'condition' affects her, and that a 'treatment' decision will affect her, but the patient must not base her treatment decision on a delusion (*Starson v. Swayze*, at para. 18).

Starson's legal capacity was upheld by the Supreme Court, and his reasons for rejecting treatment were supported, especially because the tribunal, which bore the onus of proof in finding the patient incapable, brought scant evidence of incapacity. The Court strongly noted the risks that Starson faced in treatment: 'Professor Starson stated that the medication's normalizing effect "would be worse than death for me, because I have always considered normal to be a term so boring it would be like death." The evidence indicates that the dulling effects of medication transformed Professor Starson "into a struggling-to-think 'drunk,'" a result that precluded him from pursuing scientific research. Professor Starson stated unequivocally that every drug he had previously tried had hampered his thinking' (*Starson v. Swayze, at para. 102)*.

The Court states that incapacity is, in theory, not to be equated with the rejection of illness, as Starson rejects the biomedical illness paradigm, but demonstrated by compelling evidence of a person who rejects his condition, as understood by a psychiatrist or by a psychiatric tribunal (which is generally made up of a psychiatrist, a lawyer, and a layperson). The risks of mistreatment and misdiagnosis are theoretically considered by the Supreme Court, but are ultimately left to the treating psychiatrist as issues to be weighed against other risks.

Again, the demonstrability of psychiatric theory is not as important in this decision-making process as the patient's willingness to accede to social agreement. The Court says a person must accept that she has a problem (in herself, not with others) and that some form of intervention or care (for her) would be a responsible choice. The social conflict that has led to an intervention is resolved by medical paternalism in the law. The Court is not interested in how damaging a treatment can be, as *Starson* shows, but in ensuring the individual's 'right to treatment' as a means to ensure 'public safety.' The question of the consumer's reasonableness in accepting these priorities will determine her fate (if she refuses, common sense suggests she is quixotic, indicating again that she needs treatment).

But what happens if the inmate understands and appreciates this dilemma in the way the psychiatrist presents it, yet still rejects treatment? For example, the psychiatrist and the Consent and Capacity Board had earlier decided Professor Starson was 'incapable' with respect to treatment because he did not 'understand and appreciate' his condition and the choice before him, but the Supreme Court found they had no cause (he was aware of some kind of 'condition,' just not the diagnosis he was given). It is no surprise that Starson was later imposed upon with drugs, because while the Court could rule him capable despite his disapproval of the term 'schizophrenia,' it allowed for future findings of incapacity where the patient simply did not understand his condition.

When a person's 'psychosis' interferes with her recognition of the reality of her 'condition,' this phenomenon is called 'lack of insight,' or in medical terms, 'anosognosia.' Psychiatrists have defined 'psychotic disorders' like 'schizophrenia' and 'bipolar affective disorder' as losing touch with reality ('delusion'), interfering with a person's understanding and appreciation of risk, which is arguably the same as the 'condition' perceived by the Court. So her illness, or condition, or some other word for 'it' (madness), appears to prevent her from reasonably accepting her situation. Again, psychiatrists can test for this 'insight' by asking the patient if she is aware of her condition (in practice they surmise this from the conversation, such as by asking for the correct time as a test when a person is too excited to talk of diagnostics or the way others perceive her).

But the psychiatrist's decision is not the last word. The psychiatric system extends to patients the right to challenge determinations and arrangements (the word 'appeal' is reserved for the courts), including 'involuntary status' (detention in a facility) and 'incapacity' (imposed treatments). Basic legal standards of fairness are preserved.

Until 1967 in Ontario, two psychiatrists could without any review 'certify' (declare insane), then 'commit' (incarcerate), someone the court ordered, or police forced, into 'examination.' 'Dangerousness' was not a criterion until the law was changed, in great part thanks to the Canadian Mental Health Association (formerly the Canadian National Committee on Mental Hygiene). After 1967, one psychiatrist could make the determination to incarcerate, but a dissatisfied person could have a 'hearing' at a psychiatric 'review board,' albeit without the right to appeal to the courts (Simmons, 1990).

Hospital 'review boards' acted without oversight. In 1992, when the law was split into the two acts considered in this book, further separating committal procedures from forced treatment, review boards were reformed into a 'quasi-legal' body now named the Consent and Capacity Board. The legal distinction between imposed treatment and detention did not change the criteria by which people could be forcibly treated or detained, however. A person had to be an 'imminent' danger to self or others and believed to be 'mentally ill,' as of 1967, though the 'imminence' of her threat could be interpreted to mean 'within months,' according to a former chair of the Consent and Capacity Board (Bay, 2003), one of the lead researchers in the CTO review.

As we shall see, the board has heard few challenges to CTOs. According to lawyer Suzan Fraser (personal communication, 13 June 2008), the board has been legally exempted from hearing constitutional challenges by patients, which gives us all far less opportunity to challenge the law in court, given the costs and delays involved.

Forms

[The following incident occurred in 1979, in North Bay, Ontario:] The ['deprivation'] therapy was to continue for 6 weeks, but in the fifth week, a concerned union steward went to check, observed the man in a little side room like a naked animal in a kennel. No one spoke to him. No amenities in the bare cell. A pail to urinate in, newspapers to shit on. Five weeks!

When the steward was noticed by a doctor, the result was a quick decision to release the man, bathe, shave and clothe him. A consent document for the treatment was signed – the day after his release.

– Marshall, *Madness*

Allowing for Marshall's use of the term 'madness' to explain systemic violence, we move from legal decisions to legal forms. Legal texts allow us to see the workings of institutions. Life and death decisions are made under pressure, but the only material evidence we have of them are hearsay and legal documentation. Decisions can be made to appear as though the patient's autonomy was of utmost importance, or conversely the treatment was, but the following pages will not provide anecdotes quid pro quo. My intent is to analyse the limits of the discretionary power that physicians have to make a choice in either direction.

Ontario's Mental Health Act rules are certainly not generalizable to all Canadian or external jurisdictions, but as one of the most 'progressive' examples of psychiatric law (Bay, 2003), they could be used to measure others. Their deficits will inform any reader about 'the rules' of psychiatric institutionalization as they relate to lived experience.

The Mental Health Act of Ontario provides psychiatrists with powers to detain, restrain, and impose (for therapeutic purposes), and requests that doctors provide documentation of such legal coercions using Mental Health Act forms. Additional requirements by specific facilities and institutions, as well as professional bodies, may also impinge upon doctors' decisions to use this act. The Mental Health Act regulates incarceration, among other issues, and its administrative forms determine what status a patient has, for example, 'involuntary status.' Otherwise, the Health Care Consent Act of Ontario regulates treatment-specific matters, including issues of obtaining 'consent' or assessing patient 'incapacity' to consent. Note that 'involuntary' and 'incapable' do not mean the same thing in Ontario law. In British Columbia and other provinces, a determination of 'involuntary' is taken to mean 'incapable' however, because there is no capacity law applied in the 'mental' health sector. Thus, there is generally little distinction between commitment powers and therapeutic regulation. Despite Ontario's legislative distinction between coercion and therapy the Community Treatment Order emerges in 2000 to erase the distinction. Colleagues in England suggest, as I have (Fabris, 2006), that CTOs use health regulations (as opposed to a Mental Health Act) to expedite restrictive and punitive procedures under the guise of therapeutic intent (personal communication with presenters on CTOs in Bristol University, 31 March 2010).

In my own experience, I was forcibly drugged, placed in a locked ward, told I would have to wait and see several people before being released (the 'examination'), and when I was at my worst after several days in detention (without rights advice), I was told I should sign a form, evidently indicating my wish to be a psychiatric patient. I was technically made a 'voluntary' patient (I most certainly wanted to avoid 'involuntary' status). But I was treated like everyone else, as a detainee; for example, I was told that in order to have a cigarette outside I would need to move up another level on the ward's 'privilege' ranking system. I imagine this could be excused as therapy, as could any punitive measure according to the Health Care Consent Act of Ontario. My point is that paperwork can appear to show that a patient accepts impositions made by clinicians.

From the perspective of the health care provider, not only do these administrative forms ensure some kind of governmental 'accountability' (to a taxpayer ostensibly), but they also loosely indicate directions to be taken. If the person is distressed *enough,* a psychiatrist may choose to impose or intervene with treatment. Yet, as Smith shows (1990b), such evidentiary documentation of 'rules of relation' squeeze professional conduct and regulate (or at least influence) the work of health care providers. In other words, institutional texts carry the ideology of 'extralocal' managers, who do not attend to local concerns but try to influence them all by some universal design.

In Ontario, to determine if a patient should be made 'involuntary,' a psychiatrist must check boxes and write descriptions on a 'Form 1' (called an 'Application by Physician for Psychiatric Assessment'). By doing so, the psychiatrist formally declares her 'belief' that a person should be 'assessed' (under detention) for 72 hours. This is not called an 'involuntary' status and cannot therefore be challenged at the Consent and Capacity Board. It is simply called an 'assessment' and escapes legal oversight, except by what is provided in a 'Form 42,' which is delivered to the detainee indicating her right to counsel and the indicated reasons for the assessment. But a lawyer cannot challenge medical reasons for the form, only matters external to the psychiatrist's belief that the patient needs to be monitored for 72 hours (I confess I cannot think of an example that would challenge such detention, except of course, not filling out a Form 1 and a Form 42 as required, though this happens all the time).

After this three-day period, a psychiatrist may sign a 'Form 3,' which denotes a period of 'involuntary' commitment lasting two weeks or less. A 'Form 30' is also provided to the patient, or apparently the detainee, to indicate the reasons for detention, the right to obtain legal counsel, and that a separate 'rights adviser' consultation will occur. It also says the person can fill out a 'Form 16' in order to challenge the psychiatrist's decision at the Consent and Capacity Board. There are additional forms for additional periods of detention. This assembly line of forms and procedures adds to people's problems in a place that's supposed to deliver them from stress. Advocates spend most of their time explaining these processes, ironically implemented to serve patients' rights, that is, if they have time and are available.

A Community Treatment Order is issued using a 'Form 45,' signed by a psychiatrist, who indicates reasons for the order, as well as by the patient or her substitute decision maker in her stead. The required 'community treatment plan' is developed and distributed with the Form 45 to everyone named in the plan. A 'Form 46' is also given to the detainee indicating her right to challenge the decision at the board.

Forms 1, 3, and 45 each provide checkboxes noting the possible reasons a person may be detained under the Mental Health Act. A psychiatrist can detain someone if she falls under Part A or Part B.

Part A

The Mental Health Act allows a psychiatrist to detain an individual if she believes that individual (a) attempted, attempts, threatened or threatens to cause bodily harm or self-harm, or (b) behaved or behaves 'violently,' even if only as perceived by someone else, or (c) shows inability to care for herself because she is 'apparently suffering from mental disorder of a nature or quality that likely will result in' serious harm or impairment (Mental Health Act, s. 15.1). The last of these three requirements is most broad and is all that is necessary for a psychiatrist to renew a form and extend the detention. The 'nature or quality' of the illness is not supposed to mean 'the diagnosis,' but how serious the symptoms appear (at what time is not specified). Part A is commonly called the 'dangerousness' category.

Most critics agree that this text leaves a great deal of room for determinations borne of inaccuracy or decontextualization. A man named 'R.R.' in tribunal ('Board') documents became so angry at his psychiatrist's calling the police to apprehend him, in circumstances that the psychiatrist later regretted, that R.R. demolished a nursing station. Without having to explain himself, the psychiatrist declared that the client's actions were not related to his illness and 'discharged' him promptly (*R.R., Re,* 2004 ON C.C.B.). This seemingly contradictory outcome explains the way in which perception and varied interests come into play in psychiatric determinations with limited legal oversight.

Part B

New criteria allow the psychiatrist to commit a person if she believes all of the following: the individual (a) has been treated in the past and improved as a result, (b) may, as in the past, because of her 'illness,' 'suffer substantial mental deterioration' or physical deterioration or physical impairment, and (c) is also 'incapable to consent to treatment.' Note that I have arranged the criteria in item (b) to emphasize the broadest indication first: 'substantial mental deterioration.' This criterion, lawyer Anita Szigeti has argued (personal communication, January 2001), could be adduced from any of the mental illnesses because they naturally result in 'deterioration.' So the problematic here and elsewhere is not *if and when* a mental illness might cause deterioration, but *that* mental illness causes deterioration. This makes it easier to understand why psychiatrists believe treatments work even when their patients deny it; see item (a). And because much mental illness leads to inability to recognize a need for treatment, suggesting incapacity, as the *Starson* case shows, these criteria could be applied to anyone in 'psychotic' distress as well as other diagnostic kinds of distress; see item (c).

The Community Treatment Order applies to people who fit the criteria in Part A or Part B, with some caveats. The person must also have had two 'hospitalizations,' or one lasting 30 or more days on a single occasion, within the last three years. Despite this small number of interventions, the CTO is encouraged to prevent 'chronic' readmission to hospitals (Mental Health Act, s. 33.1.3) and keep out the 'revolving door patient.' The CTO is supposed to be offered as a treatment by the psychiatrist, and the individual is then to be provided with a Rights Adviser. However, if the person is deemed 'incapable' (perhaps by use of 'Part B' criteria), a substitute decision maker will be found or appointed and *also* be provided with 'rights advice' so as to decide on the CTO (though rights advice is no longer required upon CTO renewals; CMHA, 15 April 2010). The psychiatrist is supposed to believe the SDM acts in accordance with relevant principles such as 'prior wishes' and 'best interests' set out in the Health Care Consent Act.

According to law, a CTO candidate must also be deemed by the psychiatrist to require psychiatric care and supervision while living in the community and be able to 'comply' with the treatment plan. Services in the treatment plan must be available in the community. The 'community treatment plan' may include any conceivable treatment or appointment, and may assign monitoring and information-sharing tasks to the person's family, community members, and helpers or agencies beyond the facility (usually a 'case manager' or Assertive Community Treatment team), all of whom must be consulted about the CTO.

Despite these rules, my research participants and others say health care providers do not follow standard legal 'safeguards' and 'rights provisions.' In fact, lawyer Lora Patton says they are routinely ignored (personal communication, 13 July 2008). This is not surprising given the lack of legal education for professionals and patients/detainees alone.

Patient Detainees

Now that these legal rules have been described, I will designate psychiatric patients *detainees*, if only because a person under a '72-hour assessment' is denied legal oversights or even substantive legal appellation ('patient' is simply too broad a term to explain detention for some patients, and 'inmate' is too narrow as this legal designation provides rights denied to psychiatric detainees in civil and forensic 'streams'). This is not to avail myself of the U.S. rhetoric about political prisoners that it calls detainees, but to precisely denote what is legally occurring under power of a Form 1: a detention (isolation, sequestration, containment in a controlled space or posture). But a Form 1 'assessment' is only one instantiation of legal procedures that confuse restraint with treatment, as this book attests, so anyone under compulsory psychiatric arrangements is in danger of environmental detention (isolation, sequestration) or restraint (chemical or mechanical), and is conceivable as a detainee insofar as chemical restraint impairs, limits, and constrains the body in social and physical space.[3] In some circumstances of psychiatric coercion, such as when institutionalized people are drugged into

---

3 In my prior work I used the term *inmate* in keeping with Goffman's terminology (1961) to describe people under compulsory psychiatric arrangements as well as in institutions. I also meant to suggest that if *patients* were conceived as *inmates* they might better protect their legal rights, though in practice this might not be the case. However, *detainee* more exactly describes the social location of subjects of CTOs, involuntary status, and incapable status.

a stupor without diagnosis, I believe the term could be applied without official 'patient' status. I can imagine other labels: drugner, somnolist, chemobot, but these terms have little to do with the concerns that initiated my work. I will continue to use terms like *patient* and *client* when the context calls for it, such as when a situation applies to patients of any medicinal practice, or when considering a client of advocacy services.

Decision Making

> Conditional love is no love at all.
>
> – Leonard Roy Frank, *Frankly Quoted*

I care deeply about my family, but whatever conflicts we have can be ramped up through systems of management in medicine. The role of families can be intensified under Brian's Law legislation. Family members are legally recognized as playing a role in treatment when listed in a 'community treatment plan,' making them quasi-professional health care providers. Whereas professionals work with detachment for the appearance of accountability, families in the inexplicit role of 'service providers' have prior personal relationships with their loved ones. This issue seems less important to insiders of the 'mental health industry' because of the relative closeness of all parties in a 'therapeutic alliance,' but others recognize that such arrangements bring insidious possibilities. During government consultations regarding the implementation of CTOs in Ontario (by invitation only), families became as concerned as professionals regarding their exposed liability while performing institutional functions in semi-controlled 'health care' arrangements.

Families are also sought by psychiatrists who need to obtain consent to treat someone they deem incapable, unless someone has already been chosen by the patient to act as a 'Power of Attorney for Personal Care' in treatment decisions (not to be confused with 'Power of Attorney for Personal Property'). Family members will be asked to be a substitute decision maker in order of kinship listed by the Health Care Consent Act. If someone cannot be found or no family member accepts the responsibility, a doctor can always rely on the Public Guardian and Trustee, a government office (that can also control a patient's estate if she is deemed 'incapable to manage property' whether or not she is 'involuntary' under the Mental Health Act). Only the physician's judgment regarding the family's motives (i.e., they must follow the principles of the Health Care Consent Act) will provide a check to the potential for conflict of interest, a problem mentioned by the psychiatrist who participated in this study.

In this research several participants discussed the role of families in the CTO arrangement. It was noted that in some instances doctors had overstepped a person's substitute decision maker when the SDM did not agree to treatment. Thus, even an SDM who supports a patient in refusing treatments including electroshock can be sidestepped by a psychiatrist (who convinces the tribunal that the treatment is in the patient's 'best interests').

The participant psychiatrist in this study, however, welcomed the family's involvement as a check against her own powers. She noted that detainees often felt betrayed by families who accepted a Community Treatment Order on their behalf. She had seen families that tried to have loved ones detained for monetary gain, though she said this was very rare. An informant explained that a doctor had lengthy conversations with the father of a CTO subject, but virtually no conversation with the subject himself. This father imparted stories of 'behaviours' by phone in audible range of the detainee.

Families have been written into psychiatric work. As history shows, the family has always been the first to call for therapeutic assistance. Goffman saw an alliance between family and worker that would always seek to correct loved ones who failed to fit and do well for themselves. But the experiences of psychiatric survivors without families is instructive. *Parens patrie* law, or paternal law, provides the state with parent-like powers over citizens who have no families.

6   Biocarceration

Piece by piece my body is breaking down. My tongue is thicker. Not quite attached at the root. I'll never speak again. I make myself keep talking. Concentrate on the movements each word makes even if what I'm saying doesn't sound like anything.

The nurse keeps coming by with a little white cup and a pill inside. I slur, 'No.'

– Anderson, *Code White*

From theory about 'madness' and 'illness' in chapter 3 to 'mental health' industry practices in chapter 4, to *'parens patrie'* authorization in chapter 5, we turn to the biophysical principles of chemical restraint and incarceration. Contemporary methods for achieving indefinite control of 'self' (institutionalization) will be considered in the next chapter by comparing Erving Goffman's observations inside what he called 'total institutions' to contemporary arrangements as described in this book.

Coercive community treatment provides a legal instrument by which treatment and restraint can be understood as bound together because of the absence of environmental segregation. I should point out that Community Treatment Orders and Involuntary Outpatient Committals do not come readymade with treatment prescriptions; psychiatry can deploy any drug, any procedure, or any lifestyle change considered to be therapeutic, as we saw in the last two chapters, to improve the constitution of the detained person. But CTOs are instructive in how they are most regularly used, that is, to compel the administration of psychiatric drugs called 'neuroleptics.'

We can assume that pet therapy or walks in the park are not the primary modes of treatment being ordered in CTOs. Even if they were, why commandeer such therapy? While such therapies can be added to psychiatric requirements, they act as 'complementary' treatments at best. Electroshock appointments might be ordered, but these are usually reserved for people with 'depression' rather than 'psychoses,'[1] and it is the latter that present the greatest threat to the public in commonsense discourses. So forced and coerced treatments are generally intended for treatment-resisting 'psychotics,' and the treatments most often ordered for them are neuroleptic drugs, which will be considered in this chapter.

I will argue that imposed drug treatment acts on the brain to limit the body as any restraint does, and over time as any prison does. There must be a jailer, a captor, for the idea of imprisonment to mean something to me. One cannot be detained by emotions or ideas, even if these can capture us and hold us for long periods of time. I do not use the term *incarceration* as a metaphor; it is a matter of legal or social status. My own story of incarceration continues in this chapter, a narrative of life as a tranquilized body that forgets how to resist. What is most important to my argument is that while tranquilized by neuroleptics, most bodies are susceptible to fatigue, emotional numbing, cognitive restriction, and suggestibility that make them quite manageable. This renders them less able to 'refuse treatment.' Such problems are considered unintended 'side effects' within a therapeutic or clinical paradigm.

When such methods are imposed over time, I call this a chemical incarceration. Restraint by chemical means is not just a metaphoric jailing of the 'self' or the 'mind' (as 'mental illness' is sometimes said to be), but a bodily seizure through use of the central nervous system. Over long periods, it is a detention, by seizure of the nerves. This definition assumes that the detainee resists the imposition of drugs. But a person's ability to think, about the treatment imposition, for example, may be constrained by the drug. The latter possibility can be very difficult to define for quantitative analysis, especially because the detainee can say that he or she accepts treatment while being hazed. This is not just a capitulation to authorities in 'playing the game'; this is the action of a drug on the emotional areas of a brain that leads to pacification, or simply the lack of energy to resist much at all.

---

1 However, people with depression can have psychotic breaks or features to their 'illness'; I distinguish depression from the psychotic disorders simply to indicate that not all disorders are treated with neuroleptics, or at least they are not supposed to be, from a medical orientation.

As I have argued, the appearance of voluntariness in coercive care contexts requires some interrogation. 'Offerings' like coercive treatment in exchange for release from confinement or homelessness inform the supposed consumer about what can be expected if she resists. If treatment has already been imposed on her pre-emptively, without prior consent, she may be compromised not only by false choices but also by physiological shunting of emotion, or 'affect,' as clinicians say. If the person later comes to feel positively about a drug, we can say that the erasure of choice and the hazing effect have had some influence in her decision. The past may be moot given the terrible effects expected from withdrawal. So voluntariness in coercive care is, if not illogical or meaningless, significantly compromised.

This is not to say that someone who is known to be dependent on 'antipsychotics' (who can still be lucid and wilful when the body-mind is adjusted to the toxic effect) should be prevented from taking them, probably resulting in the very behaviours the industry is bent on correcting. But with so many people already on neuroleptics who never chose to be, I am not supporting business as usual. Clinicians need to help people reduce doses wherever possible (without ignoring problems that may arise or demanding some kind of absolute abstinence). Otherwise clinics should give people more control over their drug treatment while offering support, and whatever detoxification is possible, increasing the gross capacity for voluntariness. But to prevent lifelong problems attributed to drug restraints, psychiatry needs to stop using neuroleptics pre-emptively, on 'first contact' with 'psychotics' and others (i.e., without prior instruction). Many other choices should be exhausted, even if intervention is elected.

These proposals are based on a reading of the literature on neuroleptics, as well as writings on how people have reacted to them. The effect of a drug at the cellular level is one way of explaining how drugs seem to affect people, according to themselves and others. Commonly called 'antipsychotic' drugs, neuroleptics suppress confusion or distress as 'symptoms' in a very different way than insulin suppresses dysregulation of glucose metabolism in Type 1 diabetes. Indeed, drugs can *cause* confusion or distress by creative application, if not general standards of application, as I will show, whereas sugar levels are simple to 'correct.' 'Calm' or 'ease' is induced destructively, by burdening the central nervous system with toxicity (Jackson, 2005) and by shutting down affective brain pathways. It may be possible for a person to sustain bursts of coherent activity despite this burden, which will be directed towards acceptable behaviour by others, but this does not imply a 'corrected' chemistry.[2]

In direct-to-consumer advertisements, psychiatric drugs like Zoloft™ (a seratonin reuptake inhibitor or SSRI) are said to work by preventing a chemical imbalance thought to underlie 'mental illness.' For example, by preventing the brain from reabsorbing all the seratonin it has produced (for whatever reason it does so), an SSRI leaves seratonin in the synapses between brain cells. With seratonin in our synapses, our nerves transmit more messages of elated feelings (though seratonin is linked to many other functions). Dopamine is another 'neurotransmitter' chemical that sends such messages, which can be amplified by blocking its absorption into nerve cells. Using this cellular or chemical understanding of mood, we might expect to cut madness off at the pass, improve people's feeling and functioning without any 'social' intervention (though drugging someone is certainly a kind of social act), and allowing patients to fully reimagine their relationships and the world.

There is the possibility of enhancing the brain's natural production of 'neurotransmitters,' such as by using diet, talk, pets, or any other means. Whether or not this is sustainable, why not use existing 'natural' methods to induce quick emotional 'balance.' Even under criminal charges a patient might use them to achieve chemical ease. Clinicians may not see the psychiatric ward (or the jailhouse range) as a spa, however; I suppose a patient might be deleterious in becoming balanced under orders. Clinicians turn to drugs that forcefully block neurochemicals in synapses, ultimately to instil 'recovery' and social integration.

How safe and effective is this procedure? This depends on which clinician you ask. Some will explain that psychiatric medications work just like insulin to regulate neurochemicals to balance mood. Drug company shills insist they are safe and effective. Critics like psychiatrist Peter Breggin say that neuroleptics work more like a lobotomy by destroying brain functions and rendering a patient incapable of resistance.

---

2 I do not reject neuroleptics as a 'treatment' wholesale, just as I do not reject other destructive therapies. They should be chosen by someone who is informed and not under duress (duress is a sine qua non to psychiatric detainees), and over the long term I believe general health would increase if they are reduced or avoided. These issues are quite different from the question of how people take drugs for recreational or spiritual purposes, and how the state intervenes. While any drug can be taken for medicinal purposes, its medicinal usefulness may not always apply.

To understand both sides, it is important to refer to the history of how such drugs came into use, as Scull provides (see chapter 3). This tells us that drugs were first used with very little understanding of their physiological action. The purpose of their use was to 'calm' or quell 'mad' bodies and unruly detainees.

It is not difficult to understand how an industry would simply foist drugs onto an unsuspecting public without knowing exactly how they worked. Andrew Scull (2010) recently described how industries work to influence the scientific community:

> [The pharmaceutical industry] underwrites psychiatric journals and psychiatric conferences (where the omnipresence of pharmaceutical loot startles the naive outsider). It makes psychiatric careers, and many of those whose careers it fosters become shills for their paymasters, zealously promoting lucrative off-label uses for drugs whose initial approval for prescription was awarded on quite other grounds. It ensures that when scandals surface universities will mainly turn a blind eye to the transgressions of those members of their staff who engage in these unethical practices. And it controls psychiatric knowledge in multiple ways. Its ghostwriters produce peer-reviewed 'science' that surfaces in even the most prestigious journals, with the most eminent names in the field collaborating in the deception. Researchers sign confidentiality agreements, and inconvenient data never see the light of day. The very categories within which we think about cognitive and emotional troubles are manipulated and transformed to match the requirements of the psychiatric marketplace. Side-effects, even profound, permanent, perhaps fatal side-effects, are ignored or minimized. Fines may be levied when somnolent regulators are finally prompted into action, or damages paid where aggressive class action lawyers force hitherto suppressed findings into the public arena, but the profits already booked far exceed these costs of doing business. For a historian of psychiatry to live through such revolutionary times is remarkable indeed.

A former president of the American Psychiatric Association (APA), Stephen Sharfstein (2005), admits in the Association's newsletter that psychiatry has lost its independence:

> The U.S. pharmaceutical industry is one of the most profitable industries in the history of the world, averaging a return of 17 percent on revenue over the last quarter century. Drug costs have been the most rapidly rising

element in health care spending in recent years. Antidepressant medications rank third in pharmaceutical sales worldwide, with $13.4 billion in sales last year alone. This represents 4.2 percent of all pharmaceutical sales globally. Antipsychotic medications generated $6.5 billion in revenue.

[...] In my last column, I shared with you my experience, and APA's, in responding to the antipsychiatry remarks that Tom Cruise made earlier this summer as he publicized his new movie in a succession of media interviews. One of the charges against psychiatry that was discussed in the resultant media coverage is that many patients are being prescribed the wrong drugs or drugs they don't need. These charges are true, but it is not psychiatry's fault – it is the fault of the broken health care system that the United States appears to be willing to endure. As we address these Big Pharma issues, we must examine the fact that as a profession, we have allowed the biopsychosocial model to become the bio-bio-bio model. In a time of economic constraint, a 'pill and an appointment' has dominated treatment. We must work hard to end this situation and get involved in advocacy to reform our health care system from the bottom up.

While I might argue that the biopsychosocial model is little more than a biological disease model with add-ons, and thus the 'bio-bio-bio' model is implicit to it, Sharfstein's point is that even in private practice there is a mythology about the usefulness of drugs. This is what leads to imposing drugs during economic constraint, at the expense of exploring alternatives.

Despite the largesse of this industry, it could be claimed that an ethical and scientifically valid idea has simply been debauched by greed. What is the evidence that Breggin and others use to critique the biological balancing of the brain and mood?

How do [neuroleptic drugs] 'work'? It is well known that these drugs suppress dopamine neurotransmission in the brain, directly impairing the function of the [brain's] basal ganglia and the emotion-regulating limbic system and frontal lobes and indirectly impairing the reticular activating system as well [please see more detail below]. The overall impact is a chemical lobotomy – literally so, since frontal lobe function is suppressed. The patient becomes de-energized or de-enervated. Will or volition is crushed, and passivity and docility are induced. The patient complains less and becomes more manageable. Despite the claims made for symptom cure, multiple clinical studies document a non-specific emotional flattening or blunting effect.

[. . .] Growing evidence indicates that these drugs produce tardive psychoses that are irreversible and more severe than the patients' prior problems. In children, permanent behavioral or mental disorders frequently develop as a result of the drugs . . . Many patients find themselves unable to stop taking the drugs, suggesting that we should consider them as addictive.

[. . .] [We found that] long-term neuroleptic patients were developing a largely irreversible, untreatable neurological disorder, tardive dyskinesia [he cites Crane, 1973, as does Scull]. The disease, even its mild forms, is often disfiguring [sic], with involuntary movements of the face, mouth or tongue. (Breggin, 1994)

Of course, these sorts of effects need not occur; some bodies are better at handling drugs than others (6-week drug studies are usually done on healthy white males), and some psychiatrists do not use major tranquilizers at high doses. But Breggin's point, made 15 years ago and barely registered by the psychiatric 'community,' is that some of the problems that antipsychotics are supposed to suppress, like hallucinations, are exacerbated. We will return to the issue of 'tardive psychosis.' Breggin has helped win several court judgments against pharmaceutical companies, at least one in Canada, on behalf of people with 'tardive dyskinesia': 'Since 2003, Mrs Jones has been completely disabled by a variety of motor abnormalities associated with tardive dyskinesia. In addition to the spasms of her neck, her shoulders twist severely and she has facial and abdominal spasms. Her vocal cords are impaired, producing an abnormal tone of voice. She is weakened and cannot carry out tasks requiring coordination or strength. She suffers from chronic pain. Humiliation over her appearance has caused her to be socially isolated' (Breggin, 2005). Tardive dyskinesia strikes about 5 per cent of people in their first year of neuroleptic treatment, and an additional 5 per cent each year thereafter. Breggin believes 40 to 50 per cent of everyone treated has this impairment.[3]

---

3 Tardive diseases are rarely discussed, especially 'tardive psychoses' (though psychiatrists often report disclosing them to potential patients: see, e.g., Kleinman & Schachter, 2000). People may discover the effects of 'tardives' after going off the drugs and often go back on to manage the problem. As people with tardives get older, their bodies adapt to increasingly higher neuroleptic dosages, ramping up the amount of drug required to 'stabilize' them.

I should point out that Breggin is a psychiatrist who believes in the biological basis of 'mental illness,' and from a critical perspective he does not treat physical disability with much delicacy in his texts either. However, his observations from within a clinical or therapeutic paradigm raise some of the points to be made about the usefulness of neuroleptics as restraints:

> There is no significant body of research to prove that neuroleptics have any specific effect on psychotic symptoms, such as hallucinations and delusions. To the contrary, these remain rather resistant to the drugs. The neuroleptics mainly suppress aggression, rebelliousness, and spontaneous activity in general. This is why they are effective whenever and wherever social control is at a premium, such as in mental hospitals, nursing homes, prisons, institutions for persons with developmental disabilities, children's facilities, and public clinics, as well as in Russian and Cuban psychiatric political prisons. Their widespread use for social control in such a wide variety of people and institutions makes the claim that they are specific for schizophrenia ridiculous. (Breggin, 1994)

The development of neuroleptics and their eventual adoption by psychiatry during the mid-twentieth century has been well documented by Robert Whitaker, an award-winning medical journalist (2001, 2010). He explains that those who pioneered this chemical methodology knew that brain function was not being 'balanced' by neuroleptics but, rather, grossly disrupted. As to why this might be happening, he cites a leading psychiatrist of his time, Abraham Myers, writing in a neurological journal of 1942 on the subject of brain damage and death by electroconvulsive therapy. Myers was a clinical professor of psychiatry at Harvard University: 'I think it may be true that these people have for the time being at any rate more intelligence than they can handle and that the reduction of intelligence is an important factor in the curative process, I say this without cynicism. The fact is that some of the best cures that one gets are in those individuals whom one reduces almost to amentia' (Whitaker, 2001: 73).

As to how this might be happening, the exact mechanism of neuroleptics was discovered by Arvid Carlsson in 1963, well after they were first introduced, in 1950. Using positron emission tomography (PET) scans, Carlsson found that at 'maintenance' or 'therapeutic' doses neuroleptics blocked 70 to 90 per cent of the brain's D_2 receptors (these are a kind of dopamine receptor in some nerve endings). In Parkinson's disease, about 80 per cent of such receptors are blocked. 'What neuroleptics do, then,' Whitaker says, 'is induce a pathological deficiency in dopamine transmission. They induce, in Deniker's words, a "therapeutic Parkinsonism"' (2001: 164). 'Neuroleptization' results in a hindrance of dopamine pathways, like the brain's nigrostriatal system which regulates movement. Whitaker considers this latter function a basic form of restraint.

He says neuroleptics block a second dopamine pathway called the mesolimbic system, the seat of emotional response, which allows us to respond to the world. The limbic system 'remains vigilant to environmental dangers, and if danger is seen, it mounts an emotional response. By impairing the limbic system, neuroleptics blunt this arousal response – an effect that has made the drugs useful in veterinary medicine for taming animals' (2001: 163; see also Dodman, 1999). This second clamp on the brain not only destabilizes motor control, it undercuts responses to the environment, rendering a person more agreeable or manageable – depending on how well she can still communicate.[4] This drug action leads to a disturbing disruption in the ability to know or communicate. Not only motor control and responsiveness, but also cognition is decreased.

A third dopamine pathway, called the mesocortical system, is blocked which severs communication between the frontal lobe (the seat of thinking and decision making) and older areas of the brain: 'Indeed, experiments with monkeys have shown that if the mesocortical dopaminergic system is impaired, the prefrontal cortex doesn't function well. "Depletion of dopamine in the prefrontal cortex impairs the performance of monkeys in cognitive tasks, similar to the ablating [destroying] of the prefrontal cortex" explains *Principles of Neural Science*, a modern neurology textbook' (Whitaker, 2001: 164).

In penological terms, targeting these three functions (movement, will, and consciousness), if only to destabilize them, results in a physiological hold, isolation, or incarceration. Goffman's definition (1961) of incarceration only involved the regulation of a body's movement in space and communication with others socially. My own definition

---

4 It should be noted that the oldest phenothiazines led to the development of much stronger neuroleptics, especially haldoperidol. Whitaker (2010) notes that in 1991, the heroin contaminant and neurotoxin MPTP was found to closely resemble haldoperidol and both were subsequently used to induce parkinsonism in animals for medical research.

relies on a reduced (or depreciated) internal autonomic capacity for movement in any environment and communicativity (rather than social communication). All movement and all relationships are affected, both physically and socially (and yes, it is conceivable that these two are interconnected).

I need to mention again that by using scientific data, indeed, critical examinations of psychiatric experiments, I am not suggesting that emotions and experiences are 'biologically caused' or disordered. I prefer to understand these data as describing how the body, which can be considered a convergence of many conditions, is affected by chemical impositions, as well as other limitations and errors in human management of the social.

Subjecthood under Chemobotomy

Whitaker does a great job of looking back at patient detainee accounts of being drugged. Some said drugs worked quite well for them, though one cannot expect them to say otherwise. This is not to suggest that they were lying or dupes, though that is possible in any coercive situation, but that positive responses under coercion are already suspect. Whitaker says most people had very difficult responses. 'Patients complained that the drugs turned them into "zombies" or made them feel "closed in," "mummified," "jittery," "confused," and "fearful." They described their medications as "poisons" that produced "the worst misery"' (2001: 176). But how can we rely on subjective accounts, indeed, 'mentally ill' people's accounts?

Whitaker presents two doctors' experiences of neuroleptic treatment to provide what social scientists call triangulation. Their report in the *British Journal of Psychiatry* indicated what happened on a single dose of haldoperidol: 'The effect was marked and very similar for both of us: within ten minutes a marked slowing of thinking and movement developed, along with profound inner restlessness. Neither subject [the two doctors] could continue work, and each left work for 36 hours. Each subject complained of a paralysis of volition, a lack of physical and psychic energy. The subjects felt unable to read, telephone or perform household tasks of their own will, but could perform these tasks if demanded to do so. There was no sleepiness or sedation; on the contrary, both subjects complained of severe anxiety' (2001: 179).

Over the long term, drug effects considered 'side effects,' like 'lethargy' and 'restlessness,' can become a way of life. Janet Gotkin, who with husband Paul Gotkin co-authored my favourite book by a survivor, *Too Much Anger, Too Many Tears* (1975), gave testimony at a U.S. Senate hearing:

> I became alienated from my self, my thoughts, my life, a stranger in the normal world, a prisoner of drugs and psychiatric mystification, unable to survive anywhere but in a psychiatric hospital. The anxieties and fears I had lay encased in a Thorazine [i.e., the phenothiazine called chlorpromazine] cocoon and my body, heavy as a bear's, lumbered and lurched as I tried to maneuver the curves of my outside world. My tongue was so fuzzy, so thick, I could barely speak. Always I needed water and even with it my loose tongue often could not shape the words. It was so hard to think, the effort was so great; more often than not I would fall into a stupor of not caring or I would go to sleep. In eight years I did not read an entire book, a newspaper, or see a whole movie.' (Cited in Whitaker, 2001: 176)

Whitaker provides many more examples. These are based not only on severe dosages, but 'therapeutic' doses.

If chemical restraint is conceived in physiological terms, however it might be quantified, then duration or dosage have something to do with deriving the restraining effect. When we explore the question in terms of how much or what kind of drug, I can think of contentions to my rhetoric of incarceration. First, the dosage of somnolent patients may simply be too high. A restraining or therapeutic effect might be possible from a very low dose without 'side effects.' (This is, indeed, what tends to happen when the body 'adjusts' to toxic doses.) Second, newer 'atypical' antipsychotic medications are not the same or even similar to the old phenothiazines. The new ones do not produce restraining effects like the old ones. With progress, restraint might not even be felt by the subject at all.

When I was working at the Queen Street Mental Health Centre, in 1998, I came across the pioneering work of Shitij Kapur and colleagues at the centre. They ran PET scans to find out how many dopamine receptors were being blocked by what dosage of 'antipsychotic medication.' By this time, the second-generation drugs were certainly in use, but Kapur and colleagues used haldoperidol in their study. This suggests that newer 'atypical' drugs also functioned to block dopamine in a similar way, and that this was their most important function, the 'antipsychotic' function of any neuroleptic. Kapur's team also wanted to relate the dosage used to the amount of drug in the blood ('plasma levels,' which are often monitored to prevent extreme negative effects). Clinicians would then have a simple gauge by which to treat most patients. The exact level of blockage needed for 'optimal dosing,' as Kapur found, was about 2 to 5 mg of haldoperidol per day (enough to block 60 to 80 per cent of D_2 receptors, just like in Carlsson's 1960s' studies). What was surprising was that this dose is far less than the 10 to 60 mg per day Kapur said were used routinely (Kapur et al., 1997: 151). They probably still are.

Kapur's work continues (Ginovart, 2009); the blockage of 60 to 80 per cent of D_2 receptors is still considered 'therapeutic.' So even with the advent of a second 'atypical' generation of antipsychotics like olanzapine (Zyprexa™, which is known to cause insulin-resistant Type 2 diabetes), and now a third generation, such as aripiprazole (Abilify™, which brings its own negative effects), the most important function is D_2 receptor 'occupancy,' as any scan of the literature will show. But do these newer drugs have fewer or different or additional 'side' effects?

In my discussion with my Italian friend (see above, chapter 2), I cited an impressive watershed study done by the U.S. National Institute of Mental Health (Lieberman et al., 2005), which was downplayed by some clinicians and the institute itself, according to Whitaker. It was shown that the old and new drugs had similar problems. Lieberman, who is no radical, found that among 1,493 willing patients given one of three 'atypical' neuroleptics or an old neuroleptic, about 74 per cent left each group due to negative effects or lack of improvement. Some simply left the study. In terms of the safety and efficacy of antipsychotics, Lieberman's study is a significant embarrassment.

There are counters to this analysis. For example, each patient needs a personalized neuroleptic program for treatment. Yet how should a clinician treat when a 'baseline' cannot be established, or rather the baseline that is established shows major flaws in the neuroleptic approach? Maybe the participants suffered 'severe mental illness' that was simply too much for present-day technology. By this logic, they should have stayed with their medication even if it produced negative effects because something is better than nothing. This stock argument ignores the literature on recovery (e.g., Deegan, 1997) and supposes no withdrawal effects like tardive psychoses, which defeat the purpose of symptom management. Again, while these effects are not universal (the Lieberman study indicates that they are grossly underestimated), they occur because of well-documented brain-damaging processes that occur at any dose in any body.

Thus, we have an industry that continues to manage distress using a method of treatment that induces brain dysfunction and hardly reports findings like Lieberman's as anything of consequence. What is important is that such studies require the patient's feedback. But when a patient is being treated like a detainee, her negative reports may be dismissed or even punished, and her positive reports may be influenced by duress.

So much of what we were suffering from was overlooked. The contexts of our lives were largely ignored. The professionals who worked with us had studied the science of physical objects, not human science [. . .]

But no one asked for our stories. Instead they thought our biographies as schizophrenics had already been written nearly a century before by Kraepelin and Bleuler.[5] We were told to take medications that made us slur and shake, that robbed our youthful bodies of energy and made us walk stiff like zombies.

We were told that if we stayed on these medications for the rest of our lives we could perhaps maintain some semblance of a life. They kept telling us that these medications were good for us and yet we could feel the high dose neuroleptics transforming us into empty vessels. We felt like will-less souls or the walking dead as the numbing indifference and drug induced apathy took hold. At such high dosages, neuroleptics radically diminished our personhood and sense of self.

We found ourselves undergoing that dehumanizing transformation from being a person to being an illness: 'a schizophrenic,' 'a multiple,' 'a bi-polar.' Our personhood and sense of self continued to atrophy as we were coached by professionals to learn to say, 'I am a schizophrenic'; 'I am a bi-polar'; 'I am a multiple.' And each time we repeated this dehumanizing litany our sense of being a person was diminished as 'the disease' loomed as an all powerful 'It,' a wholly Other entity, an 'in-itself' that we were taught we were powerless over.

---

5 The former psychiatrist theorized incurable cases as suffering 'dementia praecox,' a biological disorder, and at the turn of the twentieth century the latter psychiatrist reconfigured such disorder into 'the schizophrenias' and called for more communication with patients. Bentall (2003) does an excellent job of critiquing their work as lacking validity, and many others have written about the paucity of scientific evidence for a biological cause to 'madness,' see, e.g., the following: Modrow (1995), Seidel (1998), Valenstein (1998), Whitaker (2001, 2010), Joseph (2003), Greenman (2004), and Jackson (2005).

Professionals said we were making progress because we learned to equate our very selves with our illness. They said it was progress because we learned to say 'I am a schizophrenic.'

But we felt no progress in this. We felt time was standing still. The self we had been seemed to fade farther and farther away, like a dream that belonged to somebody else. The future seemed bleak and empty and promised nothing but more suffering. And the present became an endless succession of moments marked by the next cigarette and the next. (Deegan, 1992)

Medication and Education

1993. Besides the shock of being swarmed and tied down, I feel a huge ache in my leg from the injection the next day. I feel strange, like my body is wrapped up. At times I'm restless.

The requirements for my release are unknown, the rules difficult to fathom. The doors are locked, but I don't try them. The nurses say I have to wait for an appointment with my doctor; maybe one doctor will see me, maybe two or three, probably in a day or two.

None of the others talk. They do as they are told. We line up for 'medication.' They don't give me a pill, but a little paper cup with a sickly sweet juice in it. The taste doesn't seem right. It could be the drug in it, or maybe what the drug is doing to my tongue. Two professionals watch me take it.

The next day nurses give me a psychological test to fill out. It feels like doing a multiple-choice exam in a fallout shelter. The questions are all traps: 'Do you pick the chair without legs, the handle without a cup, a tree lying beside you, or a clown in a suit?' I draw a line down the middle, and a second line across the page to dissect it. Each division is a dimension. But before I can hand it in, my partner arrives for the first time since I was restrained. I am amazed that they let her in. She looks at the sheet and quietly tells me to get another one. She helps me answer the questions using the least weird choice available. We hope it will show I am sane.

After a few days, my movements are terse, limited, far less fluid. My body shakes, spasms, and sputters under the chemical stew. I ask what my medication is. They tell me I am taking loxapine (25 mg per day I would later find out). For side effects, I am being given Cogentin™ (an 'antiparkinsonian' drug). And to help me sleep, they give me Ativan™ (a minor tranquilizer).

'It will take a few weeks before you feel the benefits of the medication. The side effects will go away soon,' says one staff member when I ask about my medication again. Later, a 19-year-old girl complains and starts screaming. She is unceremoniously followed round the clean bright unit by three men. They nab her and drag her into a small room. When they lock her in, she screams loudly.

I am finally given an interview when I least expect it. Three clinicians coldly ask me questions. I admit to having strange ideas, and I cannot look at them. I start to cry. They use the moment. They bring a clipboard forward and tell me I should sign. I sign without reading the form.

Every day I am told when and where to eat, sleep, bathe. I am told to wash my underwear in the sink with hand soap. I wear a light blue patient smock with a gap in the back that shows my ass. I try to imagine how this will help me; I might learn humility, or confidence, or perspective. I just don't know what values they are trying to instil.

Obedience is most important. I learn quickly to play the role of an object like everyone else. The more the drugs work on me, the less I feel like questioning what is happening to me, the less I feel much of anything. Out there, life goes by, quickly. Inside, it seems like time is slower and slower. I want to be well. I want to be discharged. But when I ask about it, they divert me like a turtle in a maze.

My mouth is perpetually dry, my gums expand and bleed. I ask the nurse about the bleeding a couple of weeks later. 'Oh that's your mental illness, dear,' she says nicely, and gets back to her phone call. My jaw looks wider to me in the mirror, more square or blocky, as if I'm gaining weight only in my face. My skin breaks out in places it never did in my teens. I feel occasional shivers.

I fidget as the others do, to comfort my nerves and muscles. They keep wanting to move. They rumble and shake, quiver and quake. I try to talk to the others, just a bit, but they only talk about things like the weather or food shopping. If I ask about how to get out, or about what they did to get in, or about what the rules are, they go blank. One day, five of them bolt out of the room when I ask about leaving; I worry they will report me.

Feeling dispirited, I admit to my doctor in one of our weekly meetings that I feel kind of blue. I blame the rain. My doctor blames my brain, informing me that my emotionalism is a clue. I have 'bipolar affective disorder' he says.

My primary nurse confides that BAD is easier to treat than schizophrenia or schizoaffective disorder. She is darker skinned, more than me, and she confides that I look very handsome. When we are speaking privately, she explains, 'In this century, we call you mentally ill.' She does not elaborate but adds, 'Sometimes I look at these people and wonder if we're just turning them into zombies.' I appreciate her candor, and I like her, but I dare not agree under the circumstances.

My brother and his partner have flown out to Vancouver and are trying their best to console my partner, who is quite worried and lost. They try to negotiate my release but have no clue how the system works. When they see me I tell them I need to get better, that I need to work again. Perhaps because my brother has to return in a couple weeks, the staff decide to let me return with him at the last minute, as long as I will seek help from a psychiatrist in Toronto.

I am excessively grateful; I buy them flowers on my weekend pass (the highest level of privileges). Before I leave, my psychiatrist tells me I should have stayed at least another month. The nurse stands next to him and stares at me without expression, a cue to say nothing, I suppose. My psychiatrist, who told me, 'Well I've heard of a helix but not a double helix,' and who demanded in a meeting in which I was still talking, 'Do you know where you are?' is probably trying to get me going, just one last time. I wonder if everything said in this place is just a test. Or a laugh.

Segregation without Walls

Toronto is much colder than I ever remembered. I realize I am no longer the same person. I am still saying to my family, incessantly it seems, that I need to get better and hopefully reduce my medications. It is causing me to feel nothing, I say, and my thinking is too slow for me to find work.

I try to draw, and my concentration falls apart very quickly. I try to play guitar, but there's no tension in my fingers, and I can barely remember the chords to my songs. I try to write but I have nothing in me, nothing that I care about. I try to set up an action plan on finding work, but I find myself going in circles, small circles.

I meet a couple of psychiatrists, who are nice, but one of them is too smart with the symbols, and the other works in a hospital, and I can't stand the memory of the hospital. I see a dentist. He explains that the swelling of my gums, and the lack of saliva in my mouth, are a side effect that will get worse. I will have to be extra vigilant to delay the inevitable loss of my teeth.

Everything means less and less because I don't feel it long enough, if at all. Each moment is broken from the last, and without any feeling, the story ceases to impress upon me. I can speak and listen, but it's bland, empty; any emphasis is an extra effort. When I talk I have very little to say and people lose interest. I read a paragraph or two and forget what I read. I'm watching this happen. My partner and my family talk about things that matter to them, that used to matter to me, but I'm not engaged at all.

One day my roommate asks to try half a dose of my loxapine. He is 5 feet 10 inches tall, 170 pounds, a drinker and smoker. He returns in one hour saying he can't stay awake. He sleeps for 36 hours and is somewhat lost when he awakens.

Isolation from Within

I walk up the street spending my daily government allotment on a falafel. I am never noticed on the street, even though I feel like the walking dead, and I avoid being noticed. Weeks pass and nothing changes including my halting determination to get off the drugs. A psychologist friend says, 'You don't have to stay on that shit you know? They can't make you take it.' It's true. Yet my hospital education says otherwise.

I remember my doctor's word, 'relapse.' I never want to relapse, to be taken back into a hospital because I stopped taking my medication and went mad. I still think weird thoughts, but they're under control. I fantasize that, against the odds, I will live a somewhat normal life some day. Others are cheery about this prospect.

One day, four months after my hospitalization, my partner walks in and says she has to leave me. I am doing my laundry and though I hear what she's saying, I don't feel anything. I try to think back to our time together, but no image comes to mind, no conversation or event. I try to feel a connection to her, but feel nothing. My intellect is telling me this is important, but my mind tends to float to other concerns. I concern myself with the immediate task of sorting the socks. She stares at me. Sensing that she is waiting for a response, I apologize.

'Sorry, I wish I knew what to say.' My face shows undead calm. My partner of two years starts crying uncontrollably like she never has before. I remember to stay grounded like the nurse said, to not stress myself. But I empathize with her. She is a stranger who has dropped a bag of vegetables.

'I wish there was something I could say,' I repeat. It's not that I don't care. It's just that there is nothing to say. But how can I explain that? How can I tell her that I can't feel when I don't care enough to notice I can't feel? I am living in an emotional absence, aware mostly of time passing away.

After she leaves, I tell my brother and his partner, and they are genuinely concerned. I tell them like I am reporting something, an event on the news, and they are the ones who feel for me. After a moment has passed, they also get nothing from my reaction, and the conversation turns to the usual. The family goes back to discussions in which there is emotion, even riotous emotion later in the evening. I try to join in, speaking slowly or haltingly as I try to think fast.

It's not that I'm a sad figure, or too crazy to make sense of. It's not that they dislike the new me; it is 'me' after all, and they will come to accept how I am eventually. They already have in some ways. It is that I am not there. It is that I am not about me, not interested in myself. I am still playing the object, doing the work of the mental patient, which is to stay out of trouble.

My life has shrunk before my eyes. I stare with detachment at my patient self. Dishes are cleared and washed, and the television is back on. In another month my former partner will show me a pamphlet that reads 'Proud to Be Crazy,' and I will go to my first meeting with a group of psychiatric survivors. With their help I will gain the courage to ask my shrink to let me decrease the loxapine by 5 mg every three weeks. It will seem harrowing at first, as my brain starts getting environmental messages again. By August, I will have gone off all my drugs, started working, and found new friendships to last a lifetime.

7   Transinstitutionalization

'They can't get inside you,' she had said. But they could get inside you . . . 'Under the spreading chestnut tree, I sold you and you sold me.'
– George Orwell, *Nineteen Eighty-Four*

Today, 'compassion' is used by the state, it is not felt by individuals. One can kill with compassion.
– I. Jull, 'Nietzsche, Psychiatry and the State'

2005. At a friend's birthday party, people ask what my research is about. 'It's like . . .' I think about the words to use, the order of the words, the audience . . . 'people's experience of a new psychiatric legal requirement to take their medication outside the hospital.'

'What?'

'It's kind of like parole for psychiatric patients. It's very new.' I use the word 'parole' like the *Ottawa Sun* did in describing Community Treatment Orders, a newspaper Brian Smith might have read every day. It is interesting to me that psychiatric patients can be seen as rule breakers but not as criminals.

'No. That can't be right,' says a woman who is on medications.

'Why hasn't anyone heard of that?' asks a man who has never been medicated.

'They must be violent!' says another, who I have never met. He must mean CTO candidates are violent rather than all 'mad' people. But that is not a criterion for use of CTOs.

'No,' I say with not much expression. 'Anyone who's deemed ill.' There is common disbelief.

Most people think of mental patients as unruly people who cannot be detained because they are protected by the same rights as responsible people. 'The homeless' are left on the street to their own devices, 'incoherent' and 'agitated,' bothering busy people on their way to work. This seems to have nothing to do with public resource allocation or with the care institutions' function of control. Our 'problem' has been presented as rights gone wrong.

Interest has piqued and people want to know more, but someone steps in, shifts the conversation, and the party boogies on. In polite society, there is an aversion to human affairs that go awry, agonize us, shake our belief in comfort and reason. People fear loss of self-control and 'madness' almost as much as poverty and death, perhaps more because it is suffered in life, and conceived as 'suffering' itself at times.

Someone at another party asks, 'Well have you ever tried dealing with those people? I work in a hospital and it's no picnic.' The example of the 1997 subway pushing is trotted out as an example of a patient going off his meds and stuck in the cycle of violence and rehospitalization, but few are aware that he is reported to have tried getting help immediately before the incident and was not psychotic (Simmie, in Canada, 2005). Cantankerous 'screamers' on the street are taken as proof that 'behaviour' is biology, and certainly not protest. Those who take Prozac™ can despise the 'less together crazies,' reminders of their own fall from social grace. But someone wants to know what we are talking about exactly. 'What's "crazy" anyway?' And the philosophical questions begin: what is normal? what is society? what is self? what is consciousness? what is dreaming?

Who at this party would know that electroshock is more popular now than it was in the 1970s, especially as it is used on women and the elderly, sometimes involuntarily (Funk, 1998)? Would anyone suspect that lobotomies are sometimes performed today (Mashour, Walker, & Martuza, 2005; http://www.psychosurgery.org/news-opinion/is-lobotomy-performed-today/2000506)? Would they be surprised that implants have been developed to continuously deliver chemicals and electric impulses to the brain (Siegel et al., 2002; Spencer, 2005), or that animals on route to slaughterhouses are given neuroleptics to calm them (Canadian Food Inspection Agency, 2004: 38)? What would they think of former President George W. Bush's plan to test all students and workers in U.S. schools using 'mental health screening' (Lenzer, 2004), or Prime Minister Stephen Harper's matching plan (MacCharles, 2007)? What about the rush to medicate people all around the world based on Western conceptions of ill mental health (Watters, 2010)?

The term 'transinstitutional' has been used to refer to how various Western institutions of control interact to manage bodies (Maidment, 2005). The term provides a description of how various institutions (facilities) and practices (arrangements) provide 'institutionalization' through a matrix of ill-coordinated professions and workers who are legally responsible for control and care of bodies determined deviant, excessive, or degenerative. Psychiatric treatment was probably never restricted to madness houses and mental health centres. But its authorization off the ward in legal and clinical texts still anchors it in Western rationales of the social. Without mental illness as defined in psychiatric nosology, the use of drugging would be questionable as a punishment alone. With mental illness theory sustaining such practices, examples of institutional abuse are easily dismissed as exaggeration, delusion, a romanticization of 'mental illness' (an acerbic example is Brean, 2010). If people have heard of opposition to drugging, they often think of Scientology or anti-drug luddites. Many have never heard of 'psychiatric survivors,' whose claims are often seen as a brazen insult to the valiant efforts of doctors.

As we have spent some time with the theoretical issues, the practices and mechanisms of imposing medicine, this chapter will look at the broader treatment methodologies that span many custodial-curative industries, with more attention to oppressions that intersect across formal institutions (e.g., how labour, resources, education, or consumption are distributed geographically, geopolitically, in terms of biomedical statuses). Institutionalization of any kind is practised through persuasion, and coercion where this fails. Otherwise brute force on the body will do, such as the use of restraints. Before I review some of the literature on coercion, which will lead to a comparison of coercive practices then and now, I would like to discuss how psychiatric practices can be made to appear as medicinal or therapeutic rather than correctional or penological. The tools of psychiatric institutionalization have changed, but the building blocks are still evident: declaring 'madness' using contested assumptions (un/naming), incarcerating without formal contest (overpowering), and forcing unwanted 'tranquility' as 'health' (brutal silencing or re-storying).

Physical institutionalization is considered a thing of the past, especially as hospital beds are harder and harder to find. Forced treatment proponents like E.F. Torrey say 'the mentally ill' population is burgeoning as a result, being left to 'rot with their rights on' in jails (1997). Increasingly, prisons are being built in the United States and Canada, which might help to explain some of Torrey's observations. On the other hand, Whitaker (2010) uses psychiatric research to show that the increase in rates of government assistance due to 'mental illness' can be correlated to the increased use of psychiatric drug treatments. Whitaker asks why more people have not gotten better.

Containment and direction of individuals considered to be 'problems' goes back hundreds of years, but its continuation can be discerned from touted reforms by progressive governments. The Ontario government's 'mental health reform' policies, which attempt to balance the rights of individuals with the public's need for safety, are but one example: the 'Heseltine Report' in 1983, the 'Graham Report' in 1988, 'Putting People First' in 1993, 'Making It Happen' in 1999, which was followed up with Brian's Law and the CTO, 'Mental Health Implementation Task Force' in 2003, which was ignored by the succeeding government, and 'Every Door Is the Right Door,' announced in 2009 (CMHA, 2010). McCubbin (1998) says there can never be actual change given the imbalance of power between the helper and the object of help.

Throughout modern history, the imposition of medicine has been presented as a benign practice, one that helps the individual and society hold themselves together. To serve millions of potential discontents, disabled, or disorderlies in Western societies requires intensive modes of material production. This evidently includes not only the physical resources for restraint but the education of technicians charged with making those restraints 'work.' Detainees and the public must be convinced that existing practices are for the best. To persuade the public and the individual, medical theory can be brought to bear, or psychological theory, so that 'success' stories are used in madness discourse to hide away the population that is coerced or forced. If we consider restraint as the base mechanism of care, we might see why medical assistance has been associated with 'warehousing' in our age; medicine serves as an apologia and program for control. Nikolas Rose and Michel Foucault mentor us through some of these recognitions; the term *bio-power* in their work is instructive. Like Smith's relations of ruling, it provides a lexical mode of social inquiry relating to institutionalization.

In practice, psychiatric institutional sites have all but closed, yet the use of psychiatric treatment has been expanding alongside the prison complex and across borders, as Whitaker, Scull, and Watters show. It might appear that medical treatment is working on some level, at least to curb those who would be institutionalized. I argued in the last chapter that drug treatments can be imposed as a means of controlling resistance, a 'chemical incarceration' over time (partly made possible by the threat of withdrawal, which requires further restraint). The remaining psychiatric sites or 'clinics' would simply be used as points of initiation in the new geography of 'community mental health' (Montagu, 2001).

A number of psychiatric survivors like David Oaks, originator of Mind Freedom in the United States, have called outpatient committal practices 'institutions without walls.' In theory, the 'community treatment plan' in Ontario's CTO legislation is legally enforced using observation, monitoring, therapies, and chemical treatments that can be 'delivered' by clinics or mobile treatment teams. Using a 'therapeutic contract' scheme, the state offers a new 'less-restrictive' institutional site to detainees, 'the community' environment, while providing family and society with a more immediate and intimate form of oversight through the private sphere. Institutionalization shifts on its three pillars of naming, overpowering, and silencing, and produces new sites of activity by privatizing and communalizing its work, as it did with correctional industries since 'decarceration' in the West (Scull, 1984). There is a lot of research to be done on chemical institutionalization; see, for example, Lambe's work on the chemical management of children in Canadian youth services (2006).

Ontario's government presents the Community Treatment Order not as an acceptable extension of psychiatric power, as some psychiatrists have argued it is (O'Reilly, 2004), but as a less restrictive choice for the patient and a more humane choice for society, as if these ideas were quantifiable. The state benefits not only in terms of downloading costs to the family, but in masking the spectacle of coercion and force, thus streamlining the management of social 'risk.' Foucault said that people are made to manage themselves under a self-monitoring practice he called 'governmentality'; in the familial scheme governmentality is affixed to small social units as well as the individual.

Home and prison, like treatment and restraint, are co-mingled under new schemes of institutionalization. A detainee may now choose home over a locked hospital ward, or her family may choose it for her, by electing mandatory treatment. A long-institutionalized inmate can, with agreement from the Public Guardian and Trustee, be relocated to a rooming house that functions for her like a psychiatric facility, and not necessarily with a better vista. An informant tells me a 90-year-old man refused to leave an institution when he was offered a CTO because he had spent the last few decades living there and knew little of the outside world. But the old facilities were closing, and he had to go. Institutionalization is about control, not simply bricks and mortar.

Chemicalization as a method of institutionalization makes site-based detention less necessary, while the mechanics of formal institutionalization seep into familial relations. While Ontario's supposedly progressive Mental Health Act requires that CTOs be offered only to people who have been patients in the past, in practice persons have been put under CTOs on 'first contact' with the system, such as in 'early intervention for psychosis' work (Linda Carrey, of the Psychiatric Patient Advocate Office, personal communication, 28 Sept. 2007). Thus, the rules of engagement are important at the level of legality, and polity, about what constitutes a person or individual and what that person's rights will be. But the rules are bent and reshaped to ensure that the basic organizational principle of health (control) is enacted. Chemicalization allows for more latitude with coercive practices because it allows for control from within the medical 'corpus' or body.

Coercion Literature

To introduce modern and contemporary Western methods of institutionalization it is important to note how researchers discuss practices of coercion which lie between persuasion and brute force. Coercion is considered less severe than physical force, such as holding someone down while delivering an injection or electroshock, and this may seem irrelevant when someone chooses to be put on a CTO or to be restrained under certain circumstances in the future.

Coercion is examined in countless ways, from Szasz's radical concepts of pharmacracy (2004), to 'progressive' critiques of psychiatry's 'medical model' (e.g., Leifer, 2001; Allen, 1999; Caplan & Caplan, 2001) to not so critical studies of perceived coercion by 'people with severe mental illness,' 'patients,' and 'consumers' (e.g., Elbogen, Swanson, & Swartz, 2003; Canvin, Bartlett, & Pinfold, 2002; Farabee, Shen, & Sanchez, 2002; Iversen, Hoyer, Sexton & Gronli, 2002; Borum et al., 1999; Nicholson, Ekenstam & Norwood, 1996). In all these studies, a classical model of coercion is adopted in which the detainee is not conceived as part of the plan of control.

Some coercion studies deal with CTO provisions specifically (Greenberg et al., 2005). Some studies question whether the perception of coercion is based on real events (Lidz et al., 1998; Poulsen & Engberg, 2001), yet no agreement seems possible, even on such basic questions as whether involuntary status leads to a perception of coercion. Again, a classical understanding of self versus society precludes easy answers to whether therapeutic arrangements violate the individual. For example, some researchers have found that when detention or restraints are delivered respectfully, people do not perceive coercion. But the function of restraints is the same. The victim is not a dupe if restraint is all there is.

A good example of how coercion is hidden, having read Linda Smith's work (1999) on decolonization and research, is a study called 'Maori Experience of Community Treatment Orders in Otago, New Zealand' (Gibbs et al., 2004). This small study suggests that CTOs were considered helpful by Maori people in increasing patient safety and family or community (*whanau*) security. It was noted, however, that CTOs imposed drawbacks, 'particularly concerning medication and restrictions on choices' and 'reconciling [indigenous] traditional beliefs with the medical model of mental illness.' A critical study would have explored the contradiction uncovered between 'security' and a traditional way of life. This would require seeing psychiatry as doing more than 'health care.'

Nevertheless, the question of whether there is coercion in psychiatry, and whether psychiatry is not at root a coercive scheme, seems less and less ridiculous to people in my opinion. Survivors and qualitative researchers have recently entered the arena (e.g., from New Zealand; Mary O'Hagan, 2003), quite aware of psychiatric racism against Maoris (e.g., Johnstone & Read, 2000). Qualitative research attempts to name and describe the practices seen as coercive rather than to prove that they are coercive. Questions related to inducement, authority, and persuasion come into play (Wertheimer, 1993).

Generally coercion is conceived as an alternative to force or violence, not an extension of it. Diamond (1996), says coercion is common practice in 'community treatment' of any kind, especially with the homeless, ranging from 'friendly persuasion' to 'interpersonal pressure' to 'control of resources' to the 'use of force.' Dennis and Monahan find that perceptions of coercion decrease when concern and respect are used to perform psychiatric functions (1996: 13–26). In the same volume, Hiday finds that IOCs feel coercive when 'services' do not meet people's needs (29–47). Diamond says coercion is inevitable if workers reinforce dependency while simultaneously encouraging independence (51–72). Susser and Roche show that 'tolerant' approaches are discussed openly in clinical practices but not coercion which is called 'setting limits' (73–84).

In the same book, Lopez says practices of persuasion that are coercive include 'deception,' 'enticement,' and the 'extraction of concession' (85–92). Withholding crucial information, and the threat of withdrawal of services, benefits, and basic needs like housing are discussed. This supports what participants said in my research. A professional sense of 'moral rightness' to coerce, and consequently 'angst and ambivalence,' were identified by Hopper as themes of study (197–219). Thus, Dennis and Monahan (1996) provide a comprehensive account of coercion as it occurs in the community, among workers, but fail to establish a place for destructive medical practices in their analysis, perhaps because drug treatment is conceived primarily as therapy.

Directly coerced or not, surreptitiously put into food or not (Ahern, 2005; Psychiatric Patient Advocate Office, 2005), drug treatment brings physical effects of brain damage that are not only an issue of 'treatment success' or coercion, but force. Neuroleptics can be addictive and were adopted because they caused dysfunctions that were held to be 'therapeutic' by psychiatrists. Research on coercion must include destructiveness of 'treatment,' and duress under the ever-present possibility of detention, if we are to understand people's experiences in psychiatry.

Comparing Methods of Institutionalization

It is possible for a person to voluntarily choose psychiatric medications or hospitalization or even pre-arrange physical and chemical restraint. As we saw in chapter 5, the social position of the mentally ill body, conceived as needing treatment that doubles as a restraint, must be qualified as a subject of coercions. Once treatment is imposed, either pre-emptively or coercively through a therapeutic agreement like a Community Treatment Order, that person is subject to potentially long-lasting effects, and the state has implicitly committed itself to her control and care indefinitely, using chemical incarceration.

Certainly, the detainee may manage to escape or negotiate a less coercive arrangement, contingent on the effects of neuroleptization. But the detainee description does not depend on legal statuses such as criminalization, 'voluntary' or 'involuntary' designations that can be toggled at will by psychiatrists, or the 'capable' and 'incapable' designations arbitrarily ascribed.

Goffman's (1961) 'inmate' usage was descriptive. In the following excerpts, I will try to link Goffman's observations of life in the asylum to practices observable in community psychiatry today, assuming that we are moving (back before asylum institutionalization) to social control procedures that do not rely on central sites. It should be noted that Goffman did not rule out the possibility that some individuals might accept institutional control or treatments, but his descriptions put the institution's architecture, routines, and beliefs into the foreground.

In nineteenth-century texts, doctors remarked that their institutions were not nearly as violent as the public believed them to be. Rarely did they decry abuses by institutional employees (Dwyer, 1987: 23). Large institutions of the nineteenth century were a move from prior almshouses or poorhouses with rooms sometimes smaller than those in rooming houses today. The new hospitals were refitted with iron shackles and unheated basement cells. Even before poorhouses, American towns dealt with emotionally distressed people using a 'welfare' scheme of relocation; the 'mad' were sometimes provided for, but more generally beaten or sold for labour or sent on to other towns (Anonymous, 1982: 111–12). Thus, institutions were built as a remedy for violent 'community' practices. Yet to curb institutional violence, 'deinstitutionalization' has brought such practices back to some degree.[1]

Canadian-born sociologist Erving Goffman's work on mid-twentieth-century mental institutions and prisons provides a modern sociological model of what he calls 'the resocialization chamber' of 'total institutions' (1961: 163, 203). Goffman exhibited in detail barbarisms that occurred in the last days before 'deinstitutionalization.' He was no 'antipsychiatrist'; to my knowledge he never declared direct opposition to treatments such as lobotomy, which were prevalent in his time. He believed institutions would always be required by families, professionals, and governments, and that the clinical 'tinkering trade' he critiqued would always prevail, if only to 'stay somewhat the hand of the attendant' (1961: 383).

---

1 Relocation is still used by professionals today, as Victor explains in his interview: 'In [this city] for example, if a client can't fit in anywhere or can't maintain housing, they send him to [a] hospital [in a city 100 km away].' The Centre for Addictions and Mental Health in Toronto is refashioning its modernist structure into a 'neighbourhood' environment in part to combat 'stigma.'

In the first few pages of his book *Asylums: Essays on the Social Situation of Mental Patients and Other Inmates* (1961), Goffman describes an initiation of a new detainee by way of a brutal beating. The example prisoner is made to accept his new status by force, and others are made to watch as a kind of lesson. This simple education in institutionalization leads to Goffman's description of what seems like an institutional methodology, such as by 'funneling' the 'pre-inmate' into this new life. His observations and theorizations are instructive not as a fixed model, description, or analysis, but as a set of example methods of control that can be confirmed to be in use today in and outside of hospitals.

Goffman says total institutions such as prisons and religious convents manage inmates by surveillance, restriction of movement, and social distance or quarantine from the general population. These sites are 'a social hybrid, part residential community, part formal organization [. . .] forcing houses for changing persons; each is a natural experiment on what can be done to the self' (1961: 9–12). Thus, they achieve through surveillance and several other methods a restriction of movement and association for the purpose of changing a person's narratives of being.

If we contrast Goffman's descriptions with common descriptions by psychiatric survivors today, we see several overlapping institutional practices, though some practices are totally replaced by others. Goffman described 'disculturation' as the loss of one's ability to interact with others culturally after a long period in a prisonlike environment (1961: 13). Community treatment is supposed to do away with this. However, tranquilizers can suppress wilfulness and personality on the part of a detainee.

Goffman says the loss of one's full name establishes a person as less than what she was (1961: 18), and this still occurs as the 'client' is hidden from stigmatizing view by use of initials and first names in records, even in public exhibitions of writing or art, keeping the mocked and the tormentor apart (Reaume, 2000b). We see this sequestering of the subject in tribunal documents also, a crude protection of privacy by hiding patients' legal status. Similarly, CTOs hide detainees from the view of other detainees, survivors, and advocates in that they make institutional work less perceptible. While rights advice is provided at the time that a doctor is considering a CTO (not when signing), the patient may likely have little other contact with advocates after the CTO is signed. As such, detainee 'privacy' or closeting, as critics might say, is of prime importance.

Goffman says the inmate is 'stripped of his usual appearance [. . .] thus suffering a personal defacement' (1961: 20). Whether by old neuroleptics that make her tremble or new neuroleptics that cause rapid weight changes, or the physical defacement brought on by hunger, iatrogenic diseases, and other problems born of insufficient care, this method of institutionalization continues unabated. 'Disfigurement,' possibly less visible than defacement, was seen as a physical violation caused by persistent violence (1961: 21), yet interestingly, Goffman did not list electroshock 'treatments' among such disfigurements, just as most people today would not list tardive dyskinesia that makes chins jut out or fingers tremble a form of violence. Of course, we may assume electroshock is essentially a burning of brain matter (Alper, 1948), whether by application to one side of the head or both, and it continues to be practised today, sometimes but not always voluntarily.

Aside from treatment-related disfigurement, beatings and abuses are still known to occur, on and off the principal institutional sites at the hands of some psychiatric workers (e.g., Lopez, 2005). It is said that, statistically, inmates are more often victims of violence outside of hospitals than violent themselves (Wahl, 1995).

Goffman also describes methods that violate self-feeling and thus bring about the changes to the person that are so valued by institutionalization: 'The boundary that the individual places between his being and the environment is invaded and the embodiments of self profaned' (1961: 23). If detention and restriction of contact with others can profane the self, neuroleptic tranquilization and enervation will pollute the self, obtaining more than the same effect. The self may enter a period of understanding the body as 'non-self.' Thus, whereas bars and walls are phenomena to be seen and resisted by detainees, drug soma and hibernation wipe away sense-making altogether.

Besides permanent scarring, 'physical indignities' like being made to lie prostrate in silence (Goffman, 1961: 22) certainly continue to occur, such as during delivery of an injection under a CTO in the story reported by Phil (see chapter 4). Verbal slights and insults, such as talking about a detainee as though she were not present, or rudely dismissing her feelings, or asking embarrassing 'diagnostic' questions publicly, still occur in and out of psychiatric settings (1961: 23). This form of negative talk therapy is remarkably resilient, probably because the person is usually subdued by neuroleptics and defiance is not expected.

Cycling of Evidence, Biology, and Chemistry

Institutionalization depends on labelling, and how easily labels can be stuck on any conflict or perceived problem. Thus stories become the stuff of institutionalization. And I submit that stories can break us out. What I call a cycling of evidence (or biography) has been described in various ways by social researchers. Goffman mentions 'discreditable facts,' collected in a case file, to embarrass the inmate and enlist the support of her next of kin to psychiatric management (1961: 24, 156, 307). A generation later, Dorothy Smith finds that these practices continue (1990b; see also Burstow & Weitz, 1988; Burstow et al., 2005; Anderson, 2005). Smith said that the 'clinical record' is a primary method of decontextualizing and objectifying behaviours in texts using supposedly neutral medical narratives and professional protocols. The detainee's daily life may thus be qualified and offered up into what Smith calls 'the relations of ruling.' This allows for the legal management of individuals despite the possibility of contradictory stories regarding the events in question. This method, whether employed consciously or not, can also be considered in a different way using Thomas Scheff's labelling theory, which posits that people come to enact the things that are said about them in official labels. Over time, a person deemed 'incapable' will not attempt to perform to 'capacity.'

Detainees may take out anger at detention on individuals around them. Goffman says, 'the inmate's reaction to his own situation is collapsed back into the situation itself,' meaning one's desperate acts of resistance are read back to one as proof that one should be detained (1961: 37). Any agitation is conceived as 'psychological resistance' to therapy and so a feedback loop is established to enforce therapy regardless of non-therapeutic effects. Certainly, this cycling of evidence continues today. The passing of CTO legislation was itself an example on a societal scale: isolating choice actions by a few individuals to discredit a whole population as threatening public safety thus showing the need for more therapy (Corrigan et al., 2005; see also Mallan, 2000; Blizzard, 2000). Perhaps people need 'help', but what choices are offered?

Psychiatric workers also use the clinical file to discredit the detainee and uphold the biological basis of her incarceration. To elicit anger in the 'mad' conceived body not only upholds case file predictions, but also gives the body a kind of cognitive exemplar for future responses to threats. It instils 'acting out' or 'backing down'; there is also less chance of 'staff' engaging in discussion with the detainee. Biological explanations of behaviour and self-reports can reinforce 'biological' behaviours, and in this circular reasoning a cycle of biology is established, a kind of meta story that operates outside the cycle of evidence. Psychiatric workers and others view 'biologically' disordered people differently than 'psychologically' disturbed people, seeing them as uncontrollable and violent (Read & Haslam, 2004). The 'physical' story of madness is a very powerful story.

When institutional workers discharge the detainee, especially under a Community Treatment Order, her family may use the cycling of evidence and biology as other workers do. Discrediting facts multiply as more embarrassments are logged and recounted by workers and family, all in an attempt to rescue the 'normal' or 'real' self, or at least to institute a 'reformed' or 'recovered' self. The detainee may also become involved in this practice, weaving the evidence of her lack into her self-concept of 'when I am ill' versus 'when I am well.' This practice is not a lack of self, but a narrative of self. Goffman says inmates may always be 'readmitted' given their psychiatric 'history' (1961: 167), and indeed, the biological explanation makes them ever dubious to others.

To some sympathetic outsiders, an inmate's responses may appear reasonable, innocuous, or trivial given her circumstances. In a clinical setting, as in community life, a detainee charged with 'madness' cannot escape a cycling of evidence, a case file full of events that would normally be ignored by friends, who might themselves exhibit other embarrassing 'behaviours.' With the rise of popular psychology, has Western culture infused into practical language the same sort of clinical terminology? Psychologisms like 'passive aggressive' and 'denial' are taken for granted as factual descriptions of behaviour that is irrevocable or ingrained. These formulations of an individual's responses to social life make for simpler definitions of appropriate behaviour, and move all of us closer to the governmentality that institutions promote.

To defend oneself against such techniques is to admit no reaction, so the work of the mental detainee includes reading the moods and whims of her keepers without having whims, which is certainly still necessary on- and off-site: 'In total institutions, staying out of trouble is likely to require persistent conscious effort. The inmate may forego certain levels of sociability with his fellows to avoid possible incidents' (Goffman, 1961: 23). In the case of Community Treatment Orders, relationships with family or professionals may be altogether focused on 'managing illness.' Psychiatric workers in this study said detainees work extremely hard to avoid attention and to 'stay out of trouble.'

The cycling of biology is a difficult idea to capture; it is not just biological determinism though that model certainly informs it. It is more like a social expectation that biology will repeat itself. On the one hand, it is merely biological reductionism, the construction of all human acts or 'behaviours' into corporeal responses to the environment. It is an appeal from nature, imaged as unchangeable, at least from an individual human perspective. On the other hand, there is something visceral about our mental and, of course, emotional relationships to the world. This mentalized body (aspects that are considered fluid or changeable) can be pedestalized, honoured, or abused. If the cycle of biology is like a giant story among all the stories used in the cycling of evidence, the cycling of biology has a giant story of its own in psychiatry today. A very poignant example of the cycle of biology is what I call the *cycling of chemistry*.

The cycling or patterning of chemistry involves using chemical compounds to throw the body's biological processes into disarray and thus condition the sorts of behaviours that elicit psychiatric responses. For example, to spike someone's punch, to drug someone's drink, or to give someone a neurotoxin like haldoperidol as a medicine, can result in confused or 'agitated' reactions that clinicians, using biodeterministic models of behaviour, cite as cause to medicate the disorderly body. More of a drug or additional drugs can be used in the cycle of chemistry to solve the problem initiated by treatment. Thus, by using drugs to suppress one 'symptom,' additional symptoms arise (or withdrawal adds to and exacerbates them) that provide the grounds for using more drugs. At best, the body is so saturated that it behaves passively and the cycling of chemistry can be levelled or tapered according to the physician's expert opinion. At worst, extrapyramidal effects and negative effects like sudden death can be blamed on all sorts of factors including biological illness or genetic weakness.

Three cycling or accumulative practices of power are identifiable in institutionalization programs, either within a site or 'out' in the community: evidence, biology, and chemistry.

Goffman discusses several other methods of institutionalization. The physically incarcerated inmate is never alone, always accompanied by 'bars or walls' exposing him to others (1961: 25). By contrast, the drugged CTO subject leaves the bars behind. She is exposed as a psychiatric detainee only by the 'side effects' of drugs, if people notice these at all, and if they do not attribute them to 'illness.' At the same time her CTO status is hidden from view. The prison is invisible both to her and her allies. This is one of the major differences between today's practices, which are still burgeoning, and those of the modern institution. Treatments are so complete in their effects that site-based detention is usually unnecessary in everyday life.

Goffman rarely mentions 'medications,' which would have been forced in the institutional context of the late 1950s (1961: 28). But then, he also does not mention lobotomies or electric shock, so he may have felt that treatments were not specific to institutionalization or were cause for an entirely separate study. Likewise, professionals who discuss coercions never include treatments as one form among many, denying a history of chemical restraint. Perhaps Goffman, too, may have seen a composed and predictable individual to be improved, especially as many inmates would seek 'improvement,' just as I did looking for release. Improvement is achieved not only by accepting tranquility at all cost, but by 'staying out of trouble' and not 'acting up.' As an advocate, I found detainees spoke few ills about their captors, less about the cognitive effects of their medication, and almost never of its subjective effects. Such things are found mostly in the literature.

Goffman says the inmate loses control over who sees him as a 'patient' (1961: 28). For example, she is vulnerable to spot searches (29), and these issues are the same for on-site inmates and CTO subjects today. As a minor example, under the Mental Health Act of Ontario, a patient's mail can be intercepted, though this is rare today. And now, as in Goffman's era, the detainee can still be ignored even as she asks for food, or calls out in an emergency (45; see also Anderson, 2005). The detainee can still be humiliated into asking for minor items like razors, or for major needs as well (Goffman, 1961: 41). The cycling of evidence and biology turns all interactions into institutional exchanges. The individual becomes a serviceable form for others to exchange, a 'parcel,' as one Italian inmate called himself during the reforms in Italy in 1968 (White, 2007).

Some aspects of Goffman's observations apply differently to a 'CTO' context. CTOs were heralded as preventing or limiting hospital institutionalization for certain individuals. Goffman speaks of 'desegregation,' being forced to share accommodations with people one is not accustomed to, the 'other.' With CTOs, the detainee may not be placed in a boarding house with the 'other,' but still be forced to live with an abusive or manipulative family in a middle-class home. 'Privilege systems'

(Goffman, 1961: 48) or 'indulgences' (283), whereby inmates are granted ten-minute breaks for cigarettes like I was, or highly supervised group outings off hospital grounds (e.g., to the local shops, as I recall in my own experience, in which a rope was used to keep us 'together'), may have been the inspiration for the CTO itself.

Similarly, what Goffman calls less-supervised 'free places' (1961: 230) have been expanded greatly to include 'the community' altogether, yet monitored spaces now include the private domicile. The 'smart home' electronic surveillance system for 'people with schizophrenia' is considered by Stip and Rialle (2005). The 'buddy system' (Goffman, 1961: 279) may no longer be applicable if a CTO subject lives alone, yet might still be preferred in the absence of other supports. Goffman uses the word 'mortification' (1961: 34–5) to describe being forced to watch brutality performed on other inmates. This method of institutionalization is still used in hospitals today, such as when a 'Code White' is announced and orderlies run to subdue an inmate while others watch (Anderson, 2005). But this does not necessarily work to subdue inmates, as Goffman says. I was appalled when I saw a teenage girl chased and dragged by orderlies screaming into an isolation room. I was incensed when an older inmate who spoke very little English admitted to me that he did not know what was happening or what to do. Having overheard his doctor, I told him he wanted to use electricity as a treatment. I think the use of 'mortification' only encourages rebellion, which can conceivably be managed on-site, but spreads by word of mouth off-site.

Finally, inmate 'performance' under workers' expectations is the same under chemical incarceration as in institutional facilities. Goffman's work considers the making of the 'mental patient' as a kind of 'career.' He tracks the plight of the 'pre-patient' (1961: 131), who must enter and survive a 'funnel' of absurd expectations, a 'hazing' in other words. I think of the mental health industry (some of it quite helpful, I know) as being funnel shaped, the sink being biopsychiatric constraint; the 'pre-patient' today is the shy child in school or the distraught victim in a counsellor's office. In 'assessment,' the inmate is supposed to abide by 'conditions of imminent exposure and wide fluctuation in [her] regard, [pride, or honour] with little control over the granting of this regard' (164–5). Today, as then, the detainee must still perceive and respond immediately to the expectations of power handlers (120). The 'self' must be easily changed upon varying demands for the institutionalized person to perform to her healer's hopes and expectations. She may have

Table 7.1
List of Institutionalizations' Methods and Our Resistance to Them

Institutionalization	Resistance
Certification (medical arrest)	Question, challenge, appeal to second opinion
Commitment (medical incarceration)	Reticence, feign approval, appeal
Treatment (chemical incarceration)	Non-compliance, self-medication, feign approval
Restraint, isolation (physical control)	Defacement, violence, dissociation, self-injury
Illness education (indoctrination)	Parrot, challenge, research, publish

to discard or puppet the self to comply with extreme but ostensibly benign programs of erasure.

For some, the 'illness' becomes the repository of negative facts, memories, inferences, and meanings, an explanation for workers; but for other detainees, this cutting away of the self into 'ill' and acceptable parts is impossible. Patient detainees' use of institutional language (Goffman, 1961: 97), such as diagnostic categories and psychologisms for mockery or self-mastery, can threaten workers' social distance. Workers have labelled such forms of resistance as 'denial' and 'intellectualism.' Again these practices continue.

This is not an exhaustive review of Goffman's many examples of the methods used to alter the self by institutionalization. It is by no means a full demonstration of the kinds of personal violations of selfhood that continue to occur. Goffman's work is helpful because it suggests how interpersonal indignities and mechanical methods of restriction persist and blend with 'treatment' itself to institutionalize identities and bodies. While this sociologically theorized social machinery is not usually perceptible to workers, and inmates 'playing the game' to escape attention, it is traceable in material relations including legal documents (see chapter 8).

Of course, the Community Treatment Order may not be the first or only transfer of institutional power into the community. As Goffman tells us, in the 1950s institutional workers hoped to enlist the family in their work as soon as the inmate was 'admitted,' as they do today. Informants say the CTO is merely a formal exercise of power, one that has already been occurring informally through other coercions. Formal processes are often dismissed as excess legalism, but here legalism is being used to authorize historically contended practices, such as by expanding criteria for the detention of bodies based on their ability to 'take care of themselves.'

Rampancy has been the hallmark of psychiatric confinement, and it does not change as a result of moving the locus of control from the psychiatric facility to the psychiatric body. The restriction of movement and association is more fully executed through chemical institutionalization, which attacks movement, will, and consciousness. Incarceration instils institutional control through naming, overpowering, and silencing. This control is performed by industrial practices that cycle evidence, biology, and chemistry. These categorizations are certainly not all-inclusive, but serve as a means of studying how people are routinely subjugated. In the next chapter I will look more closely at how psychiatric practices of power inform other institutional industries and impinge on detainees' identities.

8   Dreams of Escape

This chapter is the longest in the book because it puts meat on the bones of prior chapters which have been concerned with structures of institutionalization, chemicalization, psychiatrization, industrialization, management, and sanism. What about oppression, poverty, and struggle? Let's explore these issues from where we left off.

Chemical institutionalization affords ways to manage greater numbers of people in society without expensive physical sites. Once again, we can look at how this methodology works across institutional settings. By looking at lived experiences in relation to concepts like 'insight,' psychiatric detainee education and identity management is considered across institutions, which participants call 'the system,' a 'transinstitutional' network. This network of industries, held together by institutionalized knowledges, professions, and workforces, provides not a perfect or universal structure that denies agency or difference, but an imagined telos, a societal goal, that is both organized and imagined through a core culture of institutional texts (Smith, 1987).

In my experience many of the ways in which survivors have resisted psychiatry have gone unnoticed, not only by authorities who discount us as unscientific or unfeeling, but also by people in other resistance movements who have reduced our quest to what can be done about the problem of personal distress and dysfunction. This includes members of antipsychiatry groups who are not 'crazy.' As more and more people come under psy regimes of ruling, I have noticed more interest in 'antipsychiatry' and 'survivor' rhetorics, at least in the last decade. How did this begin?

In the 1990s, racialized minorities became more prominent among the detainee population at Queen Street in Toronto, though financially poor whites, especially older people, women, people with non-psychiatric mental disabilities, and people in the 'criminal justice' system all figured among them as well. There were sometimes white disabled people, and sometimes openly gay, lesbian, bisexual, transsexual, transgendered, and two-spirited people, especially at the Clarke Institute.

I also noticed many more young people coming into the system, while workers talked about the need to bring mental health services to youth. With increased marketing of psychiatric drugs during the 1990s, especially for attention deficit disorder and other complaints about students, I started to see chemical institutionalization become applied to many different kinds of people but with less and less reliance on long-term stays in hospitals.

My informants talked about a number of these issues, though I did not ask about issues like racism and sexism; what some social scientists call the 'intersectional' dynamics of oppression were well known to them. I would like to provide accounts and questions centred on psychiatric, especially biochemical, methodologies of control to inform collective approaches. This does not mean that I ascribe to a linear structuralism about oppression, or see our problems as separate in simple ways, but given my experience and this book, I am interested in identifying issues beyond my own perspective, however difficult that can be.

In this chapter, I will work from experiences of chemical (trans)institutionalization to experiences of coercion and choice that pervade community mental health, especially through the Community Treatment Order. Then, from informants' perceptions, I will work back through legal documentation of survivor experiences for parallax or triangulation, and end on what is intended to be a hopeful note before the concluding chapter. Youth seems the best place to start.

TYLER (HOUSING WORKER): I've seen cases where people are entering the system
    at a young age, and it doesn't take very long for them to start acting like the
    people that have been there for ten years.
KIM (PEER WORKER): Yeah, the role that they've been expected –
TYLER: you know, and pretty soon they're in that hopeless category, and they're
    getting treated the same as those other people that are –

Youth can often manage problems themselves with some help, but when they reach out to an industry focused on immediate control, their struggle is reframed through psychiatric and psychological ideas

(Waters, 2005). Biological categories of distress are quickly applied and serviced with the usual chemical fix. June, a legal clinic worker, elaborates:

> They're still growing and they're coming in at what the medical model says is 'high susceptibility' for a mental illness, at sixteen to twenty-four, right? [. . .] Because, at sixteen they [. . .] don't keep them in the pediatrics ward. They go up where the adults are. So the behaviour and the culture gets learned very quickly, about how to survive there. All that it takes is for me to be depressed, because I might be thinking about, you know, same sex thoughts, or I might think my mother really sucks because she won't let me do this, or I'm an Indian who doesn't want to have to wear dresses to school, and I'm in a culture that doesn't support me. I don't fit in with my peers; I'm getting drunk all the time, so my parents are really pissed at me. They think I need a psychiatrist. I'm depressed, and I say one day, to somebody I trust, that I feel like killing myself. That suicidal language is a 'reaching out' language, but the medical model confines you very quickly, and I think once you're in there [. . .] that could be it. Because a lot of people give up.

June says that a lot of the problems that she has seen could be easily handled with simple information, counselling, and basic help with life skills. Add to this the systemic lack of understanding of immigrant experiences and non-European cultures, and it is easy to see how help fails. The impact of chemical treatment is quite severe on young people. June continues:

> I worked with homeless youth, and men and women who are in the criminal justice system and coming out. And so, part of what I saw with the young people – I worked a lot, I had no special training or anything, but I worked a lot with the youth – that had mental health issues (predominantly they were young men, and their issues were coming up after being incarcerated) and the trend I started to notice was most of them spent time in segregation, and most of them had taken psychiatric drugs against their will. And they were completely different. Like many of them I'd known since they were fourteen, 'cause they used to do 'youth employment,' and they had kind of travelled around and stayed in touch with me. And now I see them in the neighbourhood because that's where I used to refer them to, 'cause it has cheap housing, and some of [these kids] are just vacant. And I remember when I was there, that everybody in the front line doing

the service providing work felt, without discussion, that it was in the best interests of clients to be medicated. Now I didn't really have a critique. I was just, in general, against any kind of medication. You know, people having to take those options. But, I did think at some points, now this person would be better off with somebody making sure that they're safe, you know? 'Cause he's walking around the streets, and you know he's getting into trouble 'cause he's exposing himself. Things like that.

Youth are forcibly treated and isolated resulting in increased manageability. They can be detained in the criminal justice system as well, but chemical management is used there, too. The devastating results can seem impossible to avoid if we accept chemicalization as the best way to deal with distress or deviance. June shows how the system might help youth by using sensitivity and cultural knowledge:

But then I ran a group for six weeks, twelve weeks, and then it was so successful [a supervisor] wouldn't let me run it again. And the group was for young people who were immigrants and refugees, who had experienced some kind of economic or political violence in their country, and what came out of that was we made sure people had food. Not like sandwiches, but like rice and wheat and vegetables, because they weren't eating properly. Many were Muslim, and stuff. Their bodies could not physically adapt to the food. So, I had the Health Centre [...] working with me, and they're like on the forefront of mental health and stuff, but there were a couple of nurses in there who did kind of grassroots work, so the clients would always go there for whatever they needed. But we never forced them to take treatment.

We never forced them to see psychiatrists, because we found, if they were eating (we gave them two TTC [Toronto Transit Commission] tickets, and let them stay with us all day, because they were being kicked out of the shelters during the day) that they would be more stable the next day, and then the next day. The ones that kept going into the doctors and getting the shots and stuff – 'cause nurses used to give the shots before CTOs were in place – they were always more likely to be in and out of the system. So there was that mentality, 'Don't question. It's better.' And if you're a frontline service provider with no political analysis, or no education, 'cause they're not giving it to you in that field, right? – they just want you to hurry up, hurry up, and produce – it's very easy to buy into it. It's very easy to be brainwashed into believing it's in the best interests of the client, 'cause the client gets situated as problematic when they're not medicated. Everything is about 'they're not medicated.'

Danielle, an Assertive Community Treatment team psychiatrist, shows how mental disabilities other than psychiatric are often managed by chemical incarceration. Individuals labelled with intellectual disabilities (mentalism) can often be treated as if they were 'mad.' Lack of information about such arrangements can be understood as cognitive impairment, but Danielle says overdrugging is a more credible explanation:

ERICK: In one case, I had someone say, 'you know a lot of them don't even know they're on a CTO.' And I said, 'What do you mean?' And they said, 'Well often they're not informed that they are.' And I said, 'Well how can that be, because they have to sign something,' you know, and they said, 'Well when they come to me, they often don't know what their legal status is.' Now I'm wondering whether that's because of their cognitive ability –

DANIELLE: Yeah –

ERICK: Or what that might be, but –

DANIELLE: That's very odd. The only thing I can think of is like a sub-population of people who are either developmentally handicapped and have a psychotic illness, or because of the seriousness of their illness they have a lot of cognitive deficits and they're just very, very immersed, very passive, very – the scenario I'm thinking of in my mind is that they're living with the family, and the family is agreeing to it and it doesn't really change much. But certainly all my clients know they're on a CTO and they never let me forget it!

ERICK: [laughs] Wow, right.

DANIELLE: The only person – the one I told you who's at very high risk, the person who is developmentally handicapped – he knows he's on a CTO. I mean I don't think he can explain to you what a CTO is. He just knows if he gets into trouble the police pick him up and bring him into hospital. He knows. No, they know. And the other thing that strikes me as odd is that they get rights advice, right? So that's why I'm saying it must be a population that's very cognitively impaired.

ERICK: Hmm.

DANIELLE: Plus their mind is overmedicated, or something, 'cause you know they have no awareness.

If these reports suggest anything, it is that CTO treatment is not always viewed as a reprieve from simple detention. It can be viewed as more of a problem than detention, even to a refugee claimant who would prefer being returned to a war zone. A Community Treatment Order seems less restrictive, but the imposition can be more restrictive subjectively, coming from within the body. This forces all effects of treatment (restraint) into the conscious life of the individual. Working under somnolism, the individual moves slowly and treads lightly.

We also find that prisoners in correctional institutions generally have more rights than psychiatric detainees, but not in regard to druggings. In frustration, Kim, a consumer/survivor activist and advocacy worker, said:

> I mean there was an article in the [*Toronto*] *Star* the other day about those two family members who are going to court because there's no inquests into the deaths at psychiatric hospitals.

She explained that the criminal justice system has automatic inquests into prison inmate deaths, whereas unexpected deaths in a psychiatric facility are ignored. If the rights of prisoners in the correctional system are few, they are lessened by psychiatric druggings. Elizabeth Packard, a well-known U.S. psychiatric inmate and reformer of the late 1800s, said that psychiatric inmates often had less provision than many slaves of that era (see Geller & Harris, 1994: 58–85).[1] Packard brought a feminist voice to our movement in the nineteenth century. However, black, First Nations, and criminalized psychiatric inmates had far fewer provisions than white inmates, just as psychiatric detainees who are racialized or speak English as a second (or third or fourth) language today are not going to be provided the same options as detainees who are white or have lived in Toronto all their lives.

The systems of power that interconnect here are complex, and June is one of the few workers in the 'system' who can recognize detainees' needs because of her own experience as a racialized person in Canadian

---

1 Prolific psychiatric critic, Thomas Szasz, who rejected the 'antipsychiatry' label, called detainees 'psychiatric slaves.' This ahistorical metaphor appropriates the histories of African Canadians' histories and others. Szasz's idea, that ill-labelled bodies are exploited for profit and work, might better be taken up using contemporary feminist theorizations of women's labour as unpaid, unrecognized, and often performed in spite of male abuse. I believe someone has already suggested that avoidance of abuse is a kind of work, and survivors have long said that our bodies, our distress, are raw materials for psychiatric labour.

society. Her examples demonstrate that racialized youth will often be noticed 'acting out,' even if they may have more difficulties than others. Add to this questions like sexual identity and challenges begin to multiply. An additional challenge is a mindset of workers who have cachet in Western culture and expect detainees to have already adapted to Canadian society and to navigate it as they do. But even educated white males are just as confused about navigating a system that helps by hindering, as Rudy, a consumer/survivor agency worker and activist, says (see chapter 4).

Gender and Psychiatric Arrangements

While chemical institutionalization expands, its message of brain diseases treatable with medications is widely accepted (Caplan, 1995, 2004; Watters, 2010), especially as these claims cannot be debated in common forums. The targets of the helping professions are often those individuals who have suffered the most in a patriarchal colonial society. This book owes a lot to critical feminist sociology like that of Dorothy Smith, who studied psychiatric arrangements in regard to women's experiences.

As common targets of psychiatric interventions, women have been outspoken about their experiences of 'madness' and abuse (e.g., Grobe, 1995; Geller & Harris, 1994; Wood, 1994). As a student of Mad autobiographies, I find that women have been doing a lot of writing about psychiatry (see listings at www.qsos.ca). Women's resistance is important to the Mad movement based on that work alone. Women are more likely to be psychiatrized, and electroshocked (twice as often as men), and they will also end up in correctional sites and other institutions. June elaborates on this:

> Well you're going to go – if you're out in the street, or if you're a problem, you're going to go to one of two places. Depends how the cop feels. They either go to local hospital's emergency where the cop might wait for 12 hours – I highly doubt it. Or, you're going to be shoved off into jail and be put into 'mental health diversion court' [a judicial program that tries to redirect 'mentally ill' people charged with minor offences from jail into the psychiatric system]. Either way, whatever institution you end up in, it's likely you're going to be forcibly treated.
>
> So, aside from that I work with women that are incarcerated, and I can't tell you how awful in the last five years (we're a halfway house where

I work) – and I work with women that are in crisis, and so we advocate for women – I can't tell you how many hard medications these women are coming out of prison with. And when you read up on them, the side effects are just horrible. But since they've been in prison, their tolerance level's increasing, they get a different doctor out here who just increases the medication, and all of that is just to keep them quiet.

And 'superjails' are not delivering appropriate mental health services. People involved in the criminal justice system are jumping on the mental health bandwagon, with no infrastructure to understand mental health and their client community. So you can see how it happens.

How women are read and how their needs are ignored speaks to how Mad people are treated. As a psychiatrist, Danielle provides an example in which menopausal changes can be understood as psychiatric problems, an example of cycling of biology:

DANIELLE: There's a woman, when we first took her on, she had an illness for several years, maybe fifteen, twenty years, and for whatever reason the course of the illness changed – schizophrenia – so it became less treatable, less responsive to meds. You know that happens: the illness changes over time. Women going through menopause sometimes become less treatment responsive. Anyway, it changed. So she went from being someone who could live fairly independently, had children, had hospitalizations now and again, to someone who's chronically homeless and chronically very psychotic.
ERICK: With her children still in the community?
DANIELLE: Oh, no, no, they were apprehended.

The way in which women's resistance to psychiatry is described by a female psychiatrist makes me think it would be unnoticeable to most male workers. Danielle explains:

So by the time we met her I think she'd been homeless for about five years. You know every once in a while when she posed a public threat or whatever, she'd be hauled off by police to hospital, treated for a month or two, and released, 'til she deteriorated to the point that it started all over again, you know, a few months later. So we took her on, very, very psychotic woman, very bright, and very, very spunky. Like she just would not accept psychiatry at the time. So we followed her for a year or two with no change in pattern of illness, and she has this brother, very respectful. Like in anything, not all families are the same, right. He understood her illness, very respectful of her, but wanted to make sure the system could deliver the best of what it had to offer her.

This is a good example of how female identification is cleaved into 'spunky' or 'psychotic': which of these is responsible for the detainee's rejection of psychiatry? Is rebellion actually born of biological error or sustained by quirky independence? Cycling of biology creates such distortions; identity becomes incidental. The family member and psychiatrist, two well-meaning persons, accept the idea that this 'client' may be confrontational because of biology. Danielle continues:

> So in discussions with him [the detainee's brother], we put her on a CTO. I think we just did the sixth or seventh renewal; I think she's been on a CTO for about three years. And the CTO, what's it done for her? She's still psychotic, she still has a lot of problems, but she's housed, and for [non-medical] circumstances I won't go into, she's got way more money now. So she's got more money and more money's always good when you're in poverty. And the most important thing for me is the woman's not cured or treated by any stretch of the imagination but she's able to connect with the staff where she's living, and she's able to connect with the team members, which she never could before because she could never have any kind of conversation. So now, even though it's quite psychotic and disjointed, she's not alone in her psychosis. So it's not that same condemned level of isolation that she had before.

Treatment reorganizes a lapsing once-treated body. Or the body is mad and cannot be calmed by conversation, and we may be open to madness but not wandering distress, so treatment must be imposed. The patient detainee's decreased functioning due to drugging will make her amenable to conversation, whatever the quality of this conversation, but not confident enough to contest detention (and perhaps she is no longer wanting to be 'mad'). Her resistance, which brings the Community Treatment Order, is never understood, even when Danielle recognizes the amount of power she has. Danielle explains:

> So, my point being, every time I renew [the CTO], and every time we have a Review Board [hearing], and every time she fights it – she never accepted this – I have to know, you know (her treatment responsiveness is not great), I need to know or have some increased probability that I'm doing

the right thing. Her brother's a thoughtful person, too, and he thinks about it every time if he's doing the right thing. So I guess it decreases my unilateral power to have family members – you know if you have the PG&T, the Office of the Public Guardian and Trustee, I mean, you know, they'll do whatever the doctor wants, right? Because objectively, these people meet the criteria [for imposing a CTO] so clearly, there's nothing to discuss, but if there's family members who really know the person, and you know they know that the person wants to be autonomous, but at what price, and are really weighing the pros and cons, I feel a lot better as a clinician that I'm not making these decisions by myself.

The 'price' of autonomy is considered already to be dismal. Both of the individuals involved in determining CTO status for this woman are well-meaning, to be sure, and not naively so. They are trying to 'fix' a problem for which chemical institutionalization seems to be the only available option. Autonomy versus drugging seems an extremely small set of choices. Someone might object that intervention would be fine for stabilization, then dosage should be tapered as much as possible. Some alternative options will be introduced in chapter 9.

In Danielle's interview, she spoke of the female detainee as 'spunky,' but here she refers to a male detainee in more heroic terms. His fate, even without a family member on his side, is quite different. Danielle says:

That's right, there's a man who again had an illness, not that long actually, ten years or so, complicated by substance abuse, although that wasn't so great, but he just tends to pop whatever is around like Tylenol or whatever, and would take high doses of tranquilizers and then stop all of a sudden and have withdrawal and seizures. So, there's lots of reasons why he would meet the criteria [of a CTO]. When we first met him it was the same thing, like revolving door in and out of hospital, wouldn't maintain housing because he would get paranoid. He had this whole paranoid system that would evolve, and he'd get paranoid about the people where he was living, so he'd have to move. He couldn't even be in a shelter because the paranoid delusion system would take over the shelter. So he'd have to be on the street like under bridges and stuff.

Anyway, he's sort of an Ayn Rand kind of guy, like rugged individualist, good at getting what he needs, but he connected to the team as well as he would connect to any health care professional. Never accepted psychiatry, but we had a connection. So after a couple of years, and this is where I felt somewhat ambivalent, but after a couple of years when the inpatient doctors [at the hospital] after seeing him four or five times a year started talking CTOs, of course (and I talked to his sister, though she didn't want to be substitute decision maker 'cause she didn't want to strain the relationship, so the PG&T provided substitute consent), I went with a trial of the CTO. I think it lasted for a year in total. But this guy, and, you know good for him, got himself a good lawyer, and [went] to [the Ontario Court of Appeal] and [the CTO] was thrown out, on a technicality, nothing to do with the substance of the CTO. I could have reissued a CTO but I haven't [. . .] [H]e presented himself to emerge twice and had [a] brief hospitalization because he was feeling depressed and suicidal, which he never did before, and that was it.

But he was miserable. Very, very miserable. So we basically gave it a year, so he didn't have so much of the psychotic symptoms, but he did feel extremely dysphoric [sad], had a lot of side effects to the needle, wouldn't take oral meds. He was just miserable.

I would not want to be in Danielle's situation. Her compassion for this person is genuine. She believes medication should work, but the recovered detainee wants to be released seeking abandon to madness. It is to imagine solace in distress. While the female detainee may not have demonstrated her opposition with suicidal acts, she too was a rugged individualist and rejected psychiatry. The female detainee has her CTO renewed indefinitely, despite her vocal opposition, whereas the male's opposition is set into emotional relief in Danielle's interview. When I ask Danielle what the man himself has to say, she replies:

Well just that he feels awful, and he would never go to the psychiatric system unless he was desperate [. . .] He's not that much at risk of self-harm or harm to others really. I mean he's at risk out of self-neglect, but he did seem miserable, and he has a lot of side effects 'cause in the injectable medication you only get the old antipsychotics that come with neurological side effects [sic]. He had that restlessness and that parkinsonism, even though he was on a very low dose. So, yeah, high side effect burden, yet his voices and paranoid system wasn't as obvious for sure, but the guy was mostly miserable. But he was housed and his hospitalization rate was decreased, so if you just looked at housing and the hospitalization rate, it would be deemed a success, but in terms of his personal quality of life, he was no better. In fact, I'd say he was suffering more.

Danielle shows that the CTO's 'efficacy' based on the subject's use of services is not necessarily indicative of 'positive outcome.' Her description of 'medication' issues is in keeping with most mental health workers ('side effects,' 'parkinsonism' as unintended, etc.). But in terms of gender relations, whether we accord to her a maternalism (which might arguably be mirrored in a male psychiatrist's paternalism over female detainees, though anecdotes indicate otherwise), or whether we figure the involvement of a family member to guide her decisions, Danielle clearly recognizes a male's resistance whereas she seems to miss a female's resistance. This is not only important with regard to gender, but also with regard to other groups who show less strident or dramatic patterns of refusal. Danielle elaborates on this male individual:

> He never ever forgave me for that CTO, and basically we've lost contact with him and now he's chronically psychotic and homeless, and I've discharged him from our service hoping he would engage with other services. So anyway that's an example of a prototype that I hold in my mind about people you wouldn't put on CTOs, and I think there the lesson for me was the gradient between the treated and the untreated wasn't great enough, and there was no appreciable change in his quality of life that was important to him. He would rather die than be on a CTO. He's a rugged individual. He does not want to be controlled. He wants to do everything on his own terms. Personally, I have no problem with someone like that going to hospital four times a year for two weeks, and then the rest of the time he does the best he can. Personally, I have no problem with that. So the reason I issued the CTO was to see if it would make a difference to him.

Choice and the 'Harness'

More cross-institutional knowledge is needed to inform a Mad analysis of psychiatric intervention. But the scope of my research led me again to finding how chemical incarceration arose for particular individuals and is in some sense being 'chosen.'

To choose psychiatric interventions is an interesting problematic. Can a detainee truly 'choose' to be detained? I was able to find only one example of a person who wanted to be under a Community Treatment Order. He told people assembled at a public forum on CTOs that without drugs he would surely become violent and end up in a maximum security prison because of prior crimes. The CTO allows him to live in a much less restrictive way (assuming his meds are not upped) than in a high-security prison or forensic unit. Assuming correctional detention is a societal command response to crime, not just a 'therapeutic' detention that people can avoid with a CTO, treatment and restraint come together. Should a person be punished or treated? Which is worse? These orders can enable someone to avoid other forms of incarceration that one does not prefer, but it seemed that most people resented, rejected, hated being on CTOs.

I asked Danielle if anyone she knew accepted CTOs. Here is her answer:

> No, none of them do. [laughs] None of them do. But the one who comes closest to accepting me, [the woman discussed above], she likes me, I'm her hero, quote unquote (say that at the Review Board!) – but she hates that medication. So what do I do for her? And for her it's very much a question of it blunts her feelings, and she's a very good artist, and it just kills her drawing. So what I do is I just use the CTO as a bit of a harness for her. So she'll skip doses once or twice a week, and then we just raise the sceptre of the CTO and she gets back on, so it gives her a bit of breathing room. And prior to being on a CTO she'd been off – we'd known her for at least two to three years, and no matter how many meetings we'd have with her individually, any time you tried to bilaterally negotiate medication reduction or whatever, it would just go off and she would just do things unilaterally and stop her medication every single time. So the CTO kind of is a bit of a structure where I can then have some influence and help her to get back on her meds. But she has the room to get off the meds to feel her feelings a bit. It's like an elastic structure kind of. She's the only person I would say doesn't fight. All the others are completely against it. So I end up going to a lot of Review Boards, you know, where they contest it.

Without forgetting Danielle's view that this detainee was opposed to the CTO yet was 'not fighting' it, note the 'elastic structure' of chemical detention. It is that latitude that seems to enable clinicians in a new kind of power. Under crude chemical control, care and custody intersect, and the subject is hard pressed to understand how much her or his or their lives are actually being controlled from within. Danielle says of her male example:

Everything we've offered him is not – I guess that's it: he's experienced all the options and that's what he's quote-unquote choosing, I mean you can argue whether he's competent or not, but when you've been to the limit of what medical technology has to offer you it becomes kind of moot. Like, this is the person that you're dealing with. You can't talk about some hypothetical person, another brain. This is the person you're dealing with; this is the limit of our technology.

The psychiatrist saves souls in social danger. Medicine is meant to heal. Technology allows personhood in this narrative. Psychiatric survivors decried CTOs as 'leash laws' in 2000, and were dismissed for doing so, yet here is the same metaphor, the 'harness,' being used paternally to demonstrate exactly how control is achieved, relaxed, and reasserted. The detainee tries to escape drugging, but under the cycling of chemistry, she finds herself socially dependent and thus contained.

Moderate voices between psychiatrists and detainees attempt to rationalize and shift the locus of power to allow for 'alternative' services like 'psychosocial rehabilitation,' even 'recovery' services, which challenge the present belief in 'mental illness' as 'incurable.' Victor, an ACT peer worker, offers another example:

But I might say there might be one case, of this person I mentioned that we see every day, that [the CTO] just gets renewed. Is it out of convenience? The client has – is not saying 'I don't want to be on a CTO' – each time it comes up it seems to get renewed, and it's been renewed since I was there. It's been years. So you wonder where is it going to go? Is it serving a purpose? Is it doing anything? Is it effective? I think with CTOs [either] you're preventing this person from doing something 'really bad' or you're doing it for 'their own good' kind of, those are the two things [possible] [. . .] You make them take their medication or they're going to be [forced to do so] in the hospital. But what's the person learning from that? I mean they're going to get discharged, and then it starts all over again. I mean, it's hard sometimes. CTOs, to me, are effective with some people; with other people they're not. I think the people that they're used on are generally people that aren't in the frame of mind to say no or have the resources to fight them.

Victor is saying that treatment is either a restraint or it is actually therapeutic (improving, not just stabilizing). As a stabilizer, a CTO seems to postpone 'rehospitalization' rather than prevent it or replace it. CTO efficacy is based on coercion (restraint) alone. Indeed, postponement is rather an extension of hospitalization, and it is not always necessary:

ERICK: So even though [this person who was allowed to go off his drugs and was taken off a CTO] has these delusions, he's able to function?
VICTOR: He's able to maintain his housing and we check in with them [his housing workers] to see how he's doing. If they have any concern they can reach us.

Even if strictly social interventions are utilized (though they may still be sanist or destructive), the priorities of the psychiatric industry are to ensure imprisonment as the foundational provision. If all else fails, detain. Danielle, an ACT psychiatrist, explains:

I mean it's not that the patient – a patient like that would rather go to jail than end up in a psychiatric hospital. I have no problem with that (well, I do have a problem with that) but in this society, you're going to end up in front of a psychiatrist. That's what's going to happen. It's just the way it works. So, you know, either you play ball with me or [short pause]. Most people can, actually. It's kind of 'agree to disagree.'

The least objectionable jail may be something like the better mouse-trap. Technologies are more concrete and governable than social and interpersonal interventions insofar as they produce static 'objects' of interaction. Under the relations of ruling, a discourse of 'technology' is utilized in the hope of operationalizing a concrete and accountable program of change, of physical intervention for the 'mad' body that can be shown to bring it to earth. The CTO can integrate social response to distress. Danielle continues:

The CTO is more to make the system come together and be responsible for the patient than for the patient, if you know what I mean? It's more a System Cohesion Order. That way you've got a fixed point of responsibility, and you've got people built in around the person written into the CTO.

Before hospital closures, a detainee would receive treatment in the same place that restraints were used, in the institution, a different kind of 'wraparound.' The Community Treatment Order attempts to bind treatment and detention into a single unit again, out of the institution, supposedly for the purpose of service 'system' integrity (Dreezer & Dreezer, 2007). Thus, the logic of detention can be considered an advantageous methodology of ensuring service delivery. But what if the patient wants a more nuanced process of recovery? The CTO provided for negative therapeutic relationships in Victor's opinion:

ERICK: A lot of people say that if they're on treatment, they'll be able to do more [voluntary] therapies. But what you're saying is that because they've had choice withdrawn or taken away, they don't feel as open to other things?

VICTOR: Oh yeah, it affects the relationship. I have clients that I work with and I have good relationships with them. I have goals and I'm trying to help them with things. I just find, in my opinion, with clients who are on a CTO that we don't generally work with them on these kinds of things. It's not a good relationship for us. It's hard. I think other clients that aren't on CTOs, and they're taking medication and they're living their lives, they have a lot more choice, whereas people who are on CTOs seem to be, you know, really – it really is stigmatizing, right? No matter what anyone says, it's stigmatizing for someone.

I wonder whether detainees object to treatment or to the CTOs compulsory mechanism itself. To this question Danielle replies:

It's so hard to untangle the CTO versus choice over medication. Well, no, there are a few though [for whom] the CTO in and of itself is objectionable to them, not their medication, if that makes any sense [. . .] They're enmeshed because if you didn't mind the medication you wouldn't be on the medication anyways.

I wonder whether others who are not on CTOs generally accept medication in her practice. Danielle replies:

Or they don't! You know we talk – [laughs] I don't mind people being off medication. Sometimes they do sometimes they don't. It changes right? You know for the first few years they fight us all the way, then after a while they go through certain consequences, they might start making different decisions. It changes over time or life circumstances, whatever. It's a good question. That lack of friction you described [in which some people accept treatments without reservation]? I'd say maximum: maybe 40 per cent of our caseload. Because the people who end up with our [ACT] teams – the medication does come with a lot of cons for them. That's one issue.

This links back to the question of limited choice. The Community Treatment Order was instituted as an option one could choose instead of detention, much like neuroleptic treatment. Yet Danielle says that unless a person is detainable because of danger, or detainable because she is 'incapable' of understanding her condition, there is no reason to provide that person with a CTO and its promise of future imposition:

So, yeah, coming back to voluntary CTOs, they can only last six months anyway [because of involuntary or incapacity criteria]. I would never do a voluntary CTO. I don't understand the purpose of it other than to make it look less coercive than it is. The true application is when people are chronically incapable with a substitute decision maker. Otherwise you wouldn't need a CTO.

I think back to Danielle's using the CTO as a harness, flexing the muscles of authority without appearing to impose. Voluntary orders may be intended to give a detainee the illusion that she has the keys to her cell. Victor thinks that in the context of medical-legal arrangements, demands for control over drugging constitute an attempt at negotiation for detainee rights, not just 'treatment decisions.' He says:

I mean CTOs, when you look at it, you can't compare it with anything else in society. It's almost like you're on parole. It's basically a form of parole but you haven't committed a crime; you're being forced to – it's almost like you're being punished for mental [illness] and not taking your medication and being hospitalized. Well, why not look at another way of making the person better. I think sometimes CTOs are an 'out.' It's like they don't know what else to do with the person.

But Danielle understands coerced medicine as the best possible scheme for some individuals. Unlike Victor she does not have an experience of her own recovery and has less faith in interpersonal dialogue as a therapeutic paradigm (if society can be considered a paradigm in treatment). One's 'true' paradigm depends on one's experience:

DANIELLE: I guess to me the goal of so-called treatment is to increase people's real, true choices. It's paradoxical, I know. So I guess that's how I rationalize it for me, that they just have more true choices. So like that man I described; when he's treated he has more choices. He decides which college he goes to, he decides where he's going to live, he decides how much contact he's going to have with his father. When he's ill, he has no choice. He's constantly in hospital, his father talks for him because he can't speak for himself, and the police are all over him. Even though he won't agree with what I just said – he'll agree, but he won't make any connection to meds or CTOs. But, from my standpoint they have more true real choices. To me, that's the objective. I can give you another example of a CTO I abandoned. I don't know if that would help.

ERICK: I just want to continue this question because I'm trying to understand – you said, you know, these 'so-called treatments,' and you've talked about the possibility that these treatments don't always work as well as they're intended to, but generally I think the idea is they confer more choice, more social choice in other words, more capacity for the person to enter society, and to deal with society, really. If he's going to school rather than just being spoken for in an institution, obviously he's going to be reconnecting with soci – like when you say true choice, is that what you mean?

DANIELLE: That's what I mean, and if someone were to say to me, 'I'd rather be psychotic,' then I'd say, 'Fine, then that's your choice.' But when they're treated, the ones I'm talking about, they say they prefer the treated state even though they don't attribute it to treatment.

The Right to Be 'Ill'

Chemical institutionalization seems to be happening because common sense dictates that 'madness' is not a lifestyle. It is debilitating distress. As in Danielle's statements above, there is no denying that someone who accepts and even likes life while drugged (without consent), yet is so hapless while 'mad,' wants treatment but can't come to admit it or to conceive of restriction at such a personal level. But how do I relate that to the desire to be 'psychotic,' what might be called a Mad identity in this situation? I might say that only non-distressed experience counts as Mad, or that distress is contingent and not central to the experience, but this brings us back to the same question of how to manage distress.

Let's assume for a moment that all other methods to contain distress have failed, such as life coaching, counselling, diets, improved relationships, and so on. A more destructive option is understandable, and if distress prevents the person from communicating why should the state withhold treatment by well-meaning folk? To live in a fantasy makes one vulnerable to all sorts of predation. Whole nations have been plowed for trying to live 'differently.' Do we have a right to live 'madly'?

The drugged person communicates, the 'untreated' person seems incoherent and fearfully lost. Does 'madness' have something to say? By definition it does not. But in Danielle's account, even while drugged and supposedly happy the detainee refuses psychiatric explanation. Is this the stigma of mental illness which antipsychiatry seems to prop up with naysaying? Perhaps this is a memory of madness. Or it might be a wish to try it alone somehow, or with a coach who starts from where the client is.

The untreated person denies illness and wants to start from the self. Danielle sees this as denial rooted in illness. Perhaps this 'psychotic' experience is not valid in terms of competing interests but is only valuable at a personal level:

CARMEN (PEER WORKER): Because when he is taking medication he actually paints and draws and tries to – he's learning animation programs on the computer and, so when he's really engaged in his intense thinking process ['psychosis'], like actual production is zero, which is fine because I'm sure he's informing himself as to how he's going to proceed creatively. That's fine with me. But I'm saying for all intents and purposes, for the external observer who's not around mad people all the time, it looks – so now you've got a guy who's lost lots of weight, he's dressed in rags in the middle of winter, he's filthy dirty, he's yelling all the time, he's lost his apartment, so as far as things go on the –

ERICK: I can see what you're saying. Anyone who doesn't know him that well –

CARMEN: Who feels like they should do something, do something, do something, cause it looks like he needs something done – but at the same time I appreciate what [this person is] saying as well, that these are the best moments of his life.

ERICK: And he literally says that?

CARMEN: Yeah, except the unfortunate thing is he ends up in jail! [laughs] So can you have a best moment of your life in jail? Probably spiritually, and internally you can, right? I'm just not sure how to measure these things.

If a case can be made for letting someone suffer because it is a spiritual right, what about other people who are affected by that individual's distress? Is there any sanctuary if we decide we need to be alone, or a place we know someone will look out for us? That is why we are urged to seek help. Yet many problems with neuroleptic treatment remain, from placebo-like efficacy, to dependency and withdrawal, to reduced life expectancy, and these problems seem to exacerbate the 'danger' issue. Whatever happens to people after they are put on a cycle of chemistry and withdrawal, we often think it is caused by illness and not the meds. Carmen, a peer worker, describes one individual:

I don't know if it's a reaction to going off the medication or what that is – and it's not my job to figure it out [. . .] He had a job for ten years and he quit, and he just takes off into his own flight there that he says on the inside he doesn't feel bad at all. But on the outside he looks really distressed, [losing] his apartment, punching people in the head 'cause they piss him off or whatever, and he stops bathing or showering for months on end. His clothes turn literally into rags, like he wears exactly the same clothes all the time, right, and then winter comes and he's wearing the same clothes, no coat no gloves, you know, and arguing all the time, talking all the time, but it's not just like 'talking to himself.' It seems like he's in distress because he's saying, 'No, no, no!' and like trying to protect himself in the things that he's saying, right? And he loses tons of weight.

We might imagine a better apartment building for him, perhaps even nano-driven baths and changes of clothing, such that his 'flight' might be less disabling. But by the time the detainee is asked to choose meds or no meds, her choices have already been severely constricted. The choice to accept help is contaminated by societal and social conventions including what we hear about psychiatric intervention from others.

Leaving aside for a moment the level of choice available, compliance sometimes becomes the only way to 'fit in,' to 'relate,' and to 'negotiate' for more choice. Regardless of the value of 'madness,' this arrangement suggests to me a problematic that, like social accommodation of disabilities or constitutional protection of spirituality, demands a social and political response. As such, Mad polity does not have to mean rejecting help of any kind, but it does mean creating space beyond coercion.

Mad Polity in Context

These issues must still be related back to a situation in which we find the usual operations of force and imposed scarcity in 'the system.' June, a legal clinic worker, says:

> 'Cause you can be incompetent and be forced to take services, but if you're competent enough to say you need services, you're booted out the door, right, even though you're exhibiting crisis. So I think in general how mental health laws apply really depends on who is applying the law.

June says that 'incapacity' tends to confer services, possibly because psychiatric workers see 'incapacity,' however it is determined, as 'real need,' real 'madness.' This suggests a paradox: a person must resist services in order to obtain services.

The 'right to treatment' might be rephrased 'the right to forcible treatment.' It is at the line where the body breaks that the mandatory health system goes into action. Yet what it offers after imposing itself will make recovery impossible, according to many workers.

TYLER (HOUSING WORKER): I had a problem with the fact that they [the local ACT team] keep, uh, 'co-ordinating' their clients to the same places, so they're kind of ghettoizing them, right? They're setting up in one boarding home so it's convenient for the ACT team to go out and visit them.
KIM (PEER WORKER): Right.
TYLER: Whether it's appropriate for that person to be in that home is less important than the accessibility for the workers.
JUNE (LEGAL WORKER): Goes back to making it easier for staff.
TYLER: Yeah, definitely.

If madness and institutionalization are closely related to social class, the working class seems unaware somehow. All participants in this study reported 'convenience' driving practical decisions and medical determinations regardless of a detainee's needs. Abuses involved relocating 'clients' where they wished not to be, even landlords (who have no medical-legal authority) demanding that tenants be treated before being given housing. Some landlords have access to detainees' medical files:

TYLER: 'Cause you know, where I work they deal with for-profit housing, and
landlords, they don't have much of a political analysis about anything.
They just want their rent money, right?

KIM: And they ask if people are on their drugs, right?

TYLER: And they want compliance, and they almost always – I can't think of
one case otherwise – they assume that compliance with medication means
that the tenant will remain in good standing –

JUNE: Your organization outreaches to private landlords to house people with
mental health issues?

TYLER: Um, we have contracts with private landlords [. . .] but the landlord is
the owner operator, the person that accepts or rejects tenants.

JUNE: We get tons of tenant problems mostly when people are going through
a state of crisis. We've been fighting it by saying 'duty to accommodate.' So
we've been using that kind of accessibility language, but they eventually
get the tenants out, eventually.

ERICK: So you're saying landlords look for compliance, and then maybe even
encourage –

KIM: There's some landlords that won't accept tenants unless they're on drugs.

TYLER: Yeah, exactly.

JUNE: It's a violation of their human rights [. . .]

KIM: But somehow there's that whole piece –

JUNE: [to Tyler] – tied into the system – if they come through [your housing
organization] it's different 'cause they're identified already to the landlord
'cause they're a client of your organization.

TYLER: That's right. But the landlords have access to the client's information
from files.

JUNE: How? Oh, with you guys.

TYLER: With us. So they'll ask what kind of support they have.

JUNE: What about personal privacy laws under the Personal Health
Information [Protection] Act?

TYLER: They sign a consent form –

JUNE: The client?

TYLER: Yeah.

JUNE: Whoo –

KIM: Yeah, the whole housing piece is fucked up, royally.

Housing is understandably a most immediate concern for the detainee,
and for clinicians it is a mark of success when 'clients' keep housing. But
in this exchange we see how human rights and basic rules are evaded
so that workers' needs, which assumedly include housing their charges,

are met in a predictable fashion. Should a detainee reject her treatment, whatever may be said of its safety and efficacy, landlords know that there is likely to be trouble. And so without detainees having much say, landlords fish through housing agencies' records in search of problems, and ACT teams place their 'clients' in locations amenable to workers' designs. Though these relationships seem well-established in the minds of my informants, what seems to make them possible is the somnolence of preferred 'clients.'

The 'medicated' tenant is at least more employable than the 'untreated homeless' person. As time goes on, psychiatrists often have to play with dosages, change drugs, and add other drugs ('polypharmacy') to keep a person 'stable':

ERICK: Have you ever tried to take someone down off medication slowly?
DANIELLE: Yeah, oh yeah.
ERICK: Has that been successful?
DANIELLE: You mean ongoing? Nothing successful; eventually symptoms will resume, and then we'll have to get them back on. There's quite a few like that.
ERICK: So even though they've been dropped slowly, symptoms will resume?
DANIELLE: Yeah, just because the nature of the people – you see we end up seeing people who've had many, many psychotic episodes. So by then it's very predictable; they'll get psychotic again. So we have quite a few, I mean we let them get quite ill, like we try really hard to preserve patient autonomy.

I can only imagine how easy it is to accept a tranquilizer during a difficult time only to find one can't get off it after only a few weeks. It might be dispiriting after several attempts and some years of maturation to accept drugs for life. Some detainees come to equate treatment with passing (being taken as normal in society):

CARMEN: Like he would think that the best medication is no medication. But he also would tell you that he has to take enough to keep everybody off his back, essentially is what he's told me. And that's how he's framed it to me. Like, 'I just have to take enough to keep everybody off my back, so I don't do any of the things that, you know, I get in trouble for.' Which is, if you read the *Ottawa Citizen,* an article yesterday or today, where Scott Starson says the same thing.
ERICK: Really?

CARMEN: Yeah, 'I realize that if I want to do my [physics] work, I have to comply. I have to do what they say.'

Starson won the right to refuse drugging at the Supreme Court, but
not in real life. He later found himself being drugged on the forensic
ward, as before. His legal victory at the Supreme Court was not enough
to defend against a psychiatrist's determination of incapacity and his
substitute decision maker authorizing more treatment.

Starson's complaints about feeling 'punch drunk' under neuroleptization may explain why a lot of survivors don't stand up for their
rights, though Kim says that it is more a matter of institutionalization
and dependency as a whole:

ERICK: I'm just wondering if in your experience with 'inpatients' you've seen
that lack of understanding of rights, the understanding of where they're at,
'agency'-wise.
KIM (PEER WORKER): It's epidemic, and it's not only [. . .] just generally people
in the hospital, even people connected to the community are overmedicated, and so that affects people's physical ability to do stuff and navigate [the
'system']. Even when, beyond that, you have people who are quite strong
and serious about wanting information, or wanting something, there's
something not right. It's an overwhelming learned helplessness, and feeling
like they cannot – they don't know how to problem-solve.
Like, there's somebody that came into the office on Thursday or
Wednesday, and we had a whole conversation, 'cause this is someone who
lives in the community and is ticked off cause they have to come to the
hospital every day, and yet has psychiatrists saying, 'Why do you have to
do that? You're voluntary. You don't have to come to your shrink appointments.' [But he tells me], 'But I have my programs.' And I'm like, 'What
are your programs? Do you want to go to your programs? Like creative
crafts and recreation, whatever?' And he's like, 'No, not really, 'cause I have
them where I live as well.' [laughs] And they had no sense that they could
actually say, 'No, just no.' They don't have to come to the hospital at all.

Given the physiological and punitive effects of chemical institutionalization, the detainee requires an advocate who is not trapped in the
system to navigate it for her:

KIM: I generally say, 'Oh, actually, you know that's not okay, you have rights.'
I'll say the second time, 'That's – do you know that's a rights violation?'

And then, they'll call me up, 'Can you help me with something? I've been lowering my medication and I'm supposed to be taking 20 [mg]. I've been taking, um, 15. I have to go tell my doctor. I'm really afraid they're going to freak. I'm really afraid they're going to put me back in the hospital.' This person just got out after twenty years. I go to the shrink appointment, and – this was like actually beautiful – this person said to me, 'Okay I'm going to go to the doctor and I'll do the talking, and then I'll say everything, and then we'll see what happens, and then if you want to talk you can talk.' I thought that was brilliant. I thought that was so strong that that person could do that. Say what they needed, and then we went –

ERICK: Usually they don't suggest such things?

KIM: Not everybody's that – sometimes people are just confused, and they don't know how to bring me in [as the advocate], but I just thought it was brilliant [exceptional] that this person said, 'I will do the talking,' and then – I just thought that was what we want: for people to self-advocate in that way, for themselves.

And so I went, and they had [put] this person with some shrink, and the social worker was there, too, [and the detainee was saying] that he had lowered his drugs to 15 – 'Kay, so he's lowered his serious drug from 20 to 15, saying 'I just wanted to tell you, I-I-I-I've done this.' And they were like [screaming!] 'WHAT!?'

[Laughs] They totally were like, 'Why didn't you tell us!? You need to tell us! You need to communicate with us [so] we'll communicate with you! Why didn't you tell us!' And I said –

JUNE: 'He IS communicating!'

[Laughter]

KIM: 'He actually is, in fact, communicating with you.' And it becomes really overwhelming with the power dynamics of that scenario. This person actually had brought this up before, and they said, 'No. We'll talk about it later.' And they had a whole bunch of reasons why they wanted to talk about it later, but he needed to do it now, 'cause it was like interfering with his thinking.

Through Kim's statement, we see the detainee's sense of the negotiation. Like Starson, she has fight in her. Capacity and identity is complex and fluid. But she faces a common situation of rebuke and indifference even when asking for important things. A non-detainee, often a worker, is required as a sort of witness for the inmate and a guarantor for workers who fear reprisal and legal exposure, in order to ground any negotiation. As a non-self, the detainee can only negotiate what workers deem conceivable or possible, and often that precludes risk. But the advocate confers much needed moral support, encouraging self-empowerment, which is necessary to the presentation of a legal personhood. After the negotiation, who knows what supports can actually be found.

Lack of Insight and Violence

We move from contextual problems to textual elaborations of 'madness' as lack of awareness and dangerousness. I will use a few more observations from workers in connection with some of the existing literature. As we found in chapter 5, the ability to 'understand and appreciate' treatment choices is considered a capacity to consent. For psychiatrists to legally test for this ability, it is often enough to search for what is called 'insight.' Victor, an ACT peer worker, explains:

> Most clients who are on CTOs have poor insight into their illness. They might either have *some* insight, like 'I have schizophrenia,' but might say it's caused by something else, or we have some that don't even admit they have schizophrenia. 'I don't have schizophrenia.' I've said to them, 'I have mental illness; I take medication.' They'll say to me, 'Well you might have mental illness but I don't.' So I find because most of our clients have schizophrenia, the ones on CTOs, their insight's not that great. But that's not the reason to be on a CTO necessarily, on its own, but the reason most of them are on CTOs is because they wouldn't take their medication and would end up in the hospital.

People are said to go off psychiatric drugs not because of negative effects but because of poor 'insight':

DANIELLE (PSYCHIATRIST): Some people like the two examples I gave you, they're still not capable when they're treated.
ERICK: Oh, I see, so the treatment doesn't – [necessarily always work].
DANIELLE: Well, do you know what we call insight? They still don't have insight. What I mean is they never accept a psychiatric explanation of their experience, where they don't even remember or acknowledge the experience occurred, the experience being of psychosis. They see it as a spiritual happening, or they completely deny it happens at all, or – I don't know, they just don't buy psychiatry – which is fine with me. The problem is when they behave the way they do, they end up in the psychiatric syst –

Insight, then, can be understood as the ability to notice and acknowledge a problem in one's social, behavioural, emotional, or cognitive functioning. Danielle, a psychiatrist, has introduced us to a key aspect of consent and likewise the use of coercion and force. One must recognize one's 'mental disorder' in order to play a part in treatment. 'Insight' is a foundation of testing for capacity to consent and helps in determining whether to incarcerate. It rests on the notion that a psychiatric explanation for a detainee's experience or identity is scientifically correct and philosophically or rationally 'sound' such that detainees who reject this explanation are 'unsound.'

Scientific 'scales' are being developed to test 'insight' quantitatively (see, e.g., Beck et al., 2004). Philosophers have waded into the debate on 'insight,' one proposing a 'Wittgensteinian approach' that involves interpersonal frameworks, yet embraces biological rather than sociological conclusions (Gillett, 1994). However, some researchers question whether the concept of 'insight' is useful or meaningful in potentially alienating situations (McCabe & Quayle, 2002). With 'insight into illness' as a primary way of assessing 'capacity to consent to treatment,' the personal and intimate problem of increasing self-control is all but totally put into the clinician's hands. Capacity as a medical-legal construction has been thoroughly deconstructed by Secker (2001).

As Danielle said, a CTO is especially useful when a person denies a condition, lacks insight, but is treatable in the community environment. This brings the question of coercion back to the level of identity. According to Victor, an ACT peer worker:

It's almost as if you're trying to force – you're forcing insight on, into them. You know you can't force someone to have insight into their illness.

According to Danielle:

Even if they do [reject treatment while capable], because you know there's all kinds of reasons – nobody likes taking their medication every day. If you have an ongoing relationship with the person you can kind of work around that. You can, you know, have discussions about it, and they trust your judgment, and then you become a repository of their history, even though they'd like to kind of lose it, like you would remind them of what it was like when they reduced the dose previously. Like, it becomes, in the context of a relationship, much easier to manage.

Like 'lack of insight' is useful in constructing 'psychotic illness,' violence under duress is useful in constructing the 'dangerous mental patient' who must be detained. A research participant, Victor, said violence by 'clients' usually comes in the form of stalking, threats, or minor physical force, but it is often attributed to them because of their assumed 'neurological disorder':

> What generally happens if the person shows signs of being aggressive or being a harm to themselves, then they can give them medications against their will, and I find that hard to swallow because it's someone else's interpretation and you wonder what it could be [they've done]. I've heard of cases where someone is being forced to take medication 'cause they took their finger and made this sign of pointing a gun at someone, you know, like that's like giving someone the finger, you know?

Survivors commonly complain that an incarcerated person who becomes angry or confused may understandably threaten a well-meaning professional who has the power to detain or restrain her. In the custodial context, 'care' represents a threat that can 'escalate.' Danger is not attributed to coercion but rather to the detainee's biology.

During my time as an advocate at Queen Street Mental Health Centre, I heard reports of people ending up in 'forensic' psychiatry units for such things as slapping a doctor. The 'forensic' psychiatric system, commonly conceived as locking away the 'criminally insane,' is more intensively concealed and oppressive than the 'civil' psychiatric institution. Its inmates are imprisoned indefinitely, often for minor offences like theft (R. Pritchard, personal communication, 10 Nov. 2005). My employer was instrumental in arguing against such practices in the mid-1990s, especially as an intervener at the Supreme Court (Queen Street Outreach Society, 2002c).

While violence should not be tolerated in hospitals, psychiatric workers should consider how care, punishment, and reprisal are interwoven in contexts of control. These environments make otherwise rational workers take up imbalanced power practices, however 'soundly' rationalized. Such practices now pervade the community. Before the passage of Brian's Law, some expected that the criteria for imposition of a Community Treatment Order would be restricted to 'violent' individuals. However, in most if not all jurisdictions that has not been the case.

The Consent and Capacity Board
and Community Treatment Orders

Many of the following examples of violence come from records of the psychiatric tribunal, the Consent and Capacity Board, whose former chair was instrumental in conducting the legislated CTO review in Ontario. These examples bear the unmistakable flare that psychiatric workers come to hone in the cycling of evidence about detainee 'behaviours' and identities. Such management of facts can be applied to the whole of 'the mentally ill population,' as the CTO review illustrates.

I searched for the salient examples of violence or negligent acts by CTO subjects in decision statements published online by the Consent and Capacity Board. Here is one such example:

> R.J.A. is a 43 year old, single man, who resides in supervised housing when not in hospital. R.J.A. has had multiple contacts with the mental health system since the 1970's and has faced numerous criminal charges and convictions since the 1970's as well, many of which involve assault, forcible confinement and harm to others. He has had an ongoing relationship with CAMH-Queen [facility] since 2003. His criminal record is considered, to a large degree, to be a result of his mental disorder. R.J.A. suffers from chronic unremitting schizophrenia. (*R.J.A., Re*, 2005 ON C.C.B.)

How does a disease causing confusion predicate criminality? The board leaves much to interpretation. This decision statement neglects to provide any indication of the seriousness of R.J.A.'s assaults. As Dorothy Smith contends (1990b), psychiatric files mystify the events that lead to determinations and descriptions about an inmate. The linkage between R.J.A.'s violent temperament and the psychiatric determinations in this report are dithered. This CTO was predictably upheld.

In another example, a female CTO subject was said to be a danger to herself, but again, obfuscation in the psychiatric report prevents an examination of other explanations, such as the impact of drugs in her life. The following record also exhibits a curt solemnity that contrasts starkly with R.G.J.K.L.'s self-explanations, giving her identity a farcical air. Note the level of detail given to her seemingly absurd declarations. The text fails to account for the reactions of others to her evocative declarations. Did anyone laugh, smile, agree patronizingly, or beg for clarification?

Ms. R.G.J.K.L. was 46 years old. In introducing herself at the hearing, she said that she was the son of God, both male and female. When asked where she was born, she said the Kingdom of God. She also told the panel that she was a social worker on leave of absence, and a lawyer, namely Johnny Cochrane, working on her Bar. She said that she was very bright at school and had won Nobel prizes all over the world. For many years, Ms. R.G.J.K.L. had been receiving ODSP benefits. She lived alone in a sub-sidized apartment. (*R.G.J.K.L., Re*, 2003 ON C.C.B.)

Using the stare of psychiatric solemnity, the board dismisses R.G.J.K.L.'s candor outright and the cold facts of her solitude are left to the end of this narrative for effect. This is a common sanist rhetorical device: 'get a load of this, but look how sad in the end.' It subjugates by a false kindness.

Self-defence is also seen as impossible when you have been labelled 'deluded,' and the problem of danger to detainees as a result of their perceived social status is ignored as an explanation for their behaviour. In this example, beliefs are assiduously described in the banal stare of the case file genre, again pretending evidentiary, almost scientific certitude. Consider the following:

He believed that he designed all the computers in Canada. He also believed that he owned numerous vegetable gardens. He thought that his family owned the apartment building in which he resides. He believed that strangers from New York *banged on his door to harass him. He indicated that he would cut these people with his knife.* He also thought that the police who apprehended him were not real police in the domestic police force, but rather those from England. He felt they came to get him because they had heard that he was doing very well. He thought that he fathered chil-dren all over the world. Finally, he believed there was nothing wrong with him, and that he should be able to go home. (*S.H.M., Re*, 2004 ON C.C.B., emphasis added)

Spliced into the psychiatric evidence are clues, which I have italicized, regarding a possible reason for S.H.M.'s actions. These seem immaterial as the Consent and Capacity Board cycles through the usual litany of 'unsound' beliefs, with a predictable tendency to appeal to the imagi-nation in describing violence or threat. This narrative drowns the possibility of a survivor's understandable fear or discrimination against survivors. It pursues the demonstration of S.H.M.'s 'madness' in support of a psychiatric determination of 'mental illness.' The rules and rationale for psychiatric intervention must be defended rhetorically, with beliefs as legal evidence, however well each case is weighed using the scale of 'illness.'

Violence by the psychiatrized, though estimated to be rare over decades of research, is used to excuse oppression of survivors in social and medical-legal contexts. This final trump explains the need for psychiatry and incarceration and allows for a social abandonment of the institutionalized to a system that not only uses and abuses, but inflames detainees' violence, as in the well-publicized case of Herbert Cheung in Toronto, and more recently that of Adenir DeOliveira. Consider the following:

> Student Tom Billings said a group of people then followed the suspect down Dufferin Street to a mall. 'He was angry. He was clearly in crisis,' said Mr Billings.
>
> Mr Cormier had tried to stop the suspect in the station; he chased him for about 300 metres, then bodychecked him in front of a Pizza Hut and pinned him until police arrived.
>
> 'He started saying that he'd been at the hospital for 12 hours and nobody would talk to him, and they wouldn't give him any medication and he's sorry, he's sorry,' Mr Cormier said. (O'Toole, 2009)

As a whole, psychiatric professionals do not publicly defend their 'clients' when the media or government lashes out at them and attributes their 'dangerousness' to their 'depression' or 'bipolar affective disorder.'

Ontario's psychiatric tribunal has been known to decide in favour of a psychiatrist against a patient in more than 90 per cent of cases (Chambers, 2003). A detainee may challenge her involuntary status, and a doctor will show, by use of psychiatric case files, that the requirements for her committal were met in 'clear, cogent and compelling' ways. This phrase is utilized often at the Consent and Capacity Board to authorize psychiatrists' decisions.

The following, in the case of 'V.S.,' is representative of such evidence: 'At the time V.S. was described as exhibiting extremely paranoid ideas. He believed his various medications were poisoned. He had been spending all his time in bed, but could not sleep' (*V.S., Re*, 2004 ON C.C.B., 11 March 2004). The board is not of the opinion that V.S.'s drugs are toxic, nor do they believe that V.S.'s electroshock (ECT) 'treatments' could be contributing to his problems: 'In hospital, V.S. received 12 ECT treatments, his mood became brighter and he improved' (ibid.). Again, improvement is declared without mention of brain injury, which is known to result in 'aphasia' (or euphoria as occurs with serious head injury). Though V.S. rejected drugging, 'Dr Illivitsky believed that V.S. has shown no resistance to his anti-psychotic medication because he felt obligated to comply with the CTO. Injections are given to V.S. by a nurse in his residence' (ibid.). In other words, there is no question about V.S.'s rejection of drugging, let alone his privacy under a treatment order.

The board does admit that Community Treatment Orders weigh heavily on a person's rights, but evidently the need for medical attention is paramount:

> A CTO is a significant infringement on a person's liberty, autonomy, and right to self-determination. Although it does not restrict freedom of movement in the same way or to the same extent as involuntary detention, it nonetheless imposes substantial restrictions on a person's inherent right to live as he or she chooses, e.g., by requiring attendance at medical appointments and/or the taking of medication. For that reason, the *Mental Health Act* contains a number of important procedural and substantive safeguards, such as the requirement that a person for whom a CTO is being prepared receive advice and information about his or her legal rights. (*D.B., Re*, 2003 ON C.C.B.)

As I have suggested, these safeguards are not easily conferred in coercive arrangements, especially not through chemical incarceration due to its effects on judgment. The board hears challenges to psychiatric determinations, but of the twenty-four CTO-related decisions that I found published online in 2005, the CTO was revoked in six cases, and four of these revocations were based on minor technical problems. At present, the percentage of revocations is drastically lower, but apparently the board has not been keeping up with its mandated yearly CTO hearings (Suzan Fraser, a lawyer, personal communication, 13 June 2008). Such 'safeguards' are now being relaxed in legislative changes (Costa, 2010).

The most successful of CTO revocations was brought before the board by 'R.R.,' who was seen as capable to reject his order because he had accepted his diagnosis and was still accepting treatment. R.R. destroyed a nursing station, and this was deemed unrelated to his 'illness' by his

Table 8.1
Published Consent and Capacity Board Decisions Revoking a Community Treatment
Order in Ontario, with Date and Reason for Doing So

CTO Revoked	Date	Reason
W., Ottawa	June 2005	Missing signature
Q.S., Ottawa	March 2005	2 incarcerations but 7 years apart
E.B., Ottawa	Dec. 2004	CTO already cancelled
R.R., Toronto	Sept. 2004	Accepted his illness, drugs
L.F., Guelph	Oct. 2003	Missing signature
D.B., Toronto	May 2003	Board not available on time

psychiatrist, and R.R. was discharged. This may have influenced the board's decision to revoke the order. However, the R.R. case shows the lengths to which a survivor has to go to demonstrate acceptance of psychiatric explanations for his behaviour in order to influence his fate (*R.R., Re,* 2004 ON C.C.B.).

R.R. worked and dutifully took drugs for seven years when he started experiencing serious negative bodily effects. His psychiatrist's attempt to administer another drug resulted in further complications like 'akathisia' (restlessness, nervous tremors). He became violent and was incarcerated five times in the next five years. Only when he 'assaulted' a nurse (there is no clear record of what happened) was he put on a CTO. He accepted the conditions of his order so he could avoid the police, he stated. However, because R.R.'s treatment consisted of repeated intramuscular injections that made it painful for him to walk (though this was barely mentioned in the board's decision), he hoped to reduce and ultimately stop the drugging. The board again adopted psychiatric explanations in understanding the problems that R.R. faced. The possibility of complications from drugs leading to R.R.'s behaviour, though medically possible, was overlooked. Despite all this, R.R. 'presented' the appropriate attitude: 'R.R. did not have to give us direct evidence concerning his belief that he was capable. However, he did and the panel accepted that evidence as clear, cogent and compelling. R.R.'s ability to recognize that he suffered mental illness and that medication had helped him was important and relevant to making a treatment decision. We were also satisfied that R.R. was able at the Hearing to appreciate the reasonably foreseeable consequences of making or not making a treatment decision. As a result, R.R. has the right to take risks and to be wrong in his decisions' (*R.R., Re,* 2004 ON C.C.B.).

In this rare decision, the board favoured R.R.'s autonomy rights by dismissing a psychiatrist's belief that R.R. had no 'insight' because he could not describe his diagnosis to the psychiatrist's satisfaction. Also, R.R.'s maverick belief that he could slowly discontinue medications and get better 'on his own' was accepted, defying psychiatric sense. Definitive reasons are not given. This case is, however, extremely rare. The resources necessary to support R.R. in gaining control over his 'treatment' and life are not available to the large majority of detainees.

Finding Hope

One of the arguments against Community Treatment Orders in 2000 was the notion that a 'continuum' of supports should be put in place to make force largely unnecessary. According to Rudy, a peer worker:

> Well I think they've argued for a long time, for many years if not decades, and what the CMHA has talked about was put a much greater emphasis on supporting people, getting them adequate housing, adequate income, setting up a foundation that allows a person to experience a community at a level that isn't survival, striving to meet basic needs. I mean that's certainly very important. I think the other piece of it is types of mental health community services. There needs to be much more opportunity and options.

Survivors helping each other have slowly begun to show workers the possibilities in 'peer' based approaches (e.g., see Trainor et al., 1997). This is still an anxious endeavour in a sanist society that mostly values treatment compliance. June, a legal clinic worker, explains:

> I also teach people's rights, so when they're done a session with me, they know what the criteria for being confined is, and then they match their personal situation to that knowledge they now have acquired. So it does create a lot more fear. Maybe if I didn't do that – but that's something major, right? If I didn't do that [...] I think that the consequences – and because I disseminate information that survivors have written and produced, I think it does impact other people, how they feel about the system.

Professionals also need information on finding 'alternatives,' as these are usually hidden in a network of dominant 'services' that support drugging. Victor, an ACT team peer worker, says:

> I'd have to say, and I don't know if I'm tooting my own horn, but since I've started working there it [the ACT team] seems to have changed quite a

bit, I think. We also have new staff, too, who share my viewpoint as well since I've started. We focus more on recovery and having links to groups in the community. When I first started there weren't a lot of links to places in the community. People didn't know what was available for our clients in the community.

Moral certainty on the part of some workers might be replaced by personal curiosity. The ultimate 'alternative' may simply be identifying with Mad people, in a gesture of solidarity. Kim, who is a peer worker, explains:

I'm saying that when people in power say they're on board with want-ing to share power and be more equal, I think that's lip service. I think the actual work, the actual sweat, they don't want to do that. In fact, it's not just that it's sweaty. It's uncomfortable. You have to give something up. And you have to deal with messiness. It's dealing with messiness, the messiness of humanity, if you're not going to coerce somebody or lock them up for doing something or whatever. You're going to have to deal with somebody who doesn't completely fit into some socially created compartment of normalcy.

There are references that workers can find that deal critically with institutional power and burnout (Amundson, 1993; Hare-Mustin, 2004; Rossiter, 2001; Anderson, 1996; Alty & Mason, 1994; Caplan & Caplan, 2001; Mishler, 2005). These resources are just as important to people who have been through the system and survived, if not more because we take on a lot of responsibility in trying to change coercive practices. Even in private settings, we need to challenge our assumptions about the limits (and capacities) of our relationships and try to create space for autonomies as we listen to one another. Hopefully we can begin to co-create viable Mad spaces.

To review this chapter, in which I quote participants in a meandering path through the problems of agency and treatment, I want to begin by saying that I have often used language that takes participants' perspec-tives as evidenced elsewhere, such as in the CTO report, and this was purposeful. Traditional researchers might be tempted to say I elided their story, but some of what participants say (especially in common) is provable, observable, even in my own experience, and yet suppressed in the mental health fields. So participants' texts become *testimonio*. For example, when a worker says youth are being handled in the same way as adults, I believe it (knowing I have no positive proof), and say so in my representation of the worker's testimony, without presenting proof but based on strong evidence elsewhere. I do not insist on truth, but enjoin the reader to look into the facts.

We saw from youth detentions and deleterious treatments otherwise that chemical management of aggression and other symptoms contributed to a quick demoralization and the kinds of institutionalizations illustrated in the previous chapter. The criminalization and psychiatrization of racialized youth persists despite available alternatives in health and person-centred approaches (let alone anti-racist, anti-ableist, and anti-sexist approaches to name a few). In one psychiatric professional's practice, psychiatric arrangements ignored a woman's protest and yet could exonerate a male's protest. Cycling of biology is found in psychiatric explanation of changes to behaviour in women, such as by use of a menopausal explanation. There is cycling of evidence into spunky and psychotic behaviour categories by a professional, and an admission that overdrugging could cause someone not to know he, she, or they are on a CTO.

Choice was analysed in regard to how detainees knew that they had to elect treatment in order to be taken seriously for any rights, any housing, and other basic needs. Participants didn't know of people who liked their CTO, but there were people found in the government review who said it saved their lives. I considered the issue of choice of treatment while one is trying to prevent withdrawal reactions. This opens up a number of questions about negotiating treatment.

The care system is undergirded by punitive measures. This affects therapeutic outcomes and, in turn, ongoing treatment decisions. Danielle, a psychiatrist, feels that it is an 'agree to disagree' situation when she overrides refusal. She says CTOs are useful for systemic coherence, which is what the government review concluded also, but that they should only be used for 'chronically incapable' people. This ironically coercive procedure is supposed to increase their choices overall. People dress in rags otherwise. They scream and punch. Ultimately, they are incapable of recognizing their need for treatment. A stalemate.

Choice in the mental illness care system can be constrained, as other participants in this study told me, in which worker convenience and landlord preference for treatment compliance determine the choices given. Even when at the Supreme Court Starson wins his right to abstain from being drugged for his own good, in real life he has to accommodate his workers and family. While demanding no treatment he receives indefinite compulsory treatment. What appears like learned helplessness, that even youth exhibit, is institutionalization that only an outsider advocate can help with in the face of worker ignorance. 'He is communicating!' some participants said in unison when recognizing a common indifference to detainees. Yet the lack of insight attributed to the detainee as a result makes it impossible for self-advocacy to work. What is most desired by clinicians is the act of acquiescence. Thereafter, if a person can carry on, treatment can be considered successful.

The detainee's ability to accept the situation, acknowledge the problem in her condition, is evidence of insight. It leads to positive treatment and the possibility of response. The literature on insight suggests that this conceptualization is philosophically and sociologically questionable. Evidence of insight and its lapses is contained in a 'repository of their history,' as the psychiatrist says, so detainees are controlled by a file of behaviours out of context that may be unrecognizable. The cycles of biology (biologizing behaviours) and evidence provide cover for an abuse of rights, for coercive community treatment, and in such a context disorder is bred.

Violence was taken up again in the context of the legal decisions made by the quasi-legal Consent and Capacity Board in Ontario, which dismisses challenges to psychiatrists' decisions in more than nine out of ten decisions. I follow the board's mystification of violence as caused by mental illness, as evidenced in the presentation of the detainee's argumentation (as absurdity in the case of R.G.J.K.L. and as delusional self-defence in the case of S.H.M.). These assurances by the board that detainees need their medications because of their behaviour, let alone other kinds of needs, are made in the apparent absence of contradictory evidence of drugging mishaps and systemic abuses that can be said to relate to drugging. R.R.'s exceptional case, which required a show of solidarity from a group of local survivors and workers, shows how far we are from a systemic assurance of basic needs being considered and met. Yet this exemplar gives providers a note in terms of what might be made possible for any number of people given better distribution of resources. To deal critically with burnout and lack of system cohesion, one needs to find ways of creating new spaces of psychosocial relations between mad-labelled bodies and others.

9 In the Present

> So far in my life, I have never allowed the joy to be viewed and treated as a mental illness and no external force has insisted that it should be. I know that I have been fortunate and often reflect that it might have been otherwise.
> – Leibrich, 'Making Space: Spirituality and Mental Health'

I am now going to try to bring together the many themes in this book. On some level there is only a personalized account of the research process. On another level there is a transcription of many voices and issues in tandem, tension, and some unity. And finally there is a sense that can be made out of social relations that, while incomplete, may be useful in understanding.

This last chapter can be used as a basis with which to return to the theory of earlier chapters. In chapter 8, workers' empirical claims and authoritative texts are woven together in a transinstitutional description of chemical incarceration. Mad consciousness, used as a framework for this book's analysis, cannot be envisioned as separate from institutionalization because madness and treatment are entwined in madness discourse. When we consider institutionalization in the literature, Erving Goffman cannot be forgotten, and so we begin with a comparison of older and contemporary practices. The description of contemporary institutionalization depends on an empirical demonstration of restrictive actions like neuroleptic drugging, and the legal pronouncements made to impose them. These pronouncements depend on 'insight,' a subjective understanding that accepts psychiatric explanation. The contradictions in common standards of care leave much room for abuse, well-noticed on the ground. A methodology of inquiry that I needed as an activist required a form of ethnography that recognized institutional operations as well as everyday experiences. This went far beyond the traditional scientific framework of studying restraints, coercion, and violence. These practices suggest a deeper level of social and epistemological work, as we recognize in sanist destruction of feeling and difference in 'presentations of self,' as Goffman would say, which ultimately direct coercive paradigms of care. Thus, I have described backwards how I built up this book, and I can see the interweaving of process and argumentation, story, and demand that is necessary to any process like this.

The following narrative brings various elements together, not only to explain aspects of each chapter or issue, but also how to understand this kind of research. One way is to continue to tell our own stories, as we continue to survive in a sanist world. I will throughout the rest of this chapter, which takes up again the more scholarly tone, reflect on resistance to chemical incarceration, with a welcome to the reader to question this expository and its contents.

This book should not be used as the sole reason for any decision about care. Nor should it be considered the only text about psychiatric survivors. I have thought of it like homework that needed to be done. It is not a guide for mental health; its principles are not commands. And many of its key themes are shared, even if I describe them as I do.

Madness is conceived as a lack of mind, an absence of being, a void in social relations. By distancing myself from such discourses, I am able to reconsider a basic reason to stop forcing drugs. When I move away from negative talk, deterministic discourses, I find my own experiences. In my experience I find 'mad' is not bad, but something positive, even purposeful. The hallucinations and delusions that I have been taught to fear become something more important. Even distress has a function, but why should we expect it to have a purpose?

From that orientation, a Mad relation, I want to find out what happened to me, 'what hit me.' What I discover is a language of sanism, a religiosity about technology, an unbridled imposition of restraints, and governmental power plays to appease professionals and profiteers, but rarely the object of care, the 'patient' or 'client', in administrative talk and text.

But what hit me is expanding and changing, and this book cannot keep up. There are many ways in which the industry is marketing itself across institutions, and across international borders. It provides techniques to bring technologies of care and control, treatment, and restraint, to the troubled in the most remote parts of the world. It finds ways of excusing coercion, first by creating outcasts and moving them into institutions, and then by moving them back out, couching it all as a 'treatment' problem. How do they do this?

To understand, to communicate, I seek out other people's knowledge. As an academic I am supposed to find knowledge in published materials, peer-reviewed materials, and what I find are psychiatrists and lawyers talking about people like me, and the other 'crazies,' about how we might be managed. I also find philosophers and historians who seem more intrigued with the concepts of madness and chaos and nothingness than they are with the people who are marked by those ideas. Luckily, I find there are some professional researchers who have found methods of dealing with the distance between authorities and everyday people. Dorothy Smith and other ethnographers try to link everyday knowledge and talk to the rationalizations of rulership in texts, in legal decisions, in medical textbooks, and in the simplest of administrative forms used by practitioners.

With more aplomb, I ask workers what they notice about a new mechanism of control, a rather odd mechanism. The government finally decided to implement it when public opinion was poised against subway pushers, baby killers, and others thought to represent madness. In Ontario, those testimonies led to the use of compulsory treatments called Community Treatment Orders. Legislators promised that they would be used sparingly, that they were meant to balance our rights with the rights of an unsuspecting public, and that they would be monitored. I wanted to ask people on the ground what was happening.

What emerges is not only a picture of forced treatment under a therapeutic guise, but of an industry that is radically disoriented in assisting people. Practitioners and patients barely know the law and the paper rights it instils, or even the status of patients under the law. Treatment is often provided only after the patient succumbs to powerlessness. Part of the problem is resource allocation and the way in which money rules. But historical patterns of coercion show how deeply this coercive industry is immersed in our society and our lives. I only begin to imagine how our sanist assumptions about bodies in distress, bodies that are different, read into minds something awful. I learn to study what people say in relation to these broader concerns, and try to place them in some kind of order. Studying madness discourse is a way of distancing myself from sanist production.

This distance moves us further from conditions on the ground, which are far less forgiving of madness. In the language of the worker, coercive measures seem confusing and useless, but they are used anyway to appease a public, and certain well-funded advocates, and a new rank of worker (the Community Treatment Order Coordinator). 'Clients' ask for treatment orders merely to obtain housing, and all seems balanced in some sense. Many workers make legal decisions to serve their own interests and convenience. Some workers say the CTO program is nothing more than a bone tossed to embattled families who want more control over their 'loved ones.' Yet people abandoned to the streets or seeking refuge in Canada are also made to take treatments they don't want. To a researcher, these 'orders' show how force does not abide regulation. There is something like a pattern going on here.

Coercion is a rampant paradigm, and mandatory treatment is but a part. Workers who resist it usually consign themselves to it when they see others using it, and because they badly need work. The participants in this study were emphatic that workers must be avoiding my own research out of ambivalence. Perhaps it should not seem surprising that many mental health workers, like patients, reject critical or 'radical' ideas about the mental health industry, like the need to follow basic human rights ensconced in legislation. Lacking political capacity to establish alternatives or 'complementary services' that might prevent people from falling into the coercive pit, workers can sometimes grow thick skins. They shrug and say patients are getting something out of coercive treatment, like housing or services or attention. They'd do worse otherwise. Values are relative anyway. They should be happy.

But what about the government's own report, which was so slow to come? A public report that is shelved for two years and only released when an activist demands it in a Freedom of Information Act request should have something to hide. The report explains that Community Treatment Orders are predicated on legalized coercions that scientific research shows do not improve existing coercions or treatments. It reveals instances in which mandatory treatment is used to terrorize patients, but excuses abuses with many stories of success. It admits that constitutional safeguards are not being observed in the implementation of the new mechanism. But rather than suggest that the government stop what it is doing, the report recommends more money, more workers, more research, and more programs be erected to improve Community Treatment Orders. No one is surprised, exactly.

What is it about this new mechanism that bears an uncanny resemblance to psychiatry otherwise? What is it about mandatory treatment that explicates our contradictory patterns and desires? How is it that legally imposed mental health therapy seems so new and yet so old? Is it that law and medicine continue to exchange powers when a mad body does not seem to fit in the courtroom or in the hospital ward? Is it that workers who try to manage the mad body must be both kind and severe if they want to achieve their goals? Is it that the mad body by its very words and deeds questions order and at the same time indifference? There is something simple about CTOs, and it's not that the rules have been changed yet again with no end in sight but that the rules are being made explicit in a way that contradicts many prior rules.

The treatment, of course, is key to understanding Community Treatment Orders, psychiatry, mental health workers' frustrations, mad bodies out of whack, and almost anything to do with contemporary mental health care. That is, all kinds of treatment used, pills usually, are imposed on people who present a dilemma that cannot be solved. What is repeated ad nauseum is that these pills are not dross or poisonous toxins but safe and effective therapies to be trusted and taken each day without fail. They calm and ease suffering. They repair bodies out of whack. They prevent violence and despair. They are the only technological answer to what ails us. So much energy is spent selling such drugs, especially the kind used coercively, that there seems a kind of tension there, something needing to be said.

I was not interested in making pronouncements when I started my research. I had had enough of that. I wanted this to be a simple study, something like an outcome study, in which some people spoke about CTOs and what their effects were. But, by and by, talking to CTO subjects as they drooled and bobbed their heads and feet indicated the problem. The treatment is no treatment at all. It looks like treatment because the mad body is finally quelled, tranquilized, but the negative effects are not side effects. They are the primary effects. The intention of mandatory treatment makes sense when I recognize the way in which treatment does not allow the mad body to establish its own relation to the world, in some sympathy with others, but tries to harness it, pulling it taut every so often, and then releasing it when the appearance of ease is required. The treatment is restraint first. When it is eased, the body is eased, for a while.

I will not argue against the biological principles of mental disease that allow for this. Nor will I suggest that people should never choose a destructive or toxic pill. I can't pretend confusion and strangeness cannot get you killed, especially in a metropolitan centre. And I would avail myself of toxins to ease 'life,' and have. But where in these foundational truths about mad life is the problem turned around to question the responsibility of the public and the state? If this technological society, advanced as it pretends to be, cannot take care of the least violent yet most vulnerable among us without simply drugging away our cares, how are we to simply accept treatment? How are we to comply with antipsychotics, neuroleptics, phenothiazines, if their toxic effect is so great and their potential effectiveness negligible?

I can't mock the industry, suggest that it force placebos, insist it make detainees take care of animals for a living, because the point is that forcing care is contradictory, a result of projection onto the mad body perhaps, an insistence on the absurdity of emotion and illusion. And I can't mock the worker, who is made to impose societal desires of order on the supposedly disorderly day after day, who is kept fed and housed by such work while expected to advance from position to position, perhaps with a master's or Ph.D. degree. They often come to research as I did in my attempt to escape the system, to forget advocacy and activism in what seems like a losing game on the front lines.

But in all this study, I find myself again returning to the power of stories. By this I don't mean that stories are sure and simple, that they prove a point, or that they are to be trusted over numbers or theories, which should never be trusted naively also. Stories bring more stories. This book is a kind of story like that.

A Look Back

As a survivor of mandatory treatment, and as a social researcher, I was certainly not the first to notice the powerfully normative function of state psychiatry. Erving Goffman's 1961 book, *Asylums: Essays on the Social Situation of Mental Patients and Other Inmates*, provided inspiration for a comparison of practices of mental institutionalization past and present. The work of Dorothy Smith was also instructive in elaborating the ways in which authorized knowledge and practices reveal institutional relations of ruling. As useful as academic critiques of biocentric psychiatry may be, they often focus on poor facilities, staff indifference, inaccurate science, or negative effects of drugs. While there is no more fundamental critique of psychiatry in my opinion than the problematic reform of the 'self,' it is important how seldom critiques of psychiatry enlist the perceptions or experiences of psychiatric detainees. This is especially problematic as mad conceived writers have given us critiques through the ages. People who have not experienced forced treatment may see reform as a professional, scientific, or 'attitudinal' matter of progress. Yet, in order for such reforms to occur, the very people considered or theorized as 'mad' in common and academic discourses must be central to the concerns and practices of reform, and this is not a simple matter of token heads either. How we 'make sense' of 'nonsense' is necessary to this question. How we order our view of madness is a kind of relation.

I found more support for my argument that 'mad' people are more than anecdotes or cases or archetypes in the writings of survivors like Janet Gotkin, Judi Chamberlin, Mary O'Hagan, Irit Shimrat, and many others who had experienced psychiatric intervention. And more recently, the Mad movement, which seems to bridge the divide between psychiatric survivors and mental health consumers or users and make them more understandable to people in other movements perhaps, provided me with a means of reflecting on the question of voluntariness in coercive psychiatry as an identity question.

My personal experience of psychiatric drugging (not so much the assault but the effects of the drug) was the most frightening aspect of my psychiatrization. After fifteen years of soul searching, it led to the recognition that drugging is not a treatment but a restraint and that restraint over time is incarceration. If the 'therapeutic intent' ascribed to it is bracketed, drugging can be understood as torture, according to psychiatric survivor and lawyer Tina Minkowitz, as well as the U.N. Rapporteur on Torture. When we take the increased risk of iatrogenic disablement and decreased life spans into question, as Whitaker so carefully shows us, eugenics comes to mind as a description of structural inequities in our psychiatric societies. Brazenly called 'chemical lobotomy' by psychiatrists in the 1950s, tranquilization will not be abandoned simply by seeking 'best clinical practices.' Only a socially radical politic will enable us to see 'mad' experiences as 'real' experiences to be respected. We might listen not by throwing up our hands and saying 'anything goes' but by trying to make social structures relate to some of the least respected members of society. The most radical of such approaches are Soteria Houses.

I did not research Community Treatment Orders by directly interviewing CTO subjects, largely because they may not be in a position to speak freely about their experiences. Instead, using mental health workers' perceptions of CTO subjects' experiences, I sought to show that the CTO is not necessarily less restrictive than detention and that the treatments it usually imposes can be considered a detention 'within' or by use of the body that should be discontinued. This is not only because the CTO is a legal imposition that obliges a 'therapy' (sometimes with families written into a 'treatment plan'), but because chemical restraint imposes on the brain and body also.

I have argued, using Whitaker's and Breggin's work especially, but also survivors' experiences, that because neuroleptics act to compromise motor control, reduce feeling and will, and ultimately decrease one's capacity to conceptualize and communicate feelings and thoughts to others, this destructuring serves to coerce us into accepting intervention itself. It is also a form of imprisonment, restricting movement and association with others. I call this a chemical incarceration by use of the body, a cruel and unusual punishment, especially as major tranquilizers cause lifelong toxicity and damage that can make it impossible to discontinue usage.

This form of institutionalization has been legally enforced outside facilities in Ontario with the passage of Community Treatment Orders in 2000. Such mechanisms are now in widespread use throughout the West, and their merits are evidently argued on the basis of whether they work to impose 'treatments' (or ensure 'treatment compliance') beyond sites of incarceration. Such an institutionalization continues to name its victims, overpower them, and silence them in order to function. It does so in at least three ways, by applying evidence, biology, and chemistry of the mad body against the mad body, and using them to prove a detainee needs treatment.

It is supposed that compliance brings good things to life, though patients who are compliant are often granted basic needs only as if they were privileges. CTOs are useful in somnolizing detainees, reducing their resistance, preventing expensive hospitalizations, eradicating feelings or thoughts to prevent aggression, and of course, ensuring 'treatment compliance,' which can be used as a way of recommending 'clients' for housing. The CTO is not definable as less restrictive, even if it is used craftily by people seeking scarce resources, but in fact, it clarifies how 'treatment' is itself restrictive, how it often leads to broken wills and identities, as informants told me, making it possible for patients and others to ignore abuses and exploitation. While laws do not translate into practice, lack of oversight encourages a free for all, a lack of rights advice, a lack of systemic review.

Participants in my research discussed the abuses that they have witnessed under CTO rules, including the following: relocating 'inconvenient' detainees, imposing lifestyle regimens like frequent bathing and pregnancy tests, managing unrelated costs, failing to provide 'rights advice' information, imposing treatments on people with coercive families who monitor them, pre-emptively imposing drugs rather than using them as a last resort, preventing refugees from fleeing Canada's mental illness industry, and imposing 'treatment plans' more restrictively on women and other marginalized groups, as a few examples.

Participants' perceptions suggested that Community Treatment Orders do *not* broadly establish any of the following: 'reduced symptoms,' 'treatment compliance,' continued 'service delivery' and 'integration,' help for 'homeless' people, reduced use of police and other resources, or 'positive outcomes' as seen by detainees – in fact, virtually none of the CTO subjects known to my participants wanted to be on CTOs (though surely the government review knew of some). Two participants spoke of improved outcomes upon ceasing CTO use, which may inform the 'efficacy' researcher. One participant said, lest CTOs be used indefinitely, that they merely postpone 'rehospitalization.' I have argued that CTOs should be seen as an involuntary status under the law, rather than as simply a 'treatment' with 'consent' rules attached to it. This could provide the grounds for evacuating CTOs as a punitive measure.

CTOs punish the 'mad' self. They restrain the self altogether. Consider the possibility of an 'incapable' person made 'capable' artificially by psychotropic drugs that are forced on her in a facility, with acceptable side effects. This corrected individual is now allowed to decide upon her own release under a CTO, which is used to ensure her continued compliance. She was not capable before psychiatric intervention, nor is she truly capable afterwards, because only the CTO ensures her 'insight' by imposing 'treatment,' and tautologically 'insight' and 'compliance.' The corrected individual will never really choose, even if choice is conceivable under duress in 'hospitals'; that is, the detainee is only made capable by a treatment she could accidentally discontinue. Under the effects of major tranquilizers, this person may not be able to choose anything but what others suggest for a long period of time. But as the psychiatrist in my research suggested, voluntariness is neither necessary nor imperative in the actual application of CTOs.

Participants said touted 'rights' were often abused, and this is supported by the government's own review of CTO use. There is a general lack of information about CTOs on the part of both detainees and workers. Participants reported the following: many CTO subjects were not aware that they were under CTOs, there was little time to give proper 'rights advice,' activists didn't ask or know who was on CTOs making CTO inmates more difficult to help or inform, few CTO inmates were challenging orders at the tribunal, and detainees often could not control the method of delivery of drugs under CTOs.

Perceptions of CTO experiences provide a view of psychiatric operations of power as enabling a chemical institutionalization that supersedes, strengthens, and expands prior methodologies of incarceration. Such chemicalization erases identity, helps impose psychiatric education, and often ensures bodily restraint. My research participants elucidated experiences of the following: iatrogenic diseases, toxic and withdrawal reactions, tardive diseases masked by drugs, addiction (to psychopharmaceuticals), stupor or decreased energy labelled 'improvement,' detainee passivity and fearfulness produced by drugs and education, and inmate 'invisibility' before psychiatric workers. These 'side effects' of an institutional regime based on biological explanations of behaviour as disordered were directly related to detainee feelings of fear, rage, distrust, self-denial, lost esteem, dependence, despondency and immobility, lack of creativity, lack of feeling, lack of safety in society, lack of agency, and self-'splitting' (into healthy and ill selves).

These perceptions were compared with those in Goffman's *Asylums* (1961), in which many of the same techniques and methods used to alter 'self' in total institutions were found to be operant in chemical institutionalization, including the following: detention, demobilization, social segregation, physical abuse, monitoring, disculturation, disorientation, disfigurement, indignities, insult, making detainees beg for necessities, profaned and performed selfhoods, closeting, abuse of biographical evidence, and degrading 'privilege' systems. The last of these seemed the conceptual origin of the CTO mechanism.

With incarceration and drugging comes a suppression of self. With Community Treatment Orders comes a new method of (dis)ordering the self beyond the old site of incarceration. Institutionalization brings a psychological pressure to identify with the oppressor. This dynamic is well described in literature on interpersonal or political conflict as a form of abuse, with terms such as 'hazing,' 'capture-bonding,' 'Stockholm syndrome,' 'double bind,' and 'brainwashing.' This process is far more successful when restricting a person's movement or association with others than can be achieved by any physical process. The process of institutionalization can therefore be achieved through 'treatment' alone, if it can be enforced. Coerced drugging, legalized off-site by Community Treatment Orders, and conducted informally without them, can be argued to do what asylums have done for decades: restrict movement and free association. It also clouds judgment, making the occupied body less resistant at the level of consciousness.

However, beneath the institutionalized detainee identity, participants reported signs of resistance including strident independence, inquisitiveness, creativity, realism, reason, empathy, spirituality, sexuality, zest and esprit, and any aspects of subjectivity known to 'sound' individuals. While CTOs and other methodologies of institutionalization often result in detainee behaviours that conform rigidly to others' expectations, the self may find an abode beneath expectations. At the level of non-self, a person becomes aware of injustice at different levels.

In concluding, there is no medical or empirical evidence to support the illness model of 'madness,' or the assurance that drugging is 'therapeutic' in a corollary sense. The fact that some people do accept psychiatric drugs to prevent 'madness' (or accept interventions involving force) is understandable. This should not be used as an argument for coercing drugs on anyone else. Many people I've spoken to who choose drugs readily, who feel they benefit from their use, usually do not consider the problem of medical force directly, yet this is central to the complaints of psychiatric survivors. Perhaps a person who is confused is not expected to remember or care what happens to her until her 'reason' has been resuscitated by force. But strange experiences need not be defined and defended: we all have an inalienable right to freedom of thought, to consciousness itself.

Action

The perception of madness as violent, at least in the 'worst cases,' is used over and over to excuse chemical restraint and incarceration in standard practice. It is seldom accepted that such violence may be the product of drugging or withdrawal effects that are likely to come, especially without support services after discharge. This self-reinforcing institutional move, of blaming drug-related violence on illness, violence which as Whitaker indicates has been a growing phenomenon since the introduction of neuroleptics, will not end with arguments, with qualitative analyses, or with a few informed activists. But among those of us who are informed, without dismissing violence, there has been a long story of action for new possibilities.

The madness trade has been grandfathered into contemporary institutional regimes and industrial practices, and as such we have a long history of seeing people who are distressed in 'psychosis' as dangerous, as less than people, as units to be modified. Alternatives do exist, of course, and many studies like Mosher's Soteria House show us that they work better than coercion and containment. We might feel a need to suppress 'madness' in our midst because of our own fear of what cannot be predicted. But 'mad' people often find each other to be far from inexplicable in peer support networks and agencies. In fact, not only do people in such environments consider each other to have experienced many of the same things, and therefore may avoid denying each other's 'humanity,' but survivors have started to make interactive arrangements viable to governments (see, e.g., Clay, 2005). Destructive responses are not necessary to help 'mad' people cope in a sanist world.

The following path seems clear to me: (a) create self-sustaining refuges to meet 'basic needs'; (b) give people at least one person who they can count on in any circumstance; (c) create non-judgmental support strategies, not given or governed by those who are charged with imposing restrictions; (d) have negotiations regarding social restrictions overseen by advocates to ensure compliance with basic standards (though this is far from optional, even an adversarial court might not escape the all-versus-one dynamic of sanism); (e) encourage the use of non-destructive therapies (e.g., natural remedies) even for chemical restraint (if a person wants such restraint); (f) use non-destructive methods to intercede in violence. I can think of a few more. Such notions would require many levels of collaboration, and might be co-opted at every turn if ordered, so they are not sure bets. But they could be elaborated separately by different groups seeking different aims. Also, more general strategies could be used in the present to recognize the human work of nurturance, social support, and co-active reflection as a start.

On the other hand, for some time it will be necessary to live with psychiatry. Whether we believe we are 'mentally ill' or 'sane,' we must live with a society that neither believes 'madness' is fully human, nor wishes to divert resources from destructive treatments to enhance social responses. I imagine many ways in which 'dangerousness' might be averted, and many others have even tried unorthodox methods that have worked, but policy might at least provide a ground for the abandonment of medical force and the embracing of social reconnections that make 'madness' a part of human life.

To facilitate our movements in and out of crises we should begin to see ourselves as whole even when we are quite vulnerable. We are 'sound' even when/if we make little sense. This is not to deny the reality of distress or loss, or to defend hate and contempt. I am saying that to deploy mad violence stories as primary does not make 'mental illness' more acceptable or relatable. We may find ways of responding socially to people who we now consider 'mad' or 'psychotic,' methods of communicating that do not depend solely on the order and veracity of claims. It might even be possible for us to engage emotionally with one another without giving up our own emotional ground (the 'drain' of talking to distressed people). In other words, to find a way of relating without fear of the deep emotional scars and confusions of our many difficult pasts would allow us to respect vulnerability, even praise it as something that we all need to share. Rather than betray our weakness, our distress, we might embrace it as part of our experience and that of others. Conversely, others' disordered lives might become a constructive part of our own self-understanding. Yes, there are many exceptions.

These idealistic visions of a society that helps people live with and move through extreme experiences of self must come, if slowly. We will require more than the proper dissemination of a few principles. I feel a need to redirect my interest to our own experiences, an interest that eclipses the giddy fascination of sound minds with particularized aspects of madness. To do this requires being in touch with others going through similar experiences. A new social circle might arise out of truly flexible and creative responses.

References

Abbott, A. (2007). Against narrative: A preface to lyrical sociology. *Sociological Theory* 25(1): 67–99.

Adame, A.L. (2006). *Recovered Voices, Recovered Lives: A Narrative Analysis of Psychiatric Survivors' Experience of Recovery.* Unpublished M.A. thesis, Miami University, Oxford, Ohio.

Ahern, L. (2005). Taking issue: The irreversible damage caused by surreptitious prescribing. *Psychiatric Services* 56: 383.

Ahern, L., & Fisher, D.B. (2001). Recovery at your own PACE (Personal Assistance in Community Existence). *Journal of Psychosocial Nursing* 24: 22–32.

Allen, J.B. (1999). Ethical issues on coercion research in mental health systems. In J.P. Morrisey & J. Monahan (Eds.), *Coercion in Mental Health Service: International Perspectives.* Stamford, CT: JAI Press.

Alper, T.G. (1948). An electric shock patient tells his story. *Journal of Abnormal & Social Psychology* 43: 201–10.

Alty, A., & Mason, T. (1994). *Seclusion and Mental Health: A Break with the Past.* London: Chapman & Hall.

American Psychiatric Association. (1994). *Diagnostic and Statistical Manual of Mental Disorders (DSM IV).* (4th ed.). Washington, DC: Author.

Amundson, J. (1993). Temptations of power and certainty. *Journal of Marital & Family Therapy* 19(2): 111–23.

Anderson, D. (2005). *Code White.* Toronto: McGilligan Books.

Anderson, L. (1996). *Bedtime Stories for Tired Therapists.* Adelaide: Dulwich Centre.

Anderson, W.H., & Reeves, K.R. (1991). Chemical restraint: An idea whose time has gone. *Administration & Policy in Mental Health* 18: 3.

Anonymous. (1982). Five months in the New York State Lunatic Asylum. In D. Peterson (Ed.), *A Mad People's History of Madness*. Pittsburgh: University of Pittsburgh Press.

Appelbaum, P. (2005). Assessing Kendra's Law: Five years of outpatient commitment in New York. *Psychiatric Services* 56: 791–2.

Arboleda-Flórez, J., Holley, H.L., & Crisanti, A. (1996). *Mental Illness and Violence: Proof or Stereotype?* Ottawa: Health Canada. Retrieved 20 April 2010 from http://www.phac-aspc.gc.ca/mh-sm/pubs/mental_illness/index.htm.

Bachrach, L.L., Goering, P., & Wasylenki, D. (Eds.). (1994). *Mental Health Care in Canada*. Thousand Oaks: Jossey-Bass.

Badiou, A. (2006). *Being and Event*. London: Continuum.

Barnes, M. (2008). *Lily Pond: A Memoir of Madness, Memory, Myth and Metamorphosis*. Emeryville: Biblioasis.

Barton, R. (1959). *Institutional Neurosis*. Bristol: Wright.

Basaglia, F. (1968). *L'institution en négation: Rapport sur l'hôpital psychiatrique de Gorizia*. Trans. Louis Bonalumi. Paris: Editions du Seuil.

Bateson, G. (Ed.). (1974). *Perceval's Narrative: A Patient's Account of His Psychosis, 1830–1832*. New York: William Morrow.

Bateson, G., & Ruesch, J. (1951). *Communication: The Social Matrix of Psychiatry*. New York: W.W. Norton.

Bay, M. (2003). The evolution of mental health law in Ontario. In *Mental Health and Patients Rights in Ontario: Yesterday, Today and Tomorrow: 20th Anniversary Special Report*, 14–16. Toronto: Psychiatric Patient Advocate Office.

Beck, A.T., Baruch, E., Balter, J.M., Steer, R.A., & Warman, D.M. (2004). A new instrument for measuring insight: The Beck Cognitive Insight Scale. *Schizophrenia Research* 68(2–3): 319–29.

Beers, C.W. ([1908] 1953). *A Mind that Found Itself: An Autobiography*. Garden City, NY: Doubleday.

Belcher, W. (1997). Address to humanity: Containing, a letter to Dr Thomas Monro: A receipt to make a lunatic and seize his estate; and a sketch of a true smiling hyena, 1796. In Allen Ingram (Ed.), *Voices of Madness: Four Pamphlets, 1683–1796*, 129–35. Gloucestershire: Sutton.

Bentall, R.P. (2003) *Madness Explained: Psychosis and Human Nature*. London: Penguin.

Beresford, P., & Wallcraft, J. (1997). Psychiatric system survivors and emancipatory research: Issues, overlaps and differences. In C. Barnes & G. Mercer (Eds.), *Doing Disability Research*. Leeds: Disability Press.

Birnbaum, R. (2010). My father's advocacy for a right to treatment. *Journal of the American Academy of Psychiatry & the Law* 38(1): 115–23.

Black, B.L. (1982). *The Myth of Deinstitutionalization: Interorganizational Maintenance of the Medical Model in the Community.* Unpublished doctoral dissertation, State University of New York at Stonybrook.

Blizzard, C. (2000). Mentally ill need medical treatment. *Toronto Sun,* 1 April.

Borum, R., Swartz, M., Riley, S., Swanson, J., Hiday, V.A., & Wagner, R. (1999). Consumer perceptions of involuntary outpatient commitment. *Psychiatric Services* 50: 1489–91.

Brean, J. (2010). Mind control: Activists gather in Toronto for rare global event promoting the overthrow of psychiatry. *National Post,* 8 May.

Breggin, P.R. (1991). *Toxic Psychiatry: Why Therapy, Empathy, and Love Must Replace the Drugs, Electroshock, and Biochemical Theories of the New Psychiatry.* New York: St Martin's Press.

Breggin, P.R. (1994). Should the use of neuroleptics be severely limited? In S.A. Kirk & S.D. Einbinder (Eds.), *Controversial Issues in Mental Health.* Boston: Allyn & Bacon.

Breggin, P.R. (2003/04). Suicidality, violence and mania caused by selective serotonin reuptake inhibitors (SSRIs): A review and analysis. *International Journal of Risk & Safety in Medicine* 16: 31–49.

Breggin, P.R. (2005). *$1.6 Million Tardive Dyskinesia: Malpractice Verdict in October 2005.* Retrieved 10 Nov. 2005 from http://www.breggin.com/TDverdict.htm.

Burris, D.V. (2004). *Why the Policies of Deinstitutionalization Failed.* Unpublished M.A. thesis, State University of New York.

Burstow, B., & Weitz, D. (Eds.). (1988). *Shrink Resistant: The Struggle against Psychiatry.* Vancouver: New Star.

Burstow, B., Cohen, L., Diamond, B., & Lightman, E. (2005). *Report of the Psychiatric Drugs Panel, Toronto: Inquiry into Psychiatry.* Toronto: Coalition Against Psychiatric Assault.

Campbell, M., & Gregor, F. (2002). *Mapping the Social: A Primer in Doing Institutional Ethnography.* Aurora: Garamond.

Canada. Parliament, Senate. (2005). *Proceedings of the Standing Senate Committee on Social Affairs, Science and Technology,* 38th Parliament, 1st session, 6. (16 Feb. 2005). Retrieved 10 June 2010 from http://www.parl.gc.ca/38/1/parlbus/commbus/senate/Com-e/soci-e/06evb-e.htm?Language=E&Parl=38&Ses=1&comm_id=47.

Canadian Charter of Rights and Freedoms. (1982). Part I of the Constitution Act, 1982, RSC 1985, app. II, no. 44.

Canadian Food Inspection Agency. (2004). *Chemical Residues Manuals of Procedures.* Ottawa. Retrieved 18 Oct. 2005 from http://www.inspection.gc.ca/english/anima/heasan/man/crrc/crrce.shtml.

Canadian Mental Health Association (CMHA). (2005). *A Comparison of Persons on a Community Treatment Order (CTO) and Those Not on a CTO.* Unpublished research. Toronto: Author.

Canadian Mental Health Association (CMHA). (15 April 2010). *New Bill 16 Makes Changes to Mental Health Act and Health Care Consent Act.* Retrieved 10 June 2010 from http://www.ontario.cmha.ca/mental_health_notes_story. asp?cID=562199.

Canadian Mental Health Association (CMHA). (2010). *Chronology of Reports, Recommendations and Plans for Mental Health Care Reform.* Retrieved 20 June 2010 from http://www.ontario.cmha.ca/policy_and_research.asp?cID=23000.

Canadian Mental Health Association (CMHA), Ontario Division. (1998). *Position Paper Regarding the Use of Community Treatment Orders for People with Mental Illness.* Toronto: Author.

Canvin, K., Bartlett, A., & Pinfold, V. (2002). A 'bittersweet pill to swallow': Learning from mental health service users' responses to compulsory community care in England. *Health & Social Care in the Community* 10(5): 361–9.

Caplan, P.J. (1995). *They Say You're Crazy: How the World's Most Powerful Psychiatrists Decide Who's Normal.* New York: Perseus.

Caplan, P.J. (2004). The debate about PMDD and Sarafem: Suggestions for therapists. *Women & Therapy* 27(3–4): 55–67.

Caplan, R.B., & Caplan, G. (2001). *Helping the Helpers Not to Harm: Iatrogenic Damage and Community Mental Health.* New York: Brunner-Routledge.

Capponi, P. (1992). *Upstairs in the Crazy House: The Life of a Psychiatric Survivor.* New York: Viking.

Carey, B. (2008). Drugs offer no benefit in curbing aggression, study finds. *New York Times*, 4 Jan.

Carten, R. (2006). *The AIMS Test, Mad Pride & Other Essays.* Vancouver: Keewatin Books.

Caulfield, T., Downie J., & Flood, C. (Eds.). (2002). *Canadian Health Law and Policy* (2nd ed.). Toronto: Butterworths.

CBC News. (2000). New rules for Ontario mental health care. (5 Dec.). Retrieved 20 June 2010 from http://www.cbc.ca/news/story/2000/12/05/ ott_brianslaw001204.html.

Centre for Addictions and Mental Health (CAMH) and Canadian Mental Health Association (CMHA). (2005). *Report on the Survey of Hospitals' Use of Community Treatment Orders and Case Management Services.* Unpublished research.

Chamberlin, J. (1978). *On Our Own: Patient-Controlled Alternatives to the Mental Health System.* New York: McGraw-Hill.

Chambers, J. (1995). Patients Council wins fight for equal rights. *Psycho Magazine: Queen Street Patients Voice* 3.

Chambers, J. (2003). Empowerment in psychiatric facilities. In *Mental Health and Patients Rights in Ontario: Yesterday, Today and Tomorrow: 20th Anniversary Special Report*, 102–4. Toronto: Psychiatric Patient Advocate Office.

Chambers, S.D. (1993). *Implementing the 1987 Draft Plan to Downsize Riverview Hospital: Expanding the Social Control Network (British Columbia)*. Unpublished M.A. thesis, Simon Fraser University, Vancouver.

Chesler, P. (1972). *Women and Madness*. New York: Avon.

Church, K. (1996). *Forbidden Narratives: Critical Autobiography as Social Science*. Melbourne: Gordon & Breach.

Churchill, R., Owen, G., Singh, S., & Hotopf, M. (2007). *International Experiences of Using Community Treatment Orders*. London: Department of Health, Institute of Psychiatry, King's College. Retrieved 29 Aug. 2008 from http://www.dh.gov.uk/en/Publicationsandstatistics/Publications/PublicationsPolicyAndGuidance/DH_072730.

Clay, S. (Ed.). (2005). *On Our Own, Together: Peer Programs for People with Mental Illness*. Nashville: Vanderbilt University Press.

Cohen, O. (2001). *Psychiatric Survivor Oral Histories: Implication for Contemporary Mental Health Policy*. Amherst: University of Massachusetts, Center for Public Policy and Administration.

Community Treatment Orders: Ontario Legislated Review. (19 Nov. 2004). *CTO Project Update Blog*. Dreezer & Dreezer, Inc. Retrieved 28 May 2008 from http://www.ctoproject.ca/id11.html.

Conle, C. (1999). Why narrative? Which narrative? Struggling with time and place in life and research. *Curriculum Inquiry* 29(1): 7–32.

Conolly, J.J. (1856). *The Treatment of the Insane without Mechanical Restraints*. London: Smith Elder.

Cordileone, E. (2000). Man shot by police shunned medication. *Toronto Star*, 26 May.

Corrigan, P.W., Watson, A.C., Heyman, M.L., Warpinski, A., Gracia, G., Slopen, N., & Hall, L.L. (2005). Structural stigma in state legislation. *Psychiatric Services* 56: 557–63.

Costa, L. (2010). Government 'surreptitiously' changes rights under Mental Health Act. *ARCH Alert*. (23 June). Toronto: ARCH Disability Law Centre. Retrieved 1 Sept. 2010 from http://www.archdisabilitylaw.ca/?q=read-june-23-2010-arch-alert.

Crane, G. (1973). Clinical psychopharmacology in its 20th year. *Science* 181: 121–8.

Currier, G.W., & Allen, M.H. (2000). Emergency psychiatry: Physical and chemical restraint in the psychiatric emergency service. *Psychiatric Services* 51: 717–19.

Dawson, J., Romans, S., Gibbs, A., & Ratter, N. (2003). Ambivalence about Community Treatment Orders. *International Journal of Law & Psychiatry* 26(3): 243–55.

D.B., Re, 2003 ON C.C.B. (21 May 2003). Retrieved 14 Aug. 2005 from http://www.canlii.org/on/cas/onccb/2003/2003onccb10100.html.

Deegan, P. (1988). Recovery: The lived experience of rehabilitation. *Psychosocial Rehabilitation Journal* 11(4): 11–19.

Deegan, P. (1992). The Independent Living Movement and people with psychiatric disabilities: Taking back control over our own lives. *Psychosocial Rehabilitation Journal* 15: 3–19.

Deegan, P. (1997). Recovery and empowerment for people with psychiatric disabilities. *Journal of Social Work & Health Care* 25: 11–24.

Dennett, D.C. (1991). *Consciousness Explained.* Boston: Little, Brown.

Dennis, D., & Monahan, J. (Eds.). (1996). *Coercion and Aggressive Community Treatment: A New Frontier in Mental Health Law.* New York: Plenum.

Denzin, N.K., & Lincoln, Y.S. (1994). *Handbook of Qualitative Research.* Thousand Oaks: Sage.

Diamond, R.J. (1996). Coercion and tenacious treatment in the community: Applications to the real world. In D.L. Dennis & J. Monahan (Eds.), *Coercion and Aggressive Community Treatment: A New Frontier in Mental Health Law,* 51–72. New York: Plenum.

Dobbs, D. (2006). A revealing reflection: Mirror neurons are providing stunning insights into everything from how we learn to walk to how we empathize with others. *American Scientific Mind* 17: 2.

Dodman, N. (1999). *Dogs Behaving Badly: An A-to-Z Guide to Understanding and Curing Behavioral Problems in Dogs.* New York: Random House.

Dotinga, R. (2007). Antipsychotic drugs raise death rates in elderly. *Health Day News.* MedicineNet.com. (5 June). Retrieved 26 Dec. 2007 from http://www.medicinenet.com/script/main/art.asp?articlekey=81581.

Dreezer & Dreezer. (2007). *Report on the Legislated Review of Community Treatment Orders, Required under Section 33.9 of the Mental Health Act for the Ontario Ministry of Health and Long-Term Care.* Toronto: Queen's Printer for Ontario.

Duerr, M. (1996). *Hearing Voices: Resistance among Psychiatric Survivors and Consumers.* Unpublished M.A. thesis, California Institute of Integral Studies, San Francisco.

Dwyer, E. (1987). *Homes for the Mad: Life inside Two Nineteenth-Century Asylums.* New Brunswick, NJ: Rutgers University Press.

Eastman, N. (1994). Mental health law: Civil liberties and the principle of reciprocity. *British Medical Journal* 308: 43.

Elbogen, E.B., Swanson, J.W., & Swartz, M.S. (2003). Effects of legal mechanisms on perceived coercion and treatment adherence among persons with severe mental illness. *Journal of Nervous & Mental Disease* 191(10): 629–37.

Emerick, R.E. (1989). Group demographics in the mental patient movement: Group location, age, and size as structural factors. *Community Mental Health Journal* 25: 4.

Everett, B. (2000). *A Fragile Revolution: Consumers and Psychiatric Survivors Confront the Power of the Mental Health System.* Waterloo: Wilfrid Laurier University Press.

Everett, B. (2001). Community Treatment Orders: Ethical practice in an era of magical thinking. *Canadian Journal of Community Mental Health* 20(1): 5–20.

Fabris, E. (2006). *Identity, Inmates, Insight, Capacity, Consent: Chemical Incarceration in Psychiatric Survivor Experiences of Community Treatment Orders.* Unpublished M.A. thesis, Ontario Institute of Studies in Education, University of Toronto.

Facchi, L., Majoli, A., & Constantino, M. (2004). *Leros.* London: Trolley Books.

Fadiman, J., & Kewman, D. (Eds.). (1979). *Exploring Madness: Experience, Theory, and Research* (2nd ed.). Belmont: Wadsworth.

Failer, J.L. (2002). *Who Qualifies for Rights? Homelessness, Mental Illness, and Civil Commitment.* Ithaca: Cornell University Press.

Farabee, D., Shen, H., & Sanchez, S. (2002). Perceived coercion and treatment need among mentally ill parolees. *Criminal Justice & Behavior* 29(1): 76–86.

Fennel, P. (1996). *Treatment without Consent: Law, Psychiatry, and the Treatment of Mentally Disordered People since 1845.* New York: Routledge.

Fisher, D. (2003). People are more important than pills in recovery from mental disorder. *Journal of Humanistic Psychology* 43: 65–68.

Forrest, M., & Forrest, C. (n.d.). *Haldol.* Retrieved 12 Nov. 2005 from Alzheimer's Outreach site http://www.zarcrom.com/users/alzheimers/me-04a.html.

Foucault, M. (1965 [1961]). *Madness and Civilization: A History of Insanity in the Age of Reason.* Trans. R. Howard. London: Tavistock.

Frank, L.R. (1 Aug. 2008). *Frankly Quoted.* San Francisco: Author.

Frankish, C.J., Hwang, S.W., & Quantz, D. (2005). Homelessness and health in Canada: Research lessons and priorities. *Canadian Journal of Public Health* 96: S23–S29.

Freire, P. (1970). *Pedagogy of the Oppressed.* New York: Continuum.

Friedlander, H. (2001). The exclusion and murder of the disabled. In
    R. Gellately & N. Stoltzfus (Eds.), *Social Outsiders in Nazi Germany*, 145–64.
    Princeton: Princeton University Press.

Funk, W. 1998. *What Difference Does It Make? The Journey of a Soul Survivor.*
    Cranbrook: Wild Flower.

Geller, J.L. (1986). The quandaries of enforced community treatment and
    unenforceable outpatient commitment statutes. *Journal of Psychiatry & Law*
    14(1–2): 149–58.

Geller, J.L., & Harris, M. (1994). *Women of the Asylum: The Unheard Voices of
    America's Madwomen.* New York: Doubleday.

Georgaca, E. (2000). Reality and discourse: A critical analysis of the category
    of 'delusions.' *British Journal of Medical Psychology* 73: 227–42. Retrieved
    10 June 2010 from http://www.discourseunit.com/publications_pages/
    du_members/georgaca_papers/Georgaca%202000%20BJMP.pdf.

Gibbs, A., Dawson, J., Forsyth, H., Mullen, R., & Te Oranga Tonu Tanga.
    (2004). Maori experience of community treatment orders in Otago, New
    Zealand. *Australian & New Zealand Journal of Psychiatry* 38(10): 830–5.

Gibson, M. (1976). *The Butterfly Ward.* Toronto: Harper Collins.

Gillett, G. (1994). Insight, delusion, and belief. *Philosophy, Psychiatry, &
    Psychology* 1(4): 227–36.

Ginovart N., Wilson A.A., Hussey D., Houle S., & Kapur S. (2009). D2-receptor
    upregulation is dependent upon temporal course of D2-occupancy: A
    longitudinal [11C]-raclopride PET study in cats. *Neuropsychopharmacology*
    34(3): 662–71.

Goffman, E. (1961). *Asylums: Essays on the Social Situation of Mental Patients and
    Other Inmates.* New York: Doubleday Anchor.

Gotkin, J., & Gotkin, P. (1975). *Too Much Anger, Too Many Tears: A Personal
    Triumph over Psychiatry.* New York: Quadrangle/New York Times Books.

Grann, M., Belfrage, H., & Tengström, A. (2000). Actuarial assessment of risk
    for violence: Predictive validity of the VRAG and the historical part of the
    HCR-20. *Criminal Justice & Behavior* 27(1): 97–114.

Grant, B. (1999). *The Condition of Madness.* Lanham: University Press of America.

Gray, J.E., & O'Reilly, R.L. (2001). Clinically significant differences among
    Canadian mental health acts. *Canadian Journal of Psychiatry / Revue Canadi-
    enne de Psychiatrie* 46: 315–21.

Greenberg, D., Mazar, J., Brom, D., & Barer, Y.C. (2005). Involuntary outpatient
    commitment: A naturalistic study of its use and a consumer survey at one
    community mental health center in Israel. *Medicine & Law* 24(1): 95–110.

Greenberg, L. (8 Feb. 2008). Arenburg lawyer ponders insanity defence:
    'Review board made a mistake,' widow says. *Ottawa Citizen.*

Greenman, L. (2004). Biological markers: Search for villains in psychiatry. *Journal of Mind & Behavior* 25(3): 213–26.

Grobe, J. (Ed.). (1995). *Beyond Bedlam: Contemporary Women Psychiatric Survivors Speak Out*. Chicago: Third Side.

Harding, C. (1987). The Vermont longitudinal study of persons with mental illness I and II. *American Journal of Psychiatry* 144: 718–35.

Hare-Mustin, R.T. (2004). Discourses in the mirrored room: A postmodern analysis of therapy. *Family Process* 33(1): 19–35.

Hayes, J., & Wingrove, J. (2007). Journalist's killer arrested again: Jeffrey Arenburg, tied to Ottawa anchor's death, due in U.S. court today. *Toronto Star,* 3 Dec. Retrieved 19 April 2009 from: http://www.thestar.com/News/GTA/article/281990

Health Care Consent Aet. (1996). S.O. 1996, Chapter 2, Schedule A.

Healy, D. (2009 [2001]). *Psychiatric Drugs Explained* (5th ed.). London: Churchill, Livingston, Elsevier.

Hervey, N. (1986). Advocacy or folly: The Alleged Lunatics' Friend Society, 1845–63. *Medical History* 30(3): 245–75.

Hiday, V.A. (1996). Outpatient commitment: Official coercion in the community. In D.L. Dennis & J. Monahan (Eds.), *Coercion and Aggressive Community Treatment: A New Frontier in Mental Health Law,* 29–47. New York: Plenum.

Hiday, V.A., & Goodman, R.R. (1982). The least restrictive alternative to involuntary hospitalization, out-patient commitment: Its use and effectiveness. *Journal of Psychiatry & Law* 10: 81–96.

Hillman, J., & Ventura, M. (1992). *We've Had a Hundred Years of Psychotherapy and the World's Getting Worse*. New York: Harper Collins.

Hiltz, D., & Szigeti, A. (2005). *A Guide to Consent and Capacity Law in Ontario*. Markham: LexisNexis Butterworths.

Hopper, K. (1996). Regulation from without: The shadows shadow side of coercion. In D.L. Dennis & J. Monahan (Eds.), *Coercion and Aggressive Community Treatment: A New Frontier in Mental Health Law,* 197–219. New York: Plenum.

Human Rights Watch. (2005). Uzbekistan: Psychiatric drugs used to punish activist. Retrieved 12 Nov. 2005 from Human Rights News site http://hrw.org/english/docs/2005/10/21/uzbeki11908.htm.

Hunter, R.H. (2000). Treatment, management, and control: Improving outcomes through more treatment and less control. *New Directions for Mental Health Services* 88: 5–15. Retrieved 1 May 2010 from http://www3.inter science.wiley.com.myaccess.library.utoronto.ca/cgi-bin/fulltext/112467278/PDFSTART.

Hunter, R., & Macalpine, I. (1963). *Three Hundred Years of Psychiatry*. London: Oxford University Press.

Iversen, K.I., Hoyer, G., Sexton, H., & Gronli, O.K. (2002). Perceived coercion among patients admitted to acute wards in Norway. *Nordic Journal of Psychiatry* 56(6): 433–9.

Jackson, G.E. (2005). *Rethinking Psychiatric Drugs: A Guide for Informed Consent*. Bloomington: Authorhouse.

Jacobson, N. (2004). *In Recovery: The Making of Mental Health Policy*. Nashville: Vanderbilt University Press.

Jaynes, J. (1990). *The Origin of Consciousness in the Breakdown of the Bicameral Mind*. Boston: Houghton Mifflin.

Jibu, M. (1997). Magic without magic: Meaning of quantum brain dynamics. *Journal of Mind & Behavior* 18(2): 205–28.

Johnstone, K., & Read, J. (2000). Psychiatrists' recommendations for improving bicultural training and Maori mental health services: A New Zealand survey. *Australian & New Zealand Journal of Psychiatry* 34(1): 135–45.

Johnstone, L. (1989). *Users and Abusers of Psychiatry: A Critical Look at Traditional Psychiatric Practice*. New York: Routledge.

Joseph, J. (2003). *The Gene Illusion: Genetic Research in Psychiatry and Psychology under the Microscope*. Ross-on-Wye: PCCS Books.

Joukamaa, M., Heliövaara, M., Knekt, P., et al. (2006). Schizophrenia, neuroleptic medication and mortality. *British Journal of Psychiatry* 188: 122–7.

Jull, I. (1997). Nietzsche, psychiatry and the state. *Psycho Magazine: Queen Street Patients Council Voice, 8*. Retrieved 7 Sept. 2005 from http://www.qsos.ca/qspc/psycho/8.html.

Junginger, J., & McGuire, L. (2004). Psychotic motivation and the paradox of current research on serious mental illness and rates of violence. *Schizophrenia Bulletin* 30(1): 21–30.

Kapur, S., Zipursky, R., Roy, P., Jones, C., Remington, G., Reed, K., & Houle, S. (1997). The relationship between D2 receptor occupancy and plasma levels on low dose oral haloperidol: A PET study. *Psychopharmacology* 131: 148–52.

Kempe, M. (1982). The book of Margery Kempe. In D. Peterson (Ed.), *A Mad People's History of Madness*, 3–18. Pittsburgh: University of Pittsburgh Press.

King, T. (1993). *The Truth about Stories: A Native Narrative*. Toronto: Anansi.

Kisely, S.R., Xiao, J., & Preston, N.J. (2004). Impact of compulsory community treatment on admission rates: Survival analysis using linked mental health and offender databases. *British Journal of Psychiatry* 184: 432–8.

Kleinman, I., & Schachter, D. (2000). Obtaining informed consent of patients at risk of Neuroleptic Malignant Syndrome. *Psychiatric Services* 51: 1182–83.

Knight, T. 2009. *Beyond Belief: Alternative Ways of Working with Delusions, Obsessions and Unusual Experiences.* Berlin: Lehmann. Retrieved 10 June 2010 from http://www.peter-lehmann-publishing.com/books/beyond-belief.pdf.

Laing, R.D. (1961). *The Self and Others.* London: Tavistock.

Lambe, Y. (2006). *The Chemical Management of Canadian Systems Youth.* Ottawa: National Youth in Care Network. Retrieved 20 June 2010 from http://www.youthincare.ca/resources/show.cfm?id=19&t=1.

Lee, M.A., & Shlain, B. (1985). *Acid Dreams: The CIA, LSD, and the Sixties Rebellion.* New York: Grove.

Lehmann, P. (2004). *Coming off Psychiatric Drugs: Successful withdrawal from Neuroleptics, Antidepressants, Lithium, Carbamazepine and Tranquilizers.* Berlin: Lehmann.

Leibrich, J. (2002). Making space: Spirituality and mental health. *Mental Health, Religion & Culture,* 5, 2, 143–62. Retrieved 16 March 2008 from http://akmhcweb.org/Articles/WorldCongress2001JLeibrich.htm.

Leifer, R. (2001). A critique of medical coercive psychiatry, and an invitation to dialogue. *Ethical Human Sciences & Services* 3: 3.

Lenzer, J. (2004). Bush launches controversial mental health plan. *British Medical Journal* 329: 367.

Levy, R. (1994). Involuntary treatment: Walking the tightrope between freedom and paternalism. In C.J. Sundram (Ed.), *Choice and Responsibility: Legal and Ethical Dilemmas in Services for People with Mental Disabilities.* New York: New York State Commission on Quality of Care for the Mentally Disabled.

Liberman, A. (2007). There are more ways than one to be mad. *Oxford Etymologist.* Retrieved 4 July 2007 from http://blog.oup.com/2007/07/mad/.

Libet, B., Freeman, A., & Sutherland K. (Eds.). (1999). *The Volitional Brain: Towards a Science of Free Will.* Exeter: Imprint Academic.

Lidz, C.W., Mulvey, E.P., Hoge, S.K., Kirsch, B.L., Monahan, J., Eisenberg, M., Gardner, W., & Roth, L.H. (1998). Factual sources of psychiatric patients' perceptions of coercion in the hospital admission process. *American Journal of Psychiatry* 155: 1254–60.

Lieberman, J.A., Stroup, T.S., McEvoy, J.P., Swartz, M.S., Rosenheck, R.A., Perkins, D.O., Keefe, R.S., Davis, S.M., Davis, C.E., Lebowitz, B.D., Severe, B.D., & Hsiao, J.K., Clinical Antipsychotic Trials of Intervention Effectiveness (CATIE) Investigators. (2005). Effectiveness of antipsychotic drugs in patients with chronic schizophrenia. *New England Journal of Medicine* 353(12): 1209–23.

Lopez, M. (1996). The perils of outreach work: Overreaching the limits of persuasive tactics. In D.L. Dennis & J. Monahan (Eds.), *Coercion and Aggressive*

Community Treatment: A New Frontier in Mental Health Law, 85–92. New York: Plenum.

Lopez, S. (2005). Officials bicker as mentally ill wither. *Los Angeles Times,* 3 Aug.

M.B.G., Re, 2003 ON C.C.B. (7 July 2003). Retrieved 14 Aug. 2005 from http://www.canlii.org/on/cas/onccb/2003/2003onccb10105.html.

MacCharles, T. (2007). Mental illness focus of new strategy: Harper names experts to commission to 'lead a national campaign to erase the stigma.' *Toronto Star,* 1 Sept.

MacNeil, C. (2000). The prose and cons of poetic representation in evaluating reporting. *American Journal of Evaluation* 21(3): 239–367.

MacNeil, C., & Mead, S. (2005). A narrative approach to developing standards for trauma-informed peer support. *American Journal of Evaluation* 26(2): 231–44.

Maidment, M.R. (2005). *'Doing Time on the Outside': Transcarceration and the Social Control of Criminalized Women in the Community.* Unpublished doctoral dissertation, Carleton University, Ottawa.

Mallan, C. (23 March 2000). Mental health changes on way: New powers can force the sick into treatment. *Toronto Star.* Retrieved 10 Nov. 2005 from the No Force Coalition site http://www.qsos.ca/qspc/nfc/news.html.

Marshall, J. (1982). *Madness: An Indictment of the Mental Health Care System in Ontario.* Toronto: OPSEU.

Mashour, G.A., Walker, E.E., & Martuza, R.L. (2005). Psychosurgery: Past, present, and future. *Brain Research Reviews* 48(3): 409–19.

McCabe, R., & Quayle, E. (2002). Knowing your own mind. *Psychologist* 15(1): 14–16.

McCubbin, M. (1998). *The Political Economy of Mental Health: Power and Interests within a Complex System.* Unpublished doctoral dissertation, Université de Montréal.

McDonald, C., & Leong, M. (2009). Accused in 'unprovoked' subway pushing in court. Retrieved 1 Sept. 2010 from http://network.nationalpost.com/NP/blogs/toronto/archive/2009/02/17/accused-in-unprovoked-subway-pushing-in-court.aspx.

McNiel, D.E., Eisner, J.P., & Binder, R.L. (2001). The paradox of command hallucinations. (Letters). *Psychiatric Services* 52: 385–6.

Mental Disability Advocacy Centre. (2003). *Cage Beds Inhuman and Degrading Treatment in Four EU Accession Countries.* Budapest: Open Society Institute.

Mental Health Act, RSO (1990). Chapter M, 7.

Mental Health Act, RSBC (1996). Chapter 288.

Merleau-Ponty, M. (1964). *Sense and Non-Sense.* Trans. H.L. Dreyfus & P.A. Dreyfus. Evanston: Northwestern University Press.

Metzl, J. (2009). *The Protest Psychosis: How Schizophrenia Became a Black Disease.* Boston: Beacon Press.

Miller, R. (1982). The least restrictive alternative: Hidden meanings and agendas. *Community Mental Health Journal* 18(1): 46–55.

Miller, R. (1987). *Involuntary Commitment of the Mentally Ill in the Post Reform Era.* Springfield: Charles C. Thomas.

Minkowitz, T. (2006/07). The United Nations Convention on the Rights of Persons with Disabilities and the right to be free from nonconsensual psychiatric interventions. *Syracuse Journal of International Law and Commerce* 34: 405–28.

Mishler, E.G. (2005). Patient stories, narratives of resistance and the ethics of humane care: *A la recherche du temps perdu. Health* 9(4): 431–51.

Modrow, J. (1995). *How to Become a Schizophrenic: The Case against Biological Psychiatry* (2nd ed.). Everett: Apollyon.

Monahan, J. (1996). Violence prediction: The past twenty and the next twenty years. *Criminal Justice & Behavior* 23: 107–20.

Monahan, J., Hoge, S.K., Lidz, C.W., Eisenberg, M.M., Bennett, N.S., Gardner, W.P., Mulvey, E.P., & Roth, L.H. (1996). Coercion to inpatient treatment: Initial results and implications for assertive treatment in the community. In D.L. Dennis & J. Monahan (Eds.), *Coercion and Aggressive Community Treatment: A New Frontier in Mental Health Law,* 13–28. New York: Plenum.

Monahan, J., Bonnie, R.J., Appelbaum, P.S., Hyde, P.S., Steadman, H.J., & Swartz, M.S. (2001). Mandated Community Treatment: Beyond outpatient commitment. *Psychiatric Services* 52(9): 1198–1205.

Montagu, A. (2001). *Exploring the Spatiality of Ontario's Mental Health System.* Unpublished M.A. thesis, York University, Toronto.

Morrison, L.J. (2005). *Talking Back to Psychiatry: The Consumer/Survivor/Ex-patient Movement.* New York: Routledge.

Morrison, L.J. (2006). A matter of definition: Acknowledging consumer/survivor experiences through narrative. *Radical Psychology: A Journal of Psychology, Politics & Radicalism,* 5. Retrieved 16 Feb. 2008 from http://www.radpsynet.org/journal/vol5/Morrison.html.

Mullins v. Levy, 2005 BCSC 1217. British Columbia, Canada. (25 Aug. 2005).

Myers, C.L. (2002). *Thinking beyond Therapeutics: Human Service as Hegemony.* Retrieved 2 Oct. 2005 from Myers' site http://www.well.com/user/clmyers/therapeutics.htm.

Mulvey, E.P., Geller J.L., & Roth, L.H. (1987). The promise and peril of involuntary outpatient commitment. *American Psychologist* 42: 574–84.

New York State Office of Mental Health. (2005). *Kendra's Law: Final Report on the Status of Assisted Outpatient Treatment*. New York, NY. Retrieved 17 Sept. 2005 from http://www.omh.state.ny.us/omhweb/kendra_web/finalreport/.

Nicholson, R.A., Ekenstam, C., & Norwood, S. (1996). Coercion and the outcome of psychiatric hospitalization. *International Journal of Law & Psychiatry* 19(2): 201–17.

Nieves, E.J. (2002). The effectiveness of the assertive community treatment model. *Administration & Policy in Mental Health* 29(6): 461–80.

Oaks, D. (2000). *Drug Corporations Help Fund the Push in Canada for Forced Psychiatric Drugging of People Living in Their Own Homes out in the Community*. Retrieved 10 Nov. 2005 from http://www.straightgoods.com/item341.shtml.

O'Brien, A.M., & Farrell, S.J. (2005). Community Treatment Orders: Profile of a Canadian experience. *Canadian Journal of Psychiatry / Revue Canadienne de Psychiatrie* 50(1): 27–30.

Odette, C. (1995). Suicide: A verb. In J. Grobe (Ed.), *Beyond Bedlam: Contemporary Women Psychiatric Survivors Speak Out*. Chicago: Third Side Press.

O'Hagan, M. (1993). *Stopovers on My Way Home from Mars*. UK: Survivors Speak Out.

O'Hagan, M. (2003). *Force in Mental Health Services: International User/Survivor Perspectives*. Paper presented at the World Federation for Mental Health Biennial Congress, Melbourne, Australia.

O'Toole, M. (2009). Toronto teens shoved onto subway tracks, dodge train. *National Post*, 14 Feb. Retrieved 20 May 2010 from http://news.globaltv.com/world/story.html?id=1288062.

Ontario Legislative Assembly. (17 May 2000). Standing Committee on General Government. *Official Report of Debates*. 37th Parl., 1st Sess. Retrieved 2 Nov. 2005 from http://www.ontla.on.ca/hansard/37_parl/session1/Committees/GenGov/G013.htm.

Ontario Legislative Assembly. (21 June 2000). *Official Report of Debates (Hansard)*. 37th Parl., 1st Sess. Retrieved 2 Nov. 2005 from http://www.ontla.on.ca/hansard/house_debates/37_parl/session1/L076A.htm.

Ontario Ministry of Health and Long-Term Care. (2000). *Rights and Responsibilities: Mental Health and the Law*. Retrieved 15 June 2005 from http://www.ontla.on.ca/hansard/index.htm.

Ontario Ministry of Health and Long-Term Care. (22 March 2000). Ontario to introduce stronger mental health law this spring to help patients and protect communities. Press Release. Toronto: Province of Ontario.

O'Reilly, R.L. (1998). Mental health legislation and the right to appropriate treatment. *Canadian Journal of Psychiatry / Revue Canadienne de Psychiatrie* 43: 811–15.

O'Reilly, R.L. (2004). Why Are Community Treatment Orders controversial? *Canadian Journal of Psychiatry / Revue Canadienne de Psychiatrie* 49(9): 579–84.

Orwell, G. (1949). *Nineteen Eighty-Four*. London: Penguin.

Perlin, M.L. (2000). *The Hidden Prejudice: Mental Disability on Trial*. Washington, DC: American Psychological Association.

Pestana, M.S. (2001). Complexity theory, quantum mechanics and radically free self determination. *Journal of Mind & Behavior* 22(4): 365–88.

Pilgrim, D., & Rogers, A. (2005). The troubled relationship between psychiatry and sociology. *International Journal of Social Psychiatry* 51: 228–41.

Pinard, G.-F., & Pagani, L. (Eds.). (2001). *Clinical Assessment of Dangerousness: Empirical Contributions*. Cambridge: Cambridge University Press.

Porter, R. (2002). *Madness: A Brief History*. Oxford: Oxford University Press.

Poulsen, H.D., & Engberg, M. (2001). Validation of psychiatric patients' statements on coercive measures. *Acta Psychiatrica Scandinavia* 103: 60–5.

Psychiatric Patient Advocate Office. (2005). *Covert Medication (Medication Hidden in Food or Drink)*. Retrieved 20 Nov. 2005 from http://www.ppao.gov.on.ca/inf-cov.html

Psychiatric Patient Advocate Office. (2009). *Patient Advocate Office Annual Report 2008/2009*. Retrieved 8 June 2010 from http://www.ppao.gov.on.ca/pdfs/pub-ann-2008.pdf.

Queen Street Outreach Society. (2002a). *Queen Street Patients Council Archival Site (1992–2001): Our History*. Retrieved 5 Jan. 2005 from http://www.qsos.ca/qspc/bkgd.html.

Queen Street Outreach Society. (2002b). *QSOS Findings in Consultation with People Who Have Experienced the Mental Health System: To Our Membership and the Toronto-Peel Mental Health Implementation Task Force*. Retrieved 13 Nov. 2005 from http://www.qsos.ca/feedbackOverview.html.

Queen Street Outreach Society. (2002c). *Psycho Magazine*. Retrieved 12 June 2010 from http://www.qsos.ca/qspc/psycho.html.

Queen Street Outreach Society. (2002d). *Statement of Opposition to Community Treatment Orders and Expanded Criteria for Involuntary Admissions to Psychiatric Facilities*. Retrieved 10 June 2010 from http://www.qsos.ca/qspc/cto.html.

Quinn, S. (23 Jan. 2006). Community Treatment Order Documentary. *The Current*, CBC Radio. Retrieved 15 Jan. 2008 from http://www.cbc.ca/thecurrent/media/200601/20060123thecurrent_sec3.ram.

Read, J. (2004). Poverty, ethnicity and gender. In J. Read, J. Mosher, &
    R.P. Bentall (Eds.), *Models of Madness*, 161–94. Hove: Brunner-Routledge.
Read, J., & Haslam, N. (2004). Public opinion: Bad things happen and can
    drive you crazy. In J. Read, L. Mosher, & R.P. Bentall (Eds.), *Models of
    Madness*. Hove: Brunner-Routledge.
Reaume, G. (2000a). *Remembrance of Patients Past: Patient Life at the Toronto
    Hospital for the Insane, 1870–1940*. Don Mills: Oxford University Press.
Reaume, G. (2000b). Portraits of people with mental disorders in Canadian
    history. *Canadian Bulletin of Medical History* 17(1–2): 93–125.
Reaume, G. (2006) Teaching mad people's history. *Radical History Review*
    94: 170–82.
R.G.J.K.L., Re, 2003 ON C.C.B. (14 Feb. 2003). Retrieved 14 Aug. 2005 from
    http://www.canlii.org/on/cas/onccb/2003/2003onccb10094.html.
Richter, E.A. (2003). My schizophrenia. *Liberty* 17: 1. Retrieved 12 Aug. 2005
    from Liberty site http://libertyunbound.com/archive/2003_01/richter-
    schizo.html.
Ridgely, M.S., Borum, R., Petrila, J., RAND Health Institute for Civil Justice,
    & California, Legislature,Senate, Rules Committee. (2001). *The Effectiveness
    of Involuntary Outpatient Treatment: Empirical Evidence and the Experience of
    Eight States*. Santa Monica: RAND.
Ridgway, P. (2001). Restorying psychiatric disability: Learning from first per-
    son recovery narratives. *Psychiatric Rehabilitation Journal* 24(4): 335–43.
R.J.A., Re, 2005 ON C.C.B. (2 Feb. 2005). Retrieved 14 Aug. 2005 from http://
    www.canlii.org/on/cas/onccb/2005/2005onccb10002.html.
Romme, M., & Escher, S. (2000). *Making Sense of Voices*. London: Mind
    Publications.
Rosenberg, A.M. (2002). Pain in the butt: Pain management in the E.R. *P.A.
    Pearls from the E.R.* Retrieved 10 Nov. 2005 from http://webmedtechnology.
    com/papearls/PDF%20Files/nov2000.pdf.
Rosenfield, S. (1991). Homelessness and rehospitalization: The importance
    of housing for the chronic mentally ill. *Journal of Community Psychology*
    19: 60–9.
Rosenhan, D.L. (1973). On being sane in insane places. *Science* 179: 250–8.
Rossiter, A. (2001). Innocence lost and suspicion found: Do we educate for or
    against social work? *Critical Social Work* 2: 1.
Ruimy, J. (1999). Tories promise mental health bill. Harris favours forced treat-
    ment in some cases. *Toronto Star*, 14 May.
Russell, B. (1959). *Institutional Neurosis*. Bristol: John Wright.
R.R., Re, 2004 ON C.C.B. (24 Sept. 2004). Retrieved 12 Aug. 2005 from http://
    www.canlii.org/on/cas/onccb/2004/2004onccb10189.html.

Sailas, E.A., & Wahlbeck, K. (2005). Restraint and seclusion in psychiatric inpatient wards. *Current Opinion in Psychiatry* 18: 555–9.

Saks, E.R. (2003). *Refusing Care: Forced Treatment and the Rights of the Mentally Ill.* Chicago: University of Chicago Press.

Sass, L.A. (1994). *Paradoxes of Delusion: Wittgenstein, Schreber, and the Schizophrenic Mind.* Ithaca: Cornell University Press.

Sayce, L. (2000). *From Psychiatric Patient to Citizen: Overcoming Discrimination and Social Exclusion.* New York: Macmillan.

Scheff, T. (Ed.). (1967). *Mental Illness and Social Process.* New York: Harper & Row.

Scull, A. (1984). *Decarceration.* (2nd ed.). London: Polity.

Scull, A. (2010). A psychiatric revolution. *Lancet* 375(9722): 1246–7.

Secker, B. (2001). *Medico-Legal Jurisdiction over Human Decision-Making: A Philosophical Constructionist Analysis of Mental Competence.* Unpublished doctoral dissertation, University of Toronto.

Seidel, J. (1998). *Empirical Evidence Disconfirms the Biopsychiatric Ontology of Mental Disorders.* Unpublished doctoral dissertation, University of Denver.

Sharfstein, S.S. (2005). Big pharma and American psychiatry: The good, the bad, and the ugly. A letter from the President of the American Psychiatric Association. *Psychiatric News* 40 (19 Aug.): 16.

Shimrat, I. (1997). *Call Me Crazy: Stories from the Mad Movement.* Vancouver: Press Gang.

S.H.M., Re, 2004 ON C.C.B. (30 April 2004). Retrieved 14 Aug. 2005 from http://www.canlii.org/on/cas/onccb/2004/2004onccb10152.html.

Siegel, S.J., Winey, K.I., Gur, R.E., Lenox, R.H., Bilker, W.E., Ikeda, D., Gandhi, N., & Zhang, W. (2002). Surgically implantable long-term anti-psychotic delivery systems for the treatment of schizophrenia. *Neuropsychopharmacology* 26: 817–23.

Simmons, H. (1990). *Unbalanced: Mental Health Policy in Ontario (1930–1989).* Toronto: Wall & Thompson.

Singer, E. (2009). Thought translator knows vowels from consonants: Scientists make progress reading thoughts from the severely impaired. *Technology Review.* (21 Oct.). Massachusetts Institute of Technology. Retrieved 10 June 2010 from http://www.technologyreview.com/blog/editors/24279/.

Smith, D.E. (1987). *The Everyday World as Problematic: A Feminist Sociology.* Toronto: University of Toronto Press.

Smith, D.E. (1990a). *The Ideological Practice of Sociology, the Conceptual Practices of Power: A Feminist Sociology of Knowledge.* Toronto: University of Toronto Press.

Smith, D.E. (1990b). *K Is Mentally Iill: The Anatomy of a Factual Account, Texts, Facts and Femininity: Exploring the Relations of Ruling*. London: Routledge.

Smith, D.E. (2005). *Institutional Ethnography: A Sociology for People*. Toronto: AltaMira.

Smith, L.T. (1999). *Decolonizing Methodologies: Research and Indigenous Peoples*. London: Zed Books.

Spencer, J. (2005). The next generation of electric-shock therapy. *Wall Street Journal*, 18 Oct. Retrieved 19 Oct. 2005 from http://www.post-gazette.com/pg/05291/590591.stm.

Starson v. Swayze. (2003). 1 S.C.R. 722, 2003 SCC 32.

Steadman, H.J., Gounis, K., Dennis, D., Hopper, K., Roche, B., Swartz, M., & Robbins, P.C. (2001). Assessing the New York City involuntary outpatient commitment pilot program. *Psychiatric Services* 52(3): 330–6.

Steadman, H.J., Mulvey, E.P., Monahan, J., Robbins, P.C., Appelbaum, P.S., Grisso, T., Roth, L.H., & Silver, E. (1998). Violence by people discharged from acute psychiatric inpatient facilities and by others in the same neighborhoods. *Archives of General Psychiatry* 55: 393–401.

Stip, E., & Rialle, V. (2005). Environmental cognitive remediation in schizophrenia: Ethical implications of 'Smart Home' technology. *Canadian Journal of Psychiatry / Revue Canadienne de Psychiatrie* 50: 281–91.

Susser, E., & Roche, B. (1996). 'Coercion' and leverage in clinical outreach. In D.L. Dennis & J. Monahan (Eds.), *Coercion and Aggressive Community Treatment: A New Frontier in Mental Health Law*, 73–84. New York: Plenum.

Swartz, M.S., Wagner, H.R., Swanson, J.W., & Elbogen, E.B. (2004). Consumers' perceptions of the fairness and effectiveness of mandated community treatment and related pressures. *Psychiatric Services* 55(7): 780–5.

Switzky, H.N., & Miller, T.L. (1978). The least restrictive alternative. *Mental Retardation* 16(1): 52–4.

Szasz, T. (1960). The myth of mental illness. *American Psychologist* 15: 113–18.

Szasz, T. (2004). *Words to the Wise: A Medical-Philosophical Dictionary*. New Brunswick, NJ: Transaction.

Thomson, A. & Dimmock, G. (2007). Brian Smith's killer jailed after border guard attacked: U.S. customs officer punched in the face; widow's fears come true. *Ottawa Citizen*, 3 Dec. Retrieved 19 April 2009 from http://www2.canada.com/ottawacitizen/news/story.html?id=72c19756-ba2e-4d52-b6f8-23fce091124f&k=41328.

Torrey, E.F. (1997). *Out of the Shadows: Confronting America's Mental Illness Crisis*. New York: Wiley.

Torrey, E.F., & Zdanowicz, M. (1999). Op Ed: The right to mental illness? *New York Post*, 28 May.

Trainor, J., Shepherd, M., Boydell, K.M., Leff, A., & Crawford, E. (1997). Beyond the service paradigm: The impact and implications of consumer/survivor initiatives. *Psychiatric Rehabilitation Journal* 21: 132–40.

Treatment Advocacy Center. (2005). *Treatment Advocacy Center Briefing Paper: Assisted Outpatient Treatment.* Retrieved 6 Nov. 2005 from http://www.psychlaws.org/BriefingPapers/BP4.htm.

Valenstein, E.S. (1998). *Blaming the Brain: The Real Truth about Drugs and Mental Health.* New York: Free Press.

van Maanen, J. (1988). *Tales of the Field: On Writing Ethnography.* Chicago: University of Chicago Press.

V.S., Re, 2004 ON C.C.B. (11 March 2004). Retrieved 14 Aug. 2005 from http://www.canlii.org/on/cas/onccb/2004/2004onccb10101.html.

Wahl, O.F. (1995). *Media Madness: Public Images of Mental Illness.* New Brunswick, NJ: Rutgers University Press.

Waring, D. (1987). Review of the book *Acid Dreams: The CIA, LSD and the Sixties Rebellion* by Martin A. Lee and Bruce Shlain. 1985. *Phoenix Rising: The Voice of the Psychiatrized* 7: 2.

Waters, R. (2005). Medicating Aliah. *Mother Jones.* Retrieved 13 Nov. 2005 from http://www.motherjones.com/news/feature/2005/05/medicating_aliah.html.

Watters, E. (2010). *Crazy Like Us: The Globalization of the American Psyche.* New York: Free Press.

Weiss, E.M. (1998). Hundreds of the nation's most vulnerable have been killed by the system intended to care for them. *Hartford Courant,* 11 Oct.

Wertheimer, A. (1993). A philosophical examination of coercion for mental health issues. *Behavioral Sciences & the Law* 11(3): 239–58.

Whitaker, R. (2001). *Mad in America: Bad Science, Bad Medicine, and the Enduring Mistreatment of the Mentally Ill.* Cambridge: Perseus.

Whitaker, R. (2010). *Anatomy of an Epidemic: Magic Bullets, Psychiatric Drugs, and an Astonishing Rise in Mental Illness in America.* New York: Crown.

White, A. (2007). *A Patient Rereading of the Italian Psychiatric Reform: Franco Basaglia and the Therapeutic Community at Gorizia.* Unpublished M.A. research paper, Memorial University of Newfoundland.

White, H., Whelan, C., Barnes, J.D., & Baskerville, B. (2003). Survey of consumer and non-consumer mental health service providers on Assertive Community Treatment teams in Ontario. *Community Mental Health Journal* 39(3): 265–76.

Willing, J. (2009). Arenburg back in Canada: Man who killed Ottawa sportscaster says he won't come to capital. *Ottawa Sun,* 9 Sept. Retrieved 2 April 2010 from http://www.ottawasun.com/news/ottawa/2009/09/08/10789686.html.

Wood, M.E. (Ed.). (1994). *The Writing on the Wall: Women's Autobiography and the Asylum.* Urbana: University of Illinois Press.

World Health Organization. (2002). *Nations for Mental Health: Final Report.* Geneva: Author.

Yildiz, A., Sachs, G.S., & Turgay, A. (2003). Pharmacological management of agitation in emergency settings. *Emergency Medical Journal* 20(4): 339–46.

Index

actuarial risk assessment, 45–6. *See also* risk management
advanced directives, 7n7
advocacy, 14, 30n13, 48–50, 55, 157, 192, 198; patient advocates, 8, 41, 69, 109, 141, 146, 157, 173–5, 177, 186, 190, 198; peer advocacy/support/workers, 49–50, 60, 62, 63, 66, 70, 73, 78, 97, 151, 163, 168, 173, 175, 183–4, 198; self-advocacy, 50, 101–5, 110, 172–4, 186. *See also individual organizations*
aggression, 6, 45, 47–8, 92, 97; and chemical intervention, 3, 6, 37–8, 47–8, 92, 121, 177, 185, 194; and coercive treatment, 4, 40–1, 45; and 'madness,' 37–8, 40–1, 44–5, 47, 97; against patients, 13–14. *See also* violence
akathisia, 182
Alleged Lunatics' Friend Society, 95
Alviani, Aldo, 5n2, 101
American Psychiatric Association, 20, 118–19
anosognosia, 105. *See also* insight, lack of
antianxietants, 96

antidepressants, 96, 119, 133
Anti-Insane Asylum Society, 95
antiparkinsonian drugs, 127
antipsychiatry, 150, 155, 168
antipsychotics. *See* neuroleptics
Arenburg, Jeffery, 51
aripiprazole,125
arts informed research, 58
Assertive Community Treatment teams, 62, 63, 66–7, 70–1, 74–5, 97, 99, 110, 170, 172, 183
Assisted or Assertive Community Treatment, 97, 99
asylums, 42, 95–6, 140, 197
attention deficit disorder, 151
autonomy, 31, 34, 44, 48, 88, 89, 102–4, 107, 159, 172, 181, 182, 184

Badiou, Alain, 25–6
Barnes, Mike, 38n1
Basaglia, Franco, 96
Bay, Michael, 53
Beers, Clifford, 95–6
Bellevue study, 92
Bentall, R.P., 18, 21, 126n5
bioethics, 6, 40, 52, 118. *See also* ethics
biological determinism, 30, 34, 145

116, 165; informed, 3, 105, 175; restriction of, 138, 165–6; of treatment, 5, 185–6
Churchill review, 90
class, 10, 29n12, 73–4, 146, 170. *See also* homelessness; poverty
Coalition of Ontario Psychiatrists, 54, 55
Cochrane Collaboration review, 91, 92–3
coercion, 5–9, 39–40, 52, 61, 63, 66–70, 75, 87, 90, 93, 100, 102, 111–12, 134–7, 151, 164, 169, 176–7, 189–90, 198; classical model, 137; ineffectiveness of, 92–3; informal, 6, 85, 89, 148; legal, 85–6, 89–90, 92, 98, 107, 136–9, 188–90, 196–7; literature on, 137–9; parameters of, 137; perceived, 137–8; rationales for, 75–6; and reciprocity, 98; and respect, 138; and therapeutic relationships, 5, 53, 63, 91, 98, 165; treatment as, 5–6, 107–8, 146; voluntariness in, 116. *See also* chemical incarceration; chemical restraint; chemicalization; coercive community treatment; Community Treatment Orders; duress; restraint
coercive community treatment, 40, 57, 90–2, 99, 114, 138, 186. *See also* Community Treatment Orders
Cogentin, 127
commitment, 91, 92, 106, 107, 109–11, 136, 148; outpatient, 91–2. *See also* detention; incarceration
community mental health, 136, 151
community psychiatry, 96–7, 140
community supervision orders. *See* Community Treatment Orders

Community Treatment Orders, 6, 98, 99, 107, 109, 111n3, 114–15, 148, 189, 194; abuse, 5, 8, 10, 49, 63, 76–80, 84–5, 88, 146, 170–1, 190, 194–6; alternatives to, 183–4, 198–9; and choice, 161–7, 185–6; Consent and Capacity Board, 105, 106, 108, 109, 158, 162, 178–83; 186; coordinators, 85, 86, 98, 190; and deinstitutionalization, 136–7; effectiveness, 75–6, 85–6, 89, 91, 93, 98, 161, 163–4, 191, 195; eligibility for, 63–4; and families, 5, 53, 73–4, 102, 112–13, 136–7, 157–9, 190, 194, 195; focus group on, 60–1, 68–70; frequency of use, 5; as harness, 161–7; and incapacity, 64–6, 75, 85, 107, 110, 112, 166, 170, 185, 195; introduction in Ontario, 48–9, 51–5; as invisible prisons, 145–6; lack of transparency, 85; legal forms, 106–11; literature on, 90–3; mandatory hearings, 88; Maori study, 138; method of present study, 60–3; and non-/compliance, 69, 72–3, 76–8, 88, 91–2, 97, 169, 171, 185, 194–5; numbers of, 65; patient consent for, 65–6; versus physical detention, 137, 146, 154–5, 161–2, 165–6, 181, 194; and police, 5, 35, 79, 80, 154, 182, 195; and privacy, 141, 170–2, 181; professional ambivalence towards, 90–1; provincial review of, 56, 64–5, 70, 75, 84–90, 178, 190–1; as punitive, 6, 9n10, 107–8, 185, 195; purpose, 72–3; and race, 76–8; rationales for, 75–6; and refugees, 76–8, 155, 195; resistance